Eighteen Years of Slavery

To Sis
Joyce Sessoms
from TSrane
(1) You are a mighty woman!"
The Isles need you
737-529-1157

Eighteen Years of Slavery

MY JOURNEY THROUGH THE
AMERICAN FOSTER CARE SYSTEM

Tyrone Obaseki

Copyright © 2017 Tyrone Obaseki
All rights reserved.

ISBN: 1542771889
ISBN 13: 9781542771887
Library of Congress Control Number: 2017901377
CreateSpace Independent Publishing Platform
North Charleston, South Carolina

To every orphan, foster youth, and individual who has endured pain, I give you these words. Some of the most successful people in the world have had rough childhoods, and yet somehow, they managed to prosper despite facing numerous obstacles. It is time for you to journey beyond your doubt, pain, anger, and uncertainty. No matter what is going on in your life right now, you will see a better, brighter day. Walk with your head up high, and know that you are fully capable of overcoming each and every obstacle in your life. As you blaze the trail of life, remember that there is more to this world than what you can see with the naked eye.

Contents

Acknowledgments · ix
Note to Reader · xi

Chapter 1   'Round and 'Round · 1
Chapter 2   The Martin Luther King Jr. Center · · · · · · · · · · · · · 23
Chapter 3   The Smallest One · 33
Chapter 4   I Cannot Breathe · 46
Chapter 5   He Had to Be Restrained · · · · · · · · · · · · · · · · · · · 59
Chapter 6   Champions Treatment Center · · · · · · · · · · · · · · · · 79
Chapter 7   The Thibodauxs · 96
Chapter 8   Troubled Years · 122
Chapter 9   Running Back · 137
Chapter 10 Nightmare on Lovett Street · · · · · · · · · · · · · · · · 148
Chapter 11 Leap of Faith · 164
Chapter 12 Quicksand · 179
Chapter 13 Army Life · 193
Chapter 14 Full Circle · 201
Chapter 15 Present Day · 211
Chapter 16 Spiritual Warfare · 220
Chapter 17 Call to Action · 245
Chapter 18 Along the Way · 251

Acknowledgments

Dear Jesus,

There were days when I ran around in the orphanage while wearing a football helmet, a cape, and Superman underwear. You were right there. It hurt! The pain was excruciating! Yet every tear I cried, you caught with your hand. Looking back and knowing you were present truly made a difference. Your love reached even me, an individual who was one of the least, the labeled, and the lost. Thank you for setting me free! I will use my testimony to lead people to you Lord.

Note to Reader

THIS BOOK WAS WRITTEN TO give an account of my childhood experiences, in hopes of encouraging and empowering the world to focus on the children. The events are portrayed to the best of my memory. However, all of the names of the characters, incidents, and companies portrayed herein have been changed. Any similarities of the fictitious characters, incidents, or companies to the names, attributes, or actual backgrounds of any actual people, living or dead, or to any actual events or to any existing companies are entirely coincidental and unintentional. This book was written for mature audiences. Reader discretion is advised for strong language.

CHAPTER 1

'Round and 'Round

My mother was eight, and *this is how it all began.*

The year was 1975. There was only standing room in the little wooden church off Tidwell and Lockwood. Although my eyes were heavy with sleep, the excitement from church was keeping me awake. Daddy's Jerry curl was dripping as he yelled and clapped at Pastor Willie's preaching. The pastor gave a long and powerful sermon that day. The church was packed full, and all of the people present were sweating bullets and fanning themselves. I liked how the women wore big hats that looked like spaceships and how the men wore their nice and fancy suits. Everyone knew Sister Josephine—she always had a big mouth and always sat on the front row and yelled "Amen!" to the pastor. "You better preach now!" she would continually yell, her large church hat wiggling on her head. On that day, I knew that when the pastor started to sing the sermons and stomp his feet, the service would soon be over.

After church, Mama always put us to bed. The sun's rays would beam heavily through my window and warm my face when I awoke from my naps on Sunday evenings. On that day, I lay in bed, as was my custom. I could not help but look at the spinning ceiling fan. As the blades of the fan went 'round and 'round, I became nauseated, and my head began to spin from the unbearable weight in the center of my chest and stomach. No matter how hard I tried to fight the pain, it continued to go 'round and 'round, mimicking the motion of the fan, perpetuating the feeling relentlessly. "Why is this happening to me?" I thought, tears beginning to well up in my eyes. As I lay on my back, I felt as if everything that was pure and innocent was being sucked right out of me. Glancing to my right and out my bedroom window, I watched a bird land on a branch of a tree just outside. Shortly thereafter, the bird took to the air and vanished into the clouds. Oh, how I wished I could soar high into the sky, that I could fly far away from this very familiar feeling. The tears in my eyes welled up again, because the happy thoughts of flying away were cut short by the unbearable weight now in the center of my chest and stomach.

The pain then forced me to lie on my side; as it continued to go 'round and 'round again, I wondered if it would ever end. In an attempt to escape the present, I set my gaze on the family portrait on the wall. Something about the six brightly smiling faces in the portrait made my tears fall all the more heavily. "No one loves me," I thought to myself, salty tears flowing steadily down my cheek and neck. The pain in my chest and stomach had intensified to the point that my chest heaved up and down. As much as I wanted to cry, I could not. My throat felt like a brick as the compressed scream settled deep within me. As it continued to go 'round and 'round, my top lip began to quiver. Then my daddy flipped me onto my stomach, using his big, powerful hands. My eyes fixed directly on the headboard, and the muscles in my inner thighs began to spasm uncontrollably. I tried to grip the headboard, but my little hands were too small. In and out, 'round and 'round, went my father's tongue, drenching the sheets with saliva. As my father slid his tongue around my pussy, the nerves in my toes twitched uncontrollably. As he aggressively turned me back over, I came face to face with this heavily breathing man who was supposed to be my protector, my priest, and my provider. His beady eyes and foul breath seemed to pierce through my soul. Oh, how I hated to hear the five dreadful words that would come next because I knew what would follow.

"You know you're Daddy's favorite, Shana," he would say, unbuckling his pants.

The room always smelled bad when Daddy took his belt off and dropped his britches. On that day, he lifted my legs far behind my head, hurting my hamstrings and legs, and he deeply inhaled between my legs repeatedly before ramming his stuff in and out, in and out of me. Just as smoke vanishes in the wind, my innocence and purity dissipated into thin air.

The windows in the apartment rattled, and the lights flickered on and off as the summer rain refused to let up. The rain was pouring heavily, and my mother, Shana, was preparing to make a decision that would change the course of her life forever.

Honk! Honk!

"Hurry up, bitch! Let's go!" cried my mom's friend, who was outside blowing her car's horn and beckoning my mom to come out of the apartment.

"I'm coming, nigga. Wait a damn minute!" said my mother as she frantically threw her clothes into her suitcase. Tears beamed down her face as she struggled to keep the cigarette between her lips. With each garment that she took from her drawer, it seemed as if more tears began to fall.

"I can't believe he left me after all I did for his black African ass! Trish, go in the bathroom, and get my black makeup bag!"

"Yes, ma'am," said my oldest sister. She went and brought back the bag.

"You take care of your little sister and brother, you hear me?"

"Yes, ma'am," my sister said, tears welling up in her eyes.

"I'm going away for a while, so don't open the door for no one, you hear me? Not even your bitch-ass grandmother!"

"Yes, ma'am," my sister repeated. She wiped tears from her eyes.

My mother took a puff of her cigarette and looked down at the bed where I was lying. She then ran out of the house, yelling, "I'm coming, nigga, damn!" The door slammed shut with a loud thud.

My oldest sister, Trish, stood looking out the window. She was only seven years old at the time and was left with the burden of caring for our other sister, Tasha, and me. Tasha was four years old at the time; I was only two months old.

"Stop cry-neen," said Trish. She reached over and tried to console Tasha, who was crying in the corner. A roll of thunder blasted loudly, and lightning illuminated the room. "Tasha, stop cry-neen. It gone be OK." Trish laid Tasha's head in her lap and patted her back in an effort to rock her to sleep. "It gone be OK, Tasha."

By the time Trish rocked Tasha to sleep, I had woken and was crying heavily. As with any infant, the pangs of hunger were very uncomfortable and were making me cry. Trish got up, walked into the master bedroom, and climbed up on the bed. "Stop cry-neen, Roni," Trish said as she looked through the covers to see if our mom had left a bottle on the bed. Luckily, she found one and fed me, hoping that I would quiet down. While my oldest sister was feeding me, Tasha walked in crying. Trish crawled off the bed and helped Tasha up onto the bed. By the time Trish crawled back up, the bottle had fallen from my mouth, and I had started to cry again. "Shhh, Roni, stop cry-neen. It gone be OK," Trish said, putting the bottle back in my mouth.

Trish looked out the window from the bed, with tears blazing down her face, and she said yet again, "Stop cry-neen. It gone be OK." Trish felt sleep overcoming her, so she lay between Tasha and me. As she glanced over to see if Tasha was awake, she saw that both of our eyes were heavy with sleep. Trisha took a deep breath, but just as she closed her eyes, Tasha started to cry again and said, "I scared!" The thunder was getting louder, and the rain pelted heavily against the windows.

"Go sleep," Trish said as she patted Tasha's back.

The next morning, Trish awoke to my crying loudly for a bottle. She glanced over and saw that Tasha was awake in the bed, her thumb in her mouth, looking off as if she were daydreaming.

"Stop cry-neen, Roni," Trish said. She looked around the house for another bottle, but before she could find one, someone banged on the door.

Bam! Bam! Bam!

"Is anybody in there? This is the HPD!"

Back then, Trish was young, but she was very precocious. She remembered Mama's instructions not to open the door for anyone. Trish ran to Tasha, grabbed her by the hand, and led her to the corner of the living room. "Shhh, Tasha, don't say nothing."

Bam! Bam! Bam!

"Is anyone in there? This is the HPD! Sweetie, my name is Officer Malone. Open the door."

Trish continued to back away from the door and into the corner.

Officer Malone paged headquarters and said, "This is Officer Malone to base. I'm going to need a social worker from Child Protective Services and another officer out here at 5100 Nairn. We have two kids abandoned in an old apartment."

Dust filled the air after Officer Malone kicked down the door. Tasha began to cry even more now that a complete stranger was standing in front of her. Trish hugged Tasha tightly as Officer Malone advanced toward her. "It's OK, baby," Officer Malone said as she moved closer to Trish and Tasha. "I'm here to make sure you are safe."

Officer Malone then heard a high-pitched scream coming from the master bedroom. I began to cry again, louder than ever. I had awoken from my sleep and needed some breakfast. Officer Malone went to the master bedroom, where I was lying on my mom's bed. "Oh my God," Officer Malone said upon entering the room and recognizing that an infant was also in the apartment. "This is Officer Malone to headquarters. Correction, we have two young children and an infant abandoned in an apartment."

"Malone, this is dispatch. Harris is on the way; please stand by!"

"Copy that," said Officer Malone. She reached and picked me up. "Hey, little guy, stop crying."

By this time, I was crying loudly. Officer Malone walked into the kitchen to see if she could find a bottle and noticed that there was nothing in the refrigerator. "Who would leave three children all by themselves?" she said as she walked back into the living room, where my two sisters were waiting quietly.

"What you doing to my brother?" said Trish as she started to hit Officer Malone on the legs. "Him don't know you!" She continued to punch Officer Malone's legs.

"Hey, now! Slow your roll, Ms. Lady."

"You OK?" said Officer Harris, who had just walked into the apartment.

"Yea, I'm OK, but this one is feisty; she's already assuming the role of the overprotective, parentified child."

"Where are the parents?" asked Officer Harris.

"I don't know. I searched the house, but there's no one here."

"Who would leave two kids and an infant in an old apartment?" asked Officer Harris.

"Beats me," said Officer Malone. She then nearly dropped me as she bent over in pain. Trish was still going at her legs.

"Gimmee my brother! Him don't know you!"

Officer Harris grabbed Trish and started talking to her, and Officer Malone hailed dispatch about the social workers, but then two social workers walked in. "Hi, I'm Melanie Carson, and this is my coworker, Sandy Johnson. We're with the Department of Family and Protective Services. Sorry our getting here took so long."

"You wouldn't be part of child protective services if you weren't late and oblivious," said Officer Malone.

"We do the best we can as social workers, and we can take it from here," replied Melanie.

"Well, this one is feisty," said Officer Harris, referring to Trish.

Officer Malone handed me over to Sandy and walked out the door. Trish and Tasha were huddled in the corner together. The two social workers approached them.

"You must be Trish. My name is Melanie. We're going to take you to a new family, where you can be safe." Melanie motioned for Trish and Tasha to come forward. Trish and Tasha refused to budge.

"I bet you are hungry, huh? Let's go get some food!" said Melanie, trying again to get Trish and Tasha to come out of the corner. They still would not move. Melanie got down on her knees and looked into Trish's eyes. "How would you like your own room and a new mom and dad? Would you like that?"

Trish nodded her head and walked with Melanie to the car, along with Tasha. Once Melanie had my two sisters in the car and buckled up, she shut the car door and instructed Sandy to contact her once she made it to the residence.

Eventually, CPS could not find a family to take in a group of three siblings, so the decision was made to separate us and place us in different foster homes.

"Where my brother?" screamed Trish as the other social worker drove off with me in the car. "I want my brother!"

"Trish, it's OK. Your brother will be fine. Stop yelling and sit back; you will be with your new family soon."

The more the social worker talked, the more Trish began to scream. She screamed more and more loudly as she peered out the car window, crying and reaching for her baby brother.

For as long as I can remember, child protective services has been a part of my life. The day that my mother abandoned my two sisters and me was the day that our lives changed forever. Some would say that I was born to deal with changes and struggle because before I was born, I had almost died. My sister Trish always told me how black I was when I came out of Mom. The umbilical cord had wrapped around my neck, and I came out lifeless. Yep, life had started to kick my ass before I could get out of the womb.

My CPS records show that as of May 18, 1992, I had been placed in six foster homes and one shelter and had two relative placements with my maternal grandmother. In fact, the only time we were all together was when we were placed with our grandmother. Living with our grandmother did not last long because our mom kept coming in and out and creating problems. My grandmother told the social worker that she could not protect us from our mother and that our mother was making poor choices that hurt our well-being. By 1990, CPS had gained primary managing conservatorship, also known as full custody, over my two sisters and me. Our mom, only in her twenties, had been married several times. Around that time, my mom's name was Shana Anise Obaseki Jackson. She cooperated sporadically with CPS, but on several occasions, CPS heard from her only once a year. As of May 18,

1992, CPS had not heard from my mom since April 19, 1991. Mom had a history of psychiatric hospitalizations for a bipolar disorder and had met several criteria for a borderline personality disorder. My records show that the social workers could not find my mom.

My father's name was Roland Osagie Obaseki. Records show that my dad visited me in 1988 and expressed an interest in having me live with him. Time passed, and CPS never heard from him again. CPS continued to look for relatives to contact for placement and found my uncle Ned Obaseki. Uncle Ned expressed interest in having me in his home in July 1991, but like everyone else, he appeared to change his mind within a month. Records show that my grandmother's name was Sally Ann Jackson and that she had not contacted CPS since June 27, 1991. She kept changing her phone number. Back then, I was starting a life in a world without any relatives willing to take me home.

On July 21, 1986, I was placed in the home of Hazel Carrington. Records show that I was two months old when I was placed in her home. However, CPS took me back on August 21, 1986. On that day, I was placed with my grandmother for one day, but my mom soon threatened her, and she feared for our safety. On the evening of the day when the threats were made, my two sisters and I were taken back to the nearest CPS office. From August 21, 1986, to September 24, 1987, I lived in the foster home of Earl Richardson. According to my records, this time, I was removed for having excessive diarrhea.

From September 24, 1987, to March 3, 1988, I resided in the foster home of Lester Evans. CPS removed me from this foster home because my grandmother decided to try to take care of us again. Believe it or not, although I was two years old at the time, I remember staying with my grandmother at her apartment. Everyone called her Meme. My grandmother lived in a four-bedroom townhome in southwest Houston with my aunt Chy, my aunt Shammy, and my uncle Roy. Aunt Chy's real name is Tarie, but everyone called her Chy because she was shy when she was younger. My aunt Shammy's real name is Sabrina, and to this day, no one really knows who started calling her that. My uncle Ray's real name is Raymond, but everyone called him Ray Ray, as a way to shorten his name. Although my mom's name is Shana, everyone called her

Peaches. How my grandmother took care of a husband, four teenagers, and three grandchildren amazes me to this day.

Although my two sisters and I stayed with our biological relatives for only three months, it was enough time for my little mind to capture memories. I remember the fun times going to the beach and playing in the pool with my sisters. "Trish, go take your sister to the bathroom and wash her off," my aunts would say. Trish would take Tasha by the hand as if she were her mother and would protect her, brooding over her every move to ensure she was OK. Life with my grandmother seemed to be normal. I remember swimming in the little plastic pools that were probably bought from Walmart. I remember one day in particular; my two sisters and I were in the pool and having a blast with our toys until I peed in the water. When I committed the transgression, Trish screamed, and that was the end of our swimming session. Although I was young, I was an obnoxious little rascal.

Living with my grandmother seemed normal. However, it was cut short. On May 4, 1988, my grandmother could not handle us anymore. One day, my mom came by the house in a rage. She snatched my sister Trish out of the car and busted her lip. I do not remember the arguments, the cop cars, and all the fistfights during those years. My grandmother does, and she often tells my two sisters and me, "Baby, I loved all of you, but I couldn't stand to see you all hurt by your mother. Your mother, Peaches, was hurt when she was younger, and the drugs got hold of her mind." So our grandmother decided to let us go.

From May 4, 1988, to August 18, 1988, I was placed in the home of Louis Ferrel. My case file explained that when the social worker came, I did not cry; I just raised my hands in hopes that he would pick me up.

On August 18, 1988, I was placed in the home of Mr. and Mrs. Brown. I had to be only four or five when I was placed with the Brown family. Mr. Brown was a very stern minister, and I remember being in church the majority of the time. My foster brothers, Michael and Xavier, and I loved playing in church, and on several occasions, Mr. Brown walked right out of the pulpit while he was preaching and popped us on the leg. I remember feeling embarrassed and crying loudly. Mrs. Brown was the church's choir director and often sang solos. Mrs. Brown had a very authoritative personality and was considered the "big mama" around the neighborhood. Like most African-American big mamas, Mrs. Brown loved the Lord. Sometimes Mrs. Brown would sing and would be so passionate about what she was singing that she would just fall to her knees and cry. Mrs. Brown would sing the hymn "Blessed Assurance" or the song "Just a Closer Walk with Thee," by Mahalia Jackson, and the whole church would often roar with applause! Some members would start running and jumping. Some of the men in the church would have their hands extended toward the air, with tears in their eyes. One day, Mrs. Brown sang so well that one lady got up and started to shout and leap. The ushers came forth and created a circle around her as she continued to jump and move her feet. When Mama would sing and just fall to her knees, members of the church would come and fan her with paper to help her regain her composure.

At the young age that I was, I did not fully understand why Mrs. Brown would cry after singing and drop to her knees. I had no idea that as I grew older, I would eventually find out the meaning behind Mrs. Brown's tears. For the most part, I spent most of my time with her. She used to tell me that I talked too much. I would ask her questions like, "How come that lady was running in church?"

To such questions, she would say, "Sister Verna caught the Holy Ghost, chile; now sit back and hush!"

I would respond by muttering a simple yes, but I was such a curious and inquisitive child that five minutes later, I would ask another question: "Mama, why you fell to the floor while you was singing?"

Mrs. Brown would say, "Boy, sit back and be quiet before I put something on yo' behind!"

Fearful of a whippin', I would not say anything else. After church on some days, my foster brothers and I would sit in the middle of the living room while Mrs. Brown would sit in her rocking chair and cut coupons. Being a toddler, I became easily excited at all of the fancy pictures of diamond earrings, pearl necklaces, and fancy cars, and I would point to the pictures and say, "Oooh, Mama, I'm gone get you this!"

Mrs. Brown would continue to rock in her chair, nod her head, and say, "Hmmm…hmmm."

Sometimes she would question me about my days at school. She would say things like, "Now what did I tell you about going up there to the schoolhouse cutting up?" When Mrs. Brown spoke in that tone, I would fall silent, not wanting to tell her what I was going to buy her at that point. In such moments, I only tried to prevent myself from getting into further trouble.

"You go to the schoolhouse to learn; you hear me, chile?"

"Yes, ma'am," I would say, and she would continue to rock in her chair, and I would continue to tell her what I was going to buy her in the future. Just when I thought she had forgotten what she was talking about, she would blurt, "Let me find out you cutting up at that schoolhouse again, and I'm gone put something on yo' behind!"

"Yes, ma'am," I would say, my go-to response.

While Mrs. Brown would rock in her rocking chair, sometimes my foster brothers and I would take our shoes and pretend that they were toy cars. Mrs. Brown could not afford to buy us real toy cars, so we had to use our imaginations. "Vroom! Vroom!" we would say together as the shoe-cars sped off on the carpet. As young children, my foster brothers and I would use our imaginations in such ways because we really did not have anything else to occupy our attention.

On some weekends, all of us would travel to West Columbia to visit Grammaw. Mrs. Brown's mother lived in a trailer in the country, and boy did we have fun! One of the best parts about traveling to West Columbia was the long car ride. I remember looking up at the window and seeing the different colors of the sky. My two foster brothers and I loved to rip, run, and play in the wide-open fields from sunup to sundown. Xavier and I loved to act as if we were animals in the jungle. We would pounce on each other and wrestle all evening. I remember the grass being so tall that we could not see past what was in front of us. Everywhere we looked, there were dandelion flowers spread across the open field. Xavier and I used to pick them up and blow them just to watch all the little particles float away in the air. We played until sunset because we knew that when the sun started to set, Mama wanted us back in the house.

"Y'all come on back in the house now," she would say, peering from the trailer's door, wiping her white apron. After playing in the country fields all day, we would work up mighty appetites and would desperately need baths. Mrs. Brown would put my two foster brothers and me in the tub to clean us all at once. Afterward, she would sit us down for the best food in the world. To this day, I cannot remember what we ate, but I know that every night, we went to bed full and on cloud nine.

I remember waking up in the mornings to the best breakfasts ever! In the mornings, we would wake up to the smell of cinnamon, butter, and oatmeal all mixed into a bowl of happiness. Some mornings, Mrs. Brown's mom would make rice, butter, and sugar. Mrs. Brown had an older daughter named Debra, but everyone called her DD. Sometimes, she would come to West Columbia too. She would make grits, eggs, and pan sausage for us. We ate like kings!

DD spent most of her time away in the military, serving in Operation Desert Storm. However, when DD was home, we would have a blast. She would come home and yell, "Y'all ready to go to the park?"

"Yayyy!" we would scream excitedly, running toward her and trying to tackle her to the floor. When DD was around, my foster brothers and I were even happier than usual. I loved riding in her black Honda Accord. One of my happiest memories with DD was when she would push us on the swings. We would yell to be pushed higher and higher, and DD would laugh and send us flying into what felt like the upper reaches of the atmosphere.

Whenever we left the park, DD would stop by the corner store and buy me a Hawaiian Punch and a bag of Cool Ranch Doritos. Another happy memory that I have of DD is that she would sit me on her lap and bite my ear as we watched TV.

But the days with DD would not last.

Her taking us to the park and rocking me on her lap grew distant. Weeks would drag by, and we would hardly see DD because of her military obligations. Throughout my stay with the Brown family, the social workers would come and see me monthly. According to my state records, the social worker wrote the following:

May 8, 1990

    Mrs. Brown, foster mother for Tyrone Obaseki, mentioned that she was planning on reenrolling Tyrone into the summer pre-K program, which was offered by Head Start. Mrs. Brown stated that Tyrone did so well in the Head Start program for the fall that she felt he needed to stay in as long as possible. I talked to Tyrone about his mother's lack of progress in therapy. We also discussed about how he felt about going to school. Tyrone seems to be very excited about continuing in the school program. Tyrone seems to be doing well in care.

June 11, 1990

    I spoke with Tyrone. We discussed his plans for the summer. Tyrone looked well and in good health. His major concern was if he would be able to see his mother and sister soon. I explained to him that I have lost contact with his mother, but he would be able to see his sister for a sibling visit within two weeks. Overall, Tyrone is doing well in care.

June 25, 1990

    Tyrone was picked for a family visit today to see his sisters. The children were happy to see each other. The children's mother, Mrs. Jackson, did not show up for the family visit, not that she was expected. However, she had called and spoken to Trish a few days before and knew that there would be a family visit. Mrs. Jackson continues to avoid the agency. The sibling visit went well. At the end of it, the children were reluctant to leave each other. The children were returned to their individual foster homes.

July 9, 1990

I spoke with Tyrone about his mother's lack of progress. Tyrone didn't seem to understand what I was talking about. I spoke briefly with Tyrone's foster mother. She asked about Tyrone's dental treatment and his immunization. Mrs. Brown was concerned about whether Tyrone was scheduled for treatment or not. I told Mrs. Brown that I would check on the dates for her.

August 1, 1990

I picked Tyrone and took him to his sisters' foster home and let him have a visit with his sisters. The visit lasted about one hour and forty-five minutes. They seemed to really enjoy being with each other, especially at Ms. Walker's foster home. The agency will continue to allow Tyrone to visit his sisters in Ms. Walker's foster home.

August 12, 1990

I played catch with Tyrone as he was telling me about Mrs. Brown's oldest daughter, DD, who happens to be in the army and going overseas. Tyrone does not like the fact that DD is going overseas and was asking about ways to prevent her from going. I explained to Tyrone that I had nothing to do with her going overseas or not.

I also asked him about whether he was ready to go back to school. He said yes. Tyrone said that he was happy to walk to school with his friends. I mentioned this to Mrs. Brown, and she said no, that he is not going to be able to walk; he has to catch the bus.

I informed Tyrone that he might be staying with Mrs. Brown for a very long time. Tyrone made no reply one way or the other. Tyrone seems to have an attachment to Mr. and Mrs. Brown. He is doing well in their care.

September 23, 1990

Again, Tyrone was picked up and transported to Mrs. Walker's foster home for a sibling visit with his sisters. The visit lasted about two to two and a half hours. At the end of the visit, Tyrone was transported back to his foster home. The visit went well, and the children enjoyed being with each other.

October 10, 1990

Tyrone was tired and sleepy. I did not have too much interaction with him. He did appear to be doing fine today. The foster mother had no questions. I gave her the twenty-fifth as our next family-visit date for Tyrone. I mentioned that I still have not heard from Tyrone's biological mother and that if I hear from her, I would try to set up a visit.

October 23, 1990

Children were brought into the office. They were able to interact with each other and play with each other, and they were together about an hour and a half. No one brought up their mother; they just seemed to be elated to be with each other. At the end of the family visit, the children were returned to their foster homes.

November 6, 1990

I spoke to Mrs. Brown, foster mother for Tyrone, and we discussed Tyrone's care. She stated that Tyrone was doing well in Head Start. I talked with Tyrone and asked him how he was doing. I talked about his mother and told him that she was in the hospital. Tyrone did not have anything to say about his mother; his biggest concern was his sisters and when he was going to see them. I told Tyrone that he would see his sisters in about three weeks, around Thanksgiving.

Mrs. Brown had stated that she had received a phone call from his mother about two months ago but hadn't heard from her since. Mrs. Brown asked if I had heard anything from his mother, and I told her that I still haven't heard anything.

December 4, 1990

I spoke to Mrs. Brown and Tyrone. Tyrone was having a problem talking to me because he was in a hurry to leave. Mrs. Brown's daughter was home, and Mrs. Brown stated that Tyrone loves being with her at all times and that she was leaving to go visit some friends and that Tyrone was going with her. I spoke to Tyrone briefly before he left and told him that his mother still hadn't called me but that I would set up a visit so he could see his sisters before Christmas, and then I asked him what he was expecting to get for Christmas. Tyrone stated that he wanted a Nintendo, Ninja Turtle, basketball, and electric drums. Once Tyrone left, I stayed and talked with Mrs. Brown for a little while. She again was concerned about Tyrone's mother, but I was unable to answer all the questions. I mentioned to Mrs. Brown that since the state of Texas has permanent managing conservatorship, it looked as if Tyrone would be staying with her a long time.

Mrs. Brown said she understood and didn't mind Tyrone staying. I talked to Mrs. Brown about taking full guardianship of Tyrone, and she said she was very reluctant about that.

January 8, 1991

I spoke to Mrs. Brown and Tyrone. We discussed Tyrone's behavior in Head Start and his behavior at home. Mrs. Brown said he was doing fabulous; she's having no problems out of him. I spoke to Tyrone, and Tyrone excitedly told me about his field trip he was about to go on this month. Tyrone stated that he was going to go on a trip to the fire station and how he wanted to be a fireman. Afterward, I spoke to Mrs. Brown again, and she stated that she was a little worried about her daughter going to Saudi Arabia and how that would affect her and Tyrone too. I mentioned to Mrs. Brown that I had finally heard from Tyrone's mother, the second or third day of this month, and that she had stated that she was coming in and seeing her children on the eighteenth. I asked her to give me a call again on the fifteenth to reassure me that she was going to be here. If she is, then I would be picking up Tyrone on Friday, the eighteenth, to take him for the family visit with his mother. Mrs. Brown was happy to hear that Mrs. Jackson was finally trying to visit her son, Tyrone.

February 5, 1991

I spoke with Mrs. Brown and Tyrone. We discussed Tyrone's progress in Head Start. Mrs. Brown assured me that Tyrone was doing well in the program and that she was not having any problems with him at the home. We also discussed the progress and lack of progress of Tyrone's mother, Mrs. Jackson. I mentioned the fact that Tyrone's mother was no longer called Mrs. Jackson but Mrs. Carlyle now, due to her recent marriage. I told Mrs. Brown that I would let her know the day Tyrone's mother is available for a visit. Tyrone and I spent a few minutes together. Tyrone showed me his homework from Head Start. Mrs. Brown and I also listened to him say his ABCs and applauded him on the fact that he knew his ABCs, and we helped him count to ten.

March 1, 1991

Tyrone's mother called and asked that I set up a family visit for the sixth of March and that she would definitely be there.

March 6, 1991

The children were extremely happy to see their mother. Their mother brought in her new husband, Mr. Carlyle. He was introduced to the social worker and the children. The children were skeptical at first to socialize or to interact with Mr. Carlyle; however, after an hour or so, the visit was extended to two hours. During the visit, the worker and the mother had a conference. The mother tried to explain to the worker why she wasn't able to make previous family visits. She assured the worker that she would be in for all future visits, from this day forward. She asked for a visit in two weeks, which we scheduled for the twentieth. We also discussed the fact that she needed to go back to therapy and that I would ask for the services through Yoakum Social Services and Dr. Penya, who was her previous therapist. She agreed and went back to visit with the children.

April 16, 1991

I spoke with Mrs. Brown and Tyrone. We discussed Tyrone's progress in Head Start and Tyrone's family situation. I heard that Tyrone's father is back in Africa and that he's expected to return to the States in December of 1991. At that time, we should be able to get in contact with him. His last statement before he went back home to Africa was that upon his return, he would be willing to do whatever is needed to get his son. I mentioned to Mrs. Brown that Tyrone's mother, is now located in the psychiatric center of mental health and mental retardation in the medical center. It looks as if she might be going up to Rusk State Hospital afterward as well and staying for about five months. I also talked to Mrs. Brown about the fact that I spoke with Tyrone's grandmother and that she expressed interest in having the children stay with her again. I mentioned to Mrs. Brown that I am not sure as to whether or not the agency will let Tyrone and his sisters stay, due to the fact that she returned the children three times already. Mrs. Brown said that she hopes that it all works out and that it has been a privilege for Tyrone to stay in her home.

July 1, 1991

Worker arrived at Mrs. Brown's home. Mrs. Brown reported that she is having problems with Tyrone: he throws temper tantrums, acts up, and is starting to hurt himself when he is angry (Tyrone had stopped doing this). Mrs. Brown requested today that Tyrone be removed from her home, and she feels he needs counseling. Tyrone has been attending Head Start at the Gulf Coast Center and has received speech therapy. Mrs. Brown gave me Ned Obaseki's number (575-9458). Tyrone was not present. He was at McGregor Park, where he goes every weekday from 10:00 a.m. to 3:00 p.m. Mrs. Brown said that she was not aware of a visit today. I rescheduled the visit for July 3 at 9:00 a.m. Mrs. Brown said that Tyrone's uncle Ned, expressed an interest in having him in his home.

July 2, 1991

Telephone call to Tyrone's uncle, Ned Obaseki:

Worker called Mr. Obaseki to ask whether or not he is interested in Tyrone being placed with him. Mr. Obaseki said he was interested and agreed to meet at Mrs. Brown's residence on July 3, 1991, so he could visit with Tyrone. Mr. Obaseki also said that he does not know where Tyrone's father, Roland Obaseki, is.

July 3, 1991

I arrived at Mrs. Brown's residence and called Tyrone into the room. Tyrone was excited and very friendly toward me today. He asked me questions about my car and showed me a hat he had made in school. Tyrone told me that he likes going to the park to play during the day. Tyrone's uncle Ned was unable to come to the visit but talked to Tyrone over the phone and stated that he would make arrangements with Mrs. Brown to visit Tyrone.

July 16, 1991

Met with my immediate supervisor to talk about Tyrone and his sisters' case. Supervisor advised that the children be placed with other relatives or remain in foster care because the grandmother has returned them three times.

August 13, 1991

I called Mr. Ned Obaseki to ask if he was still interested in keeping Tyrone. He replied that he was unable to take him. I told him that I was having to change Tyrone's foster home anyway because the foster mother wants him removed due to discipline problems. At this time, Tyrone needs stability that his family is unwilling or unable to give.

August 19, 1991

I called to request a foster home for Tyrone because his foster parents want him moved because of discipline problems.

August 22, 1991

Mrs. Brown told me that she had to take Tyrone out of his MacGregor Park School because he kept leaving the park and going to another park without permission. She also said that he hits and spits at other children. I told Tyrone that he needs to obey adults and listen to them when they tell him to do something, or he could get hurt. Tyrone said that he has been playing over the summer and that he does not want to go to school. He counted to twenty and told me that he couldn't read. I told him that he will learn to read in school and that he may make some new friends there. I told Mrs. Brown that I had called Foster Home Services for a new foster home, and that I would start looking for shelters if I didn't hear from Foster Home Services soon. Tyrone will start attending Hartsfield Elementary School on August 26, 1991, until he is removed from the Browns' foster home.

Living with Mr. and Mrs. Brown had its ups and downs. What my social workers did not know was that Mr. and Mrs. Brown whooped my behind for every little thing that I did. Every child in the foster home got spankings left and right. For instance, while attending the Head Start program at

Hartsfield Elementary School, I was often bullied on the playground. One day, I mustered the courage to stand up for myself, and I threw a rock at the boy who bullied me and busted his lip. "I showed him," I thought. His teacher came out, furiously grabbed me by the arm, and made me sit out the rest of playtime.

When I got home, it seemed as if it was going to be a normal evening. Mrs. Brown fixed us dinner, Mr. Brown was in the living room (watching TV as usual), and my foster brothers and I were on the floor, pretending our shoes were toy cars. As bedtime approached, Mrs. Brown put me in the tub, and before I knew it, she burst through the door and said, "Didn't I tell you not to go to the schoolhouse cuttin' up?" Mrs. Brown was holding a switch the size of Texas, long enough to scare any child. I had thought that Mrs. Brown would not find about the incident at school—boy was I wrong! After whooping me with the switch for about ten minutes, Mrs. Brown said, "Now dry it up! You better dry those eyes right now, before I give you something else to cry about! You go to the schoolhouse to learn. You hear me, boy?"

"Yes, ma'am," I said, fighting back the tears she had forbidden. The combination of the welts from the whipping, the soap, and the warm water made it difficult not to cry further.

Mrs. Brown, however, continued to bathe me. She said, "You better dry it up right now." After the bath, I went to my bed and cried some more.

Whippings seemed to be a common thing around the Browns' foster home, yet the social worker had no idea.

I can recall another time when my foster brothers and I were playing with other children after church. All of us were outside and running around and having a good time, just frolicking and playing. When we got home, Mr. Brown bent us all over his knee, one by one, and spanked our behinds raw for playing at church.

On September 8, 1991, my days of playing at church or at the Browns' house came to an end. It was the last Sunday that I would spend with the church and Mr. and Mrs. Brown. I remember that day as clearly as ever. Mama sang her heart out, and the ushers had to come cool her down with a church fan. Daddy preached a powerful sermon. However, on our way out of the church, something was different. I remember Mrs. Brown taking me by the hand, and members were coming up to her to talk. Many of them stooped to my level and gave me a hug. I remember looking up at Mrs. Brown and wondering what was going on. What I did not know was that on Thursday, September 12, 1991, I would be leaving Mr. and Mrs. Brown's house for good.

CHAPTER 2

The Martin Luther King Jr. Center

MY STATE RECORDS DOCUMENTED THAT my social worker received a phone call about my new placement:

September 11, 1991

    Telephone call from Lisa Nicholas:

    Ms. Nicholas said that the Martin Luther King Nursery is willing to take Tyrone. I contacted Shandra Love (659-7704) at the center, and we agreed to move Tyrone tentatively on September 12, 1991, and to place him at 2:00 p.m. because the foster mother wants him removed soon.

September 12, 1991

    A social worker arrived to take me to an orphanage.

    Tyrone was playing with a bucket when I arrived. He said that he was ready to go with me and was very excited; however, he believed that he would be returning to the foster home. I explained to Tyrone that he was going to a shelter, where there were going to be other children, and that he was not going back to this foster home again. Tyrone did not appear to understand, because he mentioned again that he would be returning to the foster parent. Tyrone helped me put his things in my car and said good-bye to Mr. and Mrs. Brown, the foster parents. Tyrone and I picked up his school papers at Hartsfield Elementary School and then went to the Martin Luther King Jr. Center. The children were taking a nap when we arrived, so Tyrone was told to take one also. I said good-bye to him and told him that I would see him Monday. Tyrone appeared to be excited about his new move, not knowing that he would not return to Mr. and Mrs. Brown's house.

Although I only stayed at the Martin Luther King Jr. Center for approximately two months, I can still remember what it was like to be there. The center was an emergency shelter located in the heart of Third Ward, one of the worst neighborhoods in Houston, Texas. The center was established to temporarily house abandoned children until child protective services could find foster homes for them. Back then, the center was vibrant and filled with crying babies and active children. Peggy "Mama Peg" Bush, the founder of the organization, was a pillar in the community. She served the children at the shelter as if we were her own children. People considered her to be the big mama around the neighborhood. Also, if a person walked into the center, he or she would not have any problem finding Mama Peg, who was the short lady with the Jerry curl that made her look as if she were always sweating. Across the days, the visitors would see Mama Peg giving people instructions on what to do with kids, answering phones, transporting children to doctors' appointments, and helping with the food in the kitchen. Occasionally, the visitor would see her yell and scream at people through a phone for not doing enough to help her care for the children in the shelter.

Although the shelter was booming with action, all the kids who were supposed to go to school never missed a day. The center happened to be a couple of miles away from Mr. and Mrs. Brown's house, so I was still able to attend the Head Start program at Hartsfield Elementary School. After school, I would join all the other children in the living room, and we all would watch TV together. Supper would be served shortly after we watched TV. At night, all of the children would split into groups of threes and sleep in designated houses around the neighborhood. Overnight parents would monitor us, and

I remember having so much fun in the houses at nighttime! The night staff would give us snacks, tell us to brush our teeth, and then tuck us into bed. When the night staff closed the door, we would act as if we were going to sleep. As soon as the door closed, we would get up, jump on the bed, giggle, and play until we were exhausted.

In the mornings, I remember waking up to a radio show called *On the Phone with Tyrone*. The overnight parents would cook us breakfast, and then we would head over to the main building to join the other children. Mornings at the King Center were always fun during the week, primarily because most of us got a chance to rip, run, and play because of the lack of volunteers.

A very nice lady by the name of Ms. Love worked during the week and was always nice to be around. "Morning, baby," she would say when I ran into the building. Ms. Love had a funny way of saying things. For instance, most of the time, I would run into the building, and I would drop my backpack somewhere on the ground. Ms. Love would say, "Where is your pack-pack, baby; go get your pack-pack." Ms. Love would get up and stand by the door while I went back outside to pick up my pack-pack. Ms. Love was a heavyset lady with a big smile and a Jerry curl.

Unfortunately, not everyone was as pleasant as Ms. Love. One particular staff member on the weekends was very mean. I remember eating breakfast, and the staff member would comb my hair so fast that it hurt. Perhaps I had long hair when I was at the shelter, because my hair would fly out when she combed it. While living at the King Center, I began to realize that social workers were more a part of my life than I had known.

September 16, 1991

A social worker arrived to take me to a doctor.

Tyrone was ready for me when I arrived and was excited to be going somewhere. He was seen by Stella Myers at the clinic on 5100 SW Freeway and was pronounced healthy. During the drive back, Tyrone took a nail file out of the caseworker's purse and began to file his finger when told that he would not be getting a Coke. I took the file away and told him that he is supposed to file his fingernails, not his fingers. Tyrone asked when he was going home. I informed Tyrone that he was not going back to his old foster home and that I am trying to find him a new good home. Tyrone stated that the foster home he was in was a good one, and he told me that he should not be moved so much. I told him that his foster mother, Mrs. Brown, was taking a vacation from fostering. Tyrone seemed to accept this explanation.

Tyrone needs permanence. He also needs to be assessed for hyperactivity because he is very active. Tyrone still appears to not understand that he will not be going back to the foster home.

September 26, 1991

A social worker placed a call to verify whether a foster home had been found.

Phone call was placed to see if a foster home was found for Tyrone. Ms. Nicholas informed me that she had not found a foster home for Tyrone and that she probably would not be able to until he is psychologically evaluated. Ms. Nicholas stated that he would have to be moved to another shelter if placement was not found before October 12, 1991.

October 1, 1991

A social worker placed a call to schedule a psychological assessment.

I placed a phone call to Sydney Wright with Yoakum Psychological Services. Ms. Wright called to tell me that she has an opening for a psychological evaluation. I scheduled Tyrone for October 10, 1991, at 8:30 a.m.

October 9, 1991

A social worker placed a call to check on me.

The director of the program stated that Tyrone could stay at the shelter for another thirty-day period. She also said that Tyrone is very busy and willful. The director stated that Tyrone left the program on his Big Wheel, saying he was going to his foster home. Tyrone was found quickly with no problems. I told the director that I would be picking Tyrone up at 7:45 a.m. on October 10, 1991, for his psychological evaluation.

October 9, 1991

Yoakum Psychological Services called my social worker to reschedule the appointment.

The psychological evaluation was rescheduled to October 25, 1991, at 1:30 p.m., due to the doctor not being available.

October 15, 1991

A social worker called the CPS clinic.

I called the clinic to get information on where I could have Tyrone evaluated for hyperactivity. Brenda Murphy referred me to Bluebird (790-5046).

October 15, 1991

Telephone contact to Bluebird:

Placed call to schedule an evaluation for Tyrone. I was told they need a doctor's statement before they can schedule an appointment with Tyrone.

October 15, 1991

A social worker placed a call to request a doctor's appointment.

Ms. Murphy reviewed Tyrone's chart and said that she feels counseling should be pursued instead of testing for hyperactivity. Ms. Murphy said to wait for the results of the psychological evaluation and to follow its recommendations. She also said to send Yoakum Psychological Services a copy of the Denver Developmental Screening Test that was done on Tyrone.

October 15, 1991

    A social worker received a call from the Martin Luther King Jr. Center about my behavior.

    The director of the program said that Tyrone's teacher reported that Tyrone has been having behavior problems at school. He's trying to be good and having a hard time. He's fighting and hitting people. The director stated that she gave Tyrone some cough drops before school and feels he may have a sugar sensitivity. Tyrone's teacher stated that his behavior has gotten worse.

October 24, 1991

    A social worker had a conference with Latonia Woods, a supervisor.

    Supervisor wants me to see if I have a FACTS report in the system and to update it if I don't. Supervisor informed me to send a certified letter to Tyrone's uncle to ask about background information and to consider placing all the children in adoption. Supervisor stated that I could "wash my hands" of the maternal grandmother when I told her that Ms. Smith had changed her phone number, and it is now unlisted. Supervisor wants me to look for the address of the children's mom's new husband.

October 25, 1991

    A social worker transported me to Yoakum Psychological Services for an evaluation.

    I picked Tyrone up from school. He was ready to go. Tyrone sat fairly still in the car, but he would not be still at Yoakum. He played with toys, jumped on the couches, and opened office doors. He did not obey me when I told him to stop jumping on the couches or opening doors. Mr. Doogen, the evaluator, said that Tyrone did well in the interview but that he was active.

After the psychological evaluation, my social worker wrote the following:

I returned Tyrone to the shelter after his psychological evaluation, and Tyrone ran off to the playground and told me that he did not want to talk and that he was ready to play. Tyrone appeared to not hear me or not pay me any attention when I asked him to be still for a second. However, being still in the car, where his movement is restricted, does not seem to be a problem.

November 6, 1991

A social worker received a phone call from the shelter.

The director of the Martin Luther King Center had a question about the shelter extension, on which I had written that Tyrone hurts himself when angry. The director stated that she had never seen Tyrone hurt himself, and she was wondering where I got that from. I told the director that Tyrone's old foster mother reported this. The director stated that Tyrone is still very busy but that he appears to be more mischievous than misbehaving. The director stated that Tyrone is very nice and has started complimenting her on her hair and clothes and has asked her if she has a husband.

November 21, 1991

A social worker received a phone call from DFPS supervisor.

Supervisor told me that the shelter called about Tyrone and said that he needs to be taken out of the shelter. Supervisor stated that she has spoken with So La Ti and that I needed to consider placing Tyrone and his sisters there.

December 6, 1991

A social worker visited me at the shelter.

Tyrone was playing with toys when I arrived. He showed me a bag of toys that he had gotten at school and ran around the room, playing with a balloon. He asked me when he was going home. I said I didn't know exactly, but I hoped it would be soon. I told him that I'm trying to find him a special home. Tyrone then wrote his name on a piece of paper and wrote my name as I spelled it for him. Tyrone didn't seem to understand why he is still at the shelter. He appears to be worried about what is going to happen to him, and he may be feeling forgotten.

December 11, 1991

A supervisor takes me to visit with my two sisters.

I picked the children up from their schools. Tyrone was excited to see his sisters and gave them hugs. We came back to the office, and I gave them each a Christmas present. Trish and Tasha looked happy to get a present, but Tyrone was upset and stated, "All I got was a backpack," although he had previously asked for a backpack. I tried to show Trish and Tasha how to play a card game, but Tyrone began throwing toys and yelling, so I had to stop and sit him in my lap until he calmed down. I asked Tyrone if he wanted to play cards with us, and he said yes, but when he began losing, he got upset and threw the cards to the floor. I told him that it wasn't nice to throw cards and that he had lost since he threw all his cards away. I then sat him in my lap and asked him if he was ready to go back to school. He said no, and I told him that he needed to act better or I would end the visit and take him back to school. He said OK and calmed down a little. Trish and Tasha played the card game while I held Tyrone. The children were disappointed because they thought their mom and other family members were going to come. I told them that I did not know where their family was but that if I find them, I will arrange a visit. During the ride back to the school, Trish held Tyrone in her lap. They gave each other hugs when I dropped them off at their separate schools.

December 16, 1991

A social worker placed a phone call to check on me at the shelter.

The director of the shelter reported that Tyrone was caught stealing a wallet at school on Friday and that money had been stolen in two separate incidents from workers at the shelter over the weekend. The director stated that she does not know for sure that it was Tyrone. The director stated that Tyrone has been worried that Santa Claus won't find him to bring him presents, although she has been reassuring him that Santa Claus will find him. I told the director that I had received the psychological evaluation and sent it to a therapeutic foster home for them to review and that hopefully, I would hear from them early this week.

December 27, 1991

A social worker visited me at the shelter.

Tyrone was watching television when I arrived. He ran to me and said hello. He was still very active and ran around the room during most of the visit. He did sit still for a few minutes to write his name on some paper. Tyrone asked when he was leaving, and I said that I didn't know and that I am trying to find a foster home. Tyrone then became distracted and started playing with his Big Wheel, so I told him good-bye and left.

My days at the Martin Luther King Jr. Center were coming to an end. The days of playing as if I were asleep at night, jumping on the beds, and waking up to *On the Phone with Tyrone* would soon be over.

December 16, 1991

A social worker placed a phone call to Vicki Owunda at Peace Children's Home.

Ms. Owunda said that she had received the psychological evaluation on Tyrone and that she wants to arrange a preplacement visit. We initially said December 19, 1991 but then decided to do it after Christmas because Tyrone is worried that Santa Claus won't find him, and he's starting to feel uncomfortable about Christmas at the shelter.

December 16, 1991

A social worker placed a phone call to the director of the Martin Luther King Jr. Center:

I told Ms. Love that Ms. Owunda wants to do a preplacement visit but that we will do it after Christmas because Tyrone is worried about Santa Claus finding him. The director said that will be fine.

December 27, 1991

A social worker placed a phone call to Vicki Owunda, director of Peace Children's Home.

Spoke to Ms. Owunda about arranging a preplacement visit for Tyrone Obaseki. Ms. Owunda agreed that I could do the preplacement on December 30, 1991, and on December 31, 1991, for placement.

December 27, 1991

A social worker placed a call to the King Center to discuss preplacement.

Informed the staff at the King Center that I would be picking up Tyrone on December 30, 1991, at 10:45 a.m. for preplacement and that I would be placing him at the RTC on December 31, 1991. The staff member stated that she will pack his things and tell him tonight that he's moving.

CHAPTER 3

The Smallest One

~~

As a young child, I did not know why I was frequently moved from place to place. Whenever the social worker arrived, all I knew was that I was about to go somewhere. Just going somewhere was just enough to put a smile on my face. I would soon recognize that my next placement would be a placement like no other.

December 30, 1991

A social worker arrived to transport me to a preplacement visit at the Peace Children's Home to see if I would like it.

I picked up Tyrone from the shelter. He gave me a hug when he saw me and said that he was ready to go. It was explained to him on Friday that he was leaving. Little Tyrone helped me pack his bags. During the car ride, Tyrone followed our progress to the group home by looking at my key map, and he asked several times if we were "there yet." Tyrone also said that he was ready to go and was happy.

Ms. Owunda greeted us at the door when we arrived. She showed Tyrone his room and where he would be eating. Tyrone was excited, and he played Nintendo and foosball with the other boys.

Ms. Owunda gave me a list of paperwork that she needed, and I told her that I would bring it by tomorrow when I picked up Tyrone for his physical. Tyrone appeared to understand where he was going. He also appeared to be satisfied with the placement.

December 31, 1991

    A social worker arrived to place me at a new orphanage, the Peace Children's Home.

    I picked up Tyrone from the foster home. He came riding down the hall of the King Center on his Big Wheel. Several of the other boys in the home were helping him with his coat and the Big Wheel. Tyrone left me with no problems. He sat in the backseat and played with a backgammon game that he had brought with him. Tyrone was very active when we got inside the building, and I had to hold his hand or continually chase him because he would run down the halls. Tyrone eventually broke free of my hand and ran to the back rooms to play.

I remember arriving at Peace Children's Home as if it had happened just yesterday. Arriving at the new orphanage was a pretty fun day, as far as I can remember. At the time, I did not know that the orphanage I was being placed in was formerly an old day care. As I sat in my social worker's car, looking out the window, I wondered what the other kids were like. Excitement flooded my body—I could not wait to meet the new kids!

"Are we there yet?" I kept asking.

The social worker would say, "Almost, for the fifteenth time," counting higher each time I asked my question.

As I looked at the key map, my little feet barely reached over the seat. I could not wait to get out of the car and ride my Big Wheel. When the social worker made a right-hand turn on River Valley and into the parking lot of the shelter, she said, "We're here!"

"Yayyy!" I screamed as I waited for her to open the car door. After she did so, I remember running to a tall glass door and being greeted by a lady with a big smile.

"Hey there! My name is Mrs. O.! How are you doing?"

"My name is T-T-Tyrone!" I yelled and stuttered; then I ran through the facility, from room to room. Peace Children's Home seemed humongous to me because I was a very tiny five-year-old. I peered into one room, and the room was dark and filled with a lot of teenagers. They all seemed to be huddled around the TV.

"Don't go in there!" said Mrs. O. as she closed the door. Everywhere I went, Mrs. O. followed with a big smile on her face. The social worker brought my Big Wheel into the shelter, and I remember jumping on it and riding all throughout the facility's long hallways.

"Come on in here, baby, and sit for a second," said Mrs. O., and we walked into her office. The social worker had Mrs. O. fill out important paperwork, while I sat on the couch waiting for them to finish. Being the inquisitive child that I was, I remember simply looking around at every aspect of the office. Mrs. O. had a big metal desk in her office that was filled with papers. The large windows beamed slender rays of light onto her face as she filled out the paperwork. As Mrs. O. and the social worker finalized the paperwork, I looked from side to side, trying to figure out who was whispering. I looked behind me and noticed that there were six other boys my age pointing and whispering, trying to figure out who I was.

One of the boys waved and whispered, "What is your name?"

"My name is Tyrone," I responded, grinning widely.

Before I could ask them what their names were, Mrs. O. noticed the other boys and said, "Go back to your area—right now!"

The six little boys ran back to their area and waited for me to come to the room. Once the paperwork was signed, the social worker gave me a hug and left me to live at my new home. I remember watching the social worker leave with Mrs. O. beside me.

"Let's introduce you to the other children," said Mrs. O., and she walked me to the back. I remember the orphanage being divided into big girls, little girls, big boys, and little boys. Each area had its own shower and living room. As Mrs. O. and I approached the back area designated for the little boys, I noticed that there was a lot of tussling and noise.

"This is your area," said Mrs. O. as she walked me into a room with other boys. I noticed that they were much bigger than I, even though we were close in age. They were running around and playing, but Mrs. O. said, "Ya'll clean this mess up and listen up! This is Tyrone, and I want you to be nice to him. He's much smaller than all of you, and I don't want to see anyone hurt."

"Yes, ma'am," the boys whined.

Mrs. O. took me to the back and said, "This is where you will be sleeping."

As I looked around my bedroom, I remember seeing three sets of metal bunk beds with thin mattresses. My new room was filled with five other boys. Mrs. O. walked me back into the living room and introduced me to her two sons, Malachi and Troy. I would soon learn that Mrs. O's two children spent all their time in the little boys' unit instead of staying where the teenagers resided.

As Mrs. O. was leaving, she yelled, "Craig, put some pants on and stop running around in your underwear!"

"Awww, man!" he said, quickly running to put on some pants.

After Mrs. O. left, her son Malachi whispered to everybody, "Hold on, let me make sure Mama gone." He peeked his head out and around the doorway and said, "Clear!"

After Malachi made his declaration, all of the children started to fight and wrestle. Some of the boys pulled out makeshift swords, which they had made out of paper, and pretended to chop each other in half. Some of the boys had their shirts off and were using them to pop other boys upside the head. As I watched from the sidelines, I noticed that all of the children eventually formed a gigantic ball on the floor. Needing no instruction, I excitedly climbed on the couch and cried, "Kowabunga!" I then pounced right onto the big ball of wrestling children and landed on everybody with a loud thud. I remember that as I started to wrestle, I heard some of the boys shout, "My arm!" and "Ouch, you turd! No fair!" and other similar things. Some boys were just giggling the whole time. Being the smallest in the group, I always managed to break free from the ball of wrestling children. Every time I broke free, I would pounce on everybody all over again. Eventually, someone started to cry, so a staff member walked in and yelled, "What's going on in here?"

"He hurt my arm!"

"He bit me!"

"He cheated!"

The staff member yelled through the babble: "Stop horseplaying so you won't have these problems! If I have to come in here one more time, everyone will be on EBT for a week!"

Not knowing what EBT was led me to ask the other children what it meant. To my surprise, EBT meant early bedtime! Unfortunately, the staff's threats did not stop everyone from horseplaying. As the staff member walked out, everyone teased the kids who had started to cry, saying things like "You're a titty-witty baby!" We continued to laugh and play until dinnertime.

When the plates started to shuffle in the kitchen, we knew it was time for dinner. "All right, everyone, form a single-file line for dinner!" a staff member yelled.

Everyone lined up and went to the cafeteria excitedly. As I would find out later, everyone was always extra excited to eat because all of the units would be together.

On the first day, since I was the smallest, I thought I could go to the front of the line. Instead, I was met with a "Hey, go to the end of the line, you little turd!" As I made my way to the back of the line, I heard some commotion near the front of the building. I ran out of the line and noticed that the big boys were coming in loudly and excitedly. Wanting to tune in on the excitement, wondering what was going on, I ran up to them.

One of the boys picked me up and said, "We won the football game, little man!" I noticed the boy was smiling from ear to ear. "Hey, everyone, listen up: let's make him our little mascot!"

All of the boys huddled around, and one of the boys put his shoulder pads and helmet on me. Excited to be wearing football gear, I ran out of the room and into the cafeteria to show all of the other children. Running around with an oversized T-shirt, a football helmet, and shoulder pads, I looked somewhat funny. When I entered the cafeteria, all of the children started to point and laugh.

"Hey, look at the retard!" one of them yelled.

The cafeteria thundered with laughter. My first day at Peace Children's Home seemed to have gone well.

Overall, my days at Peace Children's Home started out fun! Being one of the youngest children in the orphanage meant I was able to get away with things that other children could not. For instance, I remember riding my

Big Wheel throughout all of the orphanage's hallways. I remember zipping around and crashing into the walls because the marble floors were so slippery.

Around the time that I arrived at Peace Children's Home, the shelter bought a big, brown Ford Econoline van, which could carry fifteen people. I remember waking up one morning and looking out the window, feeling awe at how big it was. I had never seen anything that enormous up close! Excited and inquisitive about what I was looking at, I left the window area and tried to open the front door to get a closer peek at the van.

"Boy, sit your little butt down somewhere, and stop leaving your area!" yelled Mrs. O. I ran back to the room to get my Big Wheel and continued my daily mission to turn the hallways into my personal racetrack. On some days, though, my hot-rodding was not that easy! Some of the older boys were not happy about my rolling through the halls and making loud noises on my Big Wheel. One of the residents, "Big Seth," would always push me off my Big Wheel and hold it over his head as if he were going to throw it. Of course, as any five-year-old would do, I would start to cry loudly and scream. I would yell, "Give me my b-b-bike!" or something similar. Somehow, my stuttering problem always got the best of me when I was upset.

In these situations, Big Seth would chortle. He would then tease me with some comment, such as "Say good-bye to your Big Wheel!" His long blond hair would spill over his face during his teasing gesticulations. However, Big Seth never really got around to throwing my Big Wheel—thanks to Mrs. O, who somehow always managed to stop him in time.

"Leave Tyrone alone. You know he's the baby," she would say, motioning for Big Seth to put the bike down. Mrs. O. was always my saving grace and protected me from the mean boys in the orphanage. Unfortunately, Mrs. O.'s protection would not save my Big Wheel for long.

I remember waking up one morning and hearing a lot of commotion outside. I ran outside and noticed that one of the staff members, Ms. Miriam, was being trained on how to drive the van. Ms. Miriam had the van jolting forward and backward, as if she were a teenager just learning how to drive. Other staff members were flailing their arms up and down, telling her to either stop or move forward or slow down. As I stood staring out a window,

I remember feeling as if something bad was about to happen. I looked to the other side of the parking lot and saw my Big Wheel. "I wonder how my Big Wheel got outside," I said to myself.

Before I knew it, Ms. Miriam had backed the van over my Big Wheel. I ran outside, crying and screaming. "My Big Wheel! My Big Wheel!" I cried repeatedly. (You have to understand that up to that moment, my Big Wheel had been the most important thing to me.) Mrs. O. ran outside behind me, fearing the worst after hearing my loud screaming.

"What's going on?" she yelled, looking from side to side.

I could not get my words out because I was crying so heavily. Mrs. O. looked at the van and the broken Big Wheel and said, "Hold on, Tyrone. Let's see if we can fix it."

One of the staff members, Mr. Mac, brought the broken Big Wheel and set it in front of me. He tried to place the wheel back on the frame.

"Can you fix it, Mr. Mac?" asked Mrs. O. as she stared at the Big Wheel.

Mr. Mac failed to reattach the wheel and said, "No, I believe it's broken."

I continued to cry loudly until Mrs. O. said, "Hush, child. You'll get another bike." She took me by the hand and led me back inside the facility, to where the other little boys were. Devastated, I walked with my head cast downward, rubbing my eyes in sadness.

During my first month at Peace Children's Home, my social worker was busy handling her duties to ensure that I was in a safe place. According to my state records, my social worker was now looking to move me again and heavily monitoring my behavior.

January 16, 1992

> My social worker visited with a supervisor and the Permanency Planning Board.
>
> Worker met with Belinda Wright. Mrs. Wright stated that Tyrone's current placement at Peace Children's Home is not appropriate due to the other boys being older. Tyrone needs a much more nurturing environment because he has not attached to anyone and

because Ms. Owunda is currently only licensed for boys ages six to eighteen years old (Tyrone is five years old). I was instructed to check out Cullen Bayou and the Pendleton foster home as possible placements for Tyrone. Belinda Wright agreed to check out possible MHMR placements for Tyrone.

January 21, 1992

My social worker met with a supervisor.

Supervisor and I agreed that I would present this case at the Permanency Planning Board. Informed supervisor that I needed to move Tyrone because the PAC committee does not agree with him being at Peace Children's Home. Supervisor stated that it would be best if I could move Tyrone soon, before he becomes more attached to his environment.

January 21, 1992

My social worker placed a call to Cullen Bayou to find a new placement and documented the following response:

I was told that there are no beds for boys at Tyrone's level of care but that there are beds available for level six. I replied that I did not feel Tyrone was a level six.

January 21, 1992

My social worker placed a call to a supervisor about placing me in a foster home.

Supervisor stated that she followed up with the Pendleton foster home and stated that they are full.

January 30, 1992

My social worker called Peace Children's Home.

Today, I spoke with Ms. Owunda about the placement committee's decision to move Tyrone and told her that I am trying to locate a placement for him. Ms. Owunda stated that she had spoken with my supervisor about Tyrone and did not want him to be moved. However, she understood that we have to do what's best. She also said that Tyrone has improved, but he does need more work. I told her that I would get back with her regarding my plans for Tyrone.

January 31, 1992

My social worker met with Ladessa Sayles.

It was decided that termination of parental rights is appropriate. I was given the tasks to obtain Tyrone's mother's records from Rusk State Hospital, to staff with agency attorney, to access parent locator and conduct diligent search, to locate ad litems assigned, to begin a lifebook for Tyrone, and to initiate sibling visits.

February 10, 1992

My social worker received a call from the Texas branch of CASA.

Texas CASA stated that they will be doing a diligent search.

February 13, 1992

My social worker placed a call to Peace Children's Home.

I told Ms. Owunda that Ms. Ladessa Sayles had approved Tyrone's staying in her facility, and I asked if Tyrone could be brought in for a sibling visit. Ms. Owunda said that he can come in the mornings, and we arranged for visits to occur on the third Thursday of each month, from 10:00 a.m. to 11:00 a.m., with the first visit on February 20, 1992. I asked Ms. Owunda how he was doing in school, and she said Tyrone is having problems.

Waking up in the mornings to go to school was exciting for me because I loved school! It was a chance for me to meet new people. Ms. Owunda walked in every morning and sang, "Good morning to you! Good morning to you! We're all in our places with sun-shiny faces! This is the way to start our new day!" Whenever Mrs. O. walked in singing this song, most of the boys covered their heads with their pillows. "Go away!" they would yell as they turned over in their beds. Mrs. O. would continue to sing and attempt to pull the covers off everyone, one by one.

"Wake up, people!" Mrs. O. would say, flickering the lights on and off. "T. Oba, are you woke?" she would say to me as she pulled away my covers. "Wake up, T. Oba. Off to school you go."

"Yes, m-m-ma'am, I'm woke," I would reply, rubbing my eyes.

Needing very little instruction, I would always jump up and quickly get dressed for school. The night staff washed our clothes during their shift and would place them on a table in the back of the cafeteria. Almost every day, I had to run to the cafeteria to get a pair of socks because I only had a few pairs. Whenever I ran into the cafeteria at that time, everyone in the orphanage would be at the back table looking for socks, T-shirts, and undergarments. Some of my peers would be fighting over clothes. Whenever I looked down to the floor, all I could see was rows and rows of bare feet scuffling the floor. All of the kids would try to move past the next person to get to the front, where they would retrieve their selected garments.

One day, at this time in the morning, I saw the older boys with their muscle shirts on; some of them were even shirtless. There were two boys named McKinley and Dillan; they were bigger and more muscular than everyone else. When they walked in, everyone just moved to the side and let them through. There was a rumor that McKinley beat someone up for jumping in front of him. One would think that the big girls would let the guys get their stuff first because the guys were stronger.

Wrong!

The girls were trying to push their way to the front of the line too! My small stature left me with few options. Asking one of the other big boys would not work because it was so noisy. All of the little boys who were actually much taller than I were still in the back just waking up. I tried yanking one of the boys' shorts, but the boy just scooted over. I tried jumping on my tippy toes, and that still did not work. Confused and having no further ideas, I bent down and bit one of the older boys on the ankle.

"G-g-give me some socks!" I pleaded.

The other boy reached down in pain. "Somebody get this badass kid! Man, he bit me!" he screamed.

Just before he positioned himself to push me, a girl named "Big K" yelled, "If you touch him, I'll whoop your ass!" The nickname Big K was the shorter version of "Big Katrina," and she was the tallest girl in the facility, weighing about two hundred fifty pounds.

"He bit me!" the boy screamed.

"So what, fool? He little, and you should've let him go to the front of the line anyway!" said Big K. She rolled her eyes. "Get the hell out my way," she said to the other boy after picking me up.

"Baby, what do you need?" she asked me.

"Some s-s-socks," I stuttered.

Big K reached to the table and grabbed me a pair of socks. She put me back down, and I ran out of the cafeteria, yelling, "Th-th-thank you!"

As I ran back to the little boys' unit, I noticed that some of the boys who had been sleeping were just now heading to the cafeteria to get some socks and undershirts. During the time that they were in the cafeteria, I was able to get first pick at watching cartoons. One of my favorite cartoons was called *Beast Wars*. In general, however, I never got to finish any of the episodes because the staff would rush everyone to the bus before the episodes were over.

Unfortunately, I was not able to ride the bus in the beginning. I remember a lady named Mrs. Sarena pulling me from the bus line and saying, "Tyrone, you gotta ride with me." As Mrs. Sarena led me to her car, she said, "Now don't you go to this schoolhouse and act like some of these other boys, who only try to scare all the white folks."

"Yes, m-m-ma'am," I said as she opened one of her car's doors.

Mrs. Sarena drove an old Cadillac; it was so ancient that she had to warm it up for twenty minutes before pulling out of the driveway. The plush brown seats were big enough to keep everyone in the car safe. As we pulled out of the driveway, I remember Mrs. Sarena turning up the radio to "Addicted Love" by BeBe and CeCe. I remember that I gazed happily out of the window and watched the trees and other cars filled with children heading to school. Before

I knew it, Mrs. Sarena was walking me into Smith Elementary School to enroll me in pre-K. I remember sitting in the front office for what seemed to be hours. The school had humongous windows in the front, which let large beams of sunlight into the halls. After I sat there for a while, Mrs. Sarena tied my shoes, and one of the teachers led me to my classroom. The front door said "E. Eckeroth."

As my guide led me into the classroom, I remember all of the students huddled around Mrs. Eckeroth's rocking chair. She was reading the students a story until I walked in.

"OK, class, it looks like we have a new student," said my new teacher. "What's your name?"

"M-m-my name is Tyrone," I stuttered.

My new teacher smiled happily at me and said, "Welcome to pre-K. You can sit right here as we finish story time."

I remember that my first day of pre-K at my new school was very fun! I remember a fun-filled day of coloring and laughing with some of the other children. To my surprise, preschool students did not stay at school the whole day.

Since I could not ride the bus, Mrs. Sarena picked me up from school. "How was school?" she asked, looking at me in the rearview mirror.

"I c-c-colored," I said, and I showed her my picture.

Mrs. Sarena nodded her head and said that I did a good job. When she and I arrived back at the orphanage, she fixed me a peanut-butter-and-jelly sandwich and said, "When you get done, go in the back and take a nap."

Hearing the word *nap* made me upset. "I don't wanna take a nap!" I screamed. After I ate my sandwich, I made an attempt to run and hide from Mrs. Sarena.

"Boy, you got five minutes to get your little butt back over here so you can take a nap!" said Mrs. Sarena. She hustled through the halls, looking for me, hearing nothing but my little feet running around. "Boy, you better get to this room and lie down!" she yelled. After about five minutes, Mrs. Sarena eventually caught me making a beeline toward the door to go back outside. "Gotcha!" she said as she threw me over her shoulder.

I yelled and kicked and said, "I don't wanna take a nap!"

"Fine, if you don't wanna take a nap, then you sitting with me! I'm not missing my stories because of you." (Mrs. Sarena would watch *The Young and the Restless* and *All My Children* devotedly each day.) As Mrs. Sarena sat on the couch and watched her stories, she held me in her arms, and I wiggled and cried for her to let me go.

The little minidrama just described became our habitual routine. What is funny in retrospect was that I did not want to go to bed and that I did not want her to hold me in her lap. I was not stronger than Mrs. Sarena, so every day, I would end up crying myself to sleep in her arms. Once I fell asleep, Mrs. Sarena would place me in my bed in the other room.

After my naps, I would wake up to loud noises due to all of the other boys returning from school. Some boys would always fall into wrestling, and other boys who wanted to watch afternoon cartoons would scream for everyone to hush so that they could hear the TV. The routine usually followed the same pattern as the scene described next.

One day, a boy named George yelled, "Come on! *Spiderman* is on! Cut it out!" to the wrestlers. He leaned closer to the TV. George was the husky one in the group, and he loved superheroes. George never wrestled unless he absolutely had to.

"Oh shut up, fat ass," a boy named Eduardo said, chucking a pencil at George.

"Cut it out, asswipe!" George yelled, chucking the pencil back.

Before I knew it, Eduardo had tackled George, and everyone was in a big ball on the floor and wrestling. Although I had just woken up, I knew exactly what time it was! I ran, climbed on the couch, and jumped off screaming, "Kowabunga!" I landed right on the ball of wrestling children. As usual, all of the children in the little boys' unit wrestled until a staff member came in to take us to dinner.

Life at Peace Children's Home seemed to be the average life of an orphan.

CHAPTER 4

I Cannot Breathe

ON SOME DAYS AFTER SCHOOL, I was greeted by my social worker. My case file says the following:

February 24, 1992

My social worker visited me at Peace Children's Home. Tyrone was watching cartoons when I arrived. He asked when he was supposed to see his sisters, and I told him that he could see them next week maybe. Tyrone also asked for my phone number, and I told him that Ms. Owunda has it and that he can ask her when he wants to call me. Tyrone had several spots on his face and arms from chicken pox. Ms. Owunda said that his behavior is improving and that they have had to be firm with him and take away privileges when he disobeys. She said that he is doing well otherwise.

Time was passing by, and it seemed as if CPS was ignoring the fact that Peace Children's Home was not conducive to my growth and development. Peace Children's Home was a level-six facility for children with extreme behavior problems, and as time progressed, I noticed changes at the orphanage. Traumatic things started to happen, and these things frightened me as a child. I remember waking up one morning and sitting in the corner, playing with my Ninja Turtles. Suddenly, I heard a loud door slam. Like a flash, one of the older boys darted out of the back door. As the back door flew open, a loud noise like a siren went off, and two other staff members ran after him.

"We got a runner!" one of the staff members said as he took off behind the "runner."

Excited and wanting to know what was going on, I ran out the back door to see what was happening! The staff members ran after him, and before the boy could get to the fence, they tackled him in the open field. Both of the staff members had the boy pinned by the arms; they forced him back into the shelter.

"Let go of my arm! I hate this fucking place!" the boy said, trying to break free from the staff members' tight grips. Once the staff members got him back inside, they threw the boy on the floor, folded his arms behind his back as if he were being arrested, and shoved his arms as close as they could up to his head. The boy screamed loudly in a high-pitched voice, saying, "I can't breathe!" His face was twisted in agony.

The staff members kept repeating, "We need you to calm down!"

"OK! OK!" the boy yelled. His face was pressed firmly on the tile floor, and blood, pouring from his bloody nose, started to pool around his mouth. The most peculiar thing about what was taking place was that as the staff members asked him to calm down, they continued to push his arms up toward his head; it seemed as if they were purposefully inflicting pain.

I remember being horrified yet captivated by the scene. Before I could start screaming, one of the other boys from my unit pulled me aside and into the room. He put his hand over my mouth and said, "Are you crazy?"

"N-n-no," I stuttered.

"Then you better stay in here when a person is being restrained."

"OK," I said.

We sat down and watched cartoons. Little did I know that one day soon, I would be on the floor, crying out in agony, restrained in a similar manner to the runner. As I sat playing with my Ninja Turtles and watching cartoons, a frustrated child was being physically abused and fighting to breathe.

As days passed, more and more traumatic things began to happen. Traumatic things happened on days that seemed to be poignant in a child's life—for instance, getting a haircut. I remember getting my first haircut at Peace Children's Home by Mr. Mac, who was a youthful man and had a great way of engaging everyone. I remember waking up one Saturday morning and wondering where all my peers were. I ran to the big boys' side and saw everyone—that is, all of the boys and girls—in the same room being loud. The boys were getting haircuts, and the girls were getting perms on their heads. As I walked around, I heard a musical mix of DJ Quick, Arrested Development, and Onyx playing on the radio. As the music blasted, I saw one group of boys throwing dice over a pile of money on the floor. Another group of boys were playing Nintendo on the TV, and some of the girls were huddled around two other girls who were about to get into a fight. I remember watching Mr. Mac cut one boy's hair.

"You didn't cut it right! I want a flattop swooped to the side, like Gumby's," said the upset teenager.

"All right, sit back. I got you," said Mr. Mac.

When Mr. Mac finished the haircut, the boy looked in the mirror, smiled, and said, "Man, I'm so fly."

Some of the boys laughed and smacked him in the back of the head. One boy said, "Yeah, right…you fly like a shaved bird!"

Everyone around laughed uncontrollably.

Eventually, my turn came to get a haircut, and Mr. Mac beckoned for me to come to the chair. I would not budge, so one of the teenagers placed me on the telephone books on the seat.

"Let's take a look at that head," said Mr. Mac.

Reluctantly, I waited in the chair, balancing on the telephone books, not knowing what was about to take place. Mr. Mac threw a towel around me and told me to hold still and not to wiggle.

As the clippers zoomed over my head, I cried not because it hurt but because the noise was loud. By the time Mr. Mac had finished, my Afro was gone, and I had a flattop and a ducktail at the back of my head. I crawled out of the chair, still crying and shocked because my hair had been cut for the first time.

One of the older girls in the facility, Porsha, took a liking to me and put me on her lap. "Stop crying, bubba. It's just a haircut!" she said.

By the time I settled down, Mr. Mac put his clippers up and told everyone it was time to roll out.

"Where is everyone going all of a sudden?" I thought.

Everyone ran out the door and went outside to get into "Big Dookie"—that is, our fifteen-passenger Ford Econoline.

"I got front seat!" someone yelled.

"Not if I get there first!"

I ran toward the door too but was stopped by Mr. Mac. "You can't go, little guy. Mrs. O. wants you to stay here."

"W-w-where is everyone else going, and why can't I go?" I said angrily.

Mr. Mac replied, "We're going on an outing right now, so stay here with Mrs. Sarena."

To be honest, I hated to stay with Mrs. Sarena, who was Mrs. O's very stern sister. She never took crap from anyone. There was a rumor going around the facility: Mrs. Sarena could restrain two people at one time! Everyone in Peace Children's Home knew that Mrs. Sarena did not play.

Mr. Mac switched the TV's channel to one showing cartoons and went back to one of the rooms where another resident was on restriction. I peered into the room and noticed that it was the same boy who had tried to run away the other day—we called him "Pookie." After speaking with the young man, Mr. Mac hurried out of the room and looked at his watch. I looked at Pookie, noticing that he was starting to get out of his bed. I turned my attention back to the TV and continued to watch *Looney Toons*. Before I could get back into the cartoon, my vision was obscured by Pookie.

"What's up, little guy?" he said with a mischievous grin. "Do you know what a dick is?"

"N-n-no," I said, stuttering.

Before I could blink my eyes, Pookie pulled out his wiener and said, "Well, s-s-suck this! It tastes just like cherries."

I sat there, confused, and it seemed as if the longer I sat there, the more impatient he became.

"I'll give you some candy if you suck this," he said, grinning mischievously. I remember coughing a little because the stench was unbearable!

"Go ahead and suck it," Pookie persisted, wiggling his private part closer to my face. The closer he got, the more I started to notice that there was a strange liquid oozing from his private part. He proceeded to rub his hand ferociously over his private part, and I sat there, feeling clueless as to what he was doing. I continued to cough more, because the stench smelled like raw fish.

My little mind began to think about candy, and just before I got up to open my mouth, Mrs. Sarena yelled, "Pookie, don't let me come in there and find you out of your room!" She was running into the office to answer the phone.

"Yes, ma'am," Pookie said, sliding his wiener back into his pants. As he ran back to his room, he whispered, "If you say something, I'll beat your bitch ass."

As I sat gazing at the TV, I found it hard to concentrate on the cartoons. For some reason, *Looney Toons* no longer captivated my attention. I started to cry, so I did the only thing a child was supposed to do. I crawled off the couch, walked into the office, and screamed, "P-P-Pookie p-p-pulled he pants down and told me to s-s-suck it!"

Mrs. Sarena cried, "Pookie did *what*!"

"P-P-Pookie pulled he pants down and told me to s-s-suck it!" I repeated.

Mrs. Sarena slammed the file cabinet shut and said, "Stay in here, chile." She left and then came back into the office to give me some coloring books and crayons. "Stay put. I'll be back in a bit."

I tried to color, but all I could think about was Pookie's sardonic grin and that putrid smell. Mrs. Sarena walked back in with Mrs. O, and they asked me once again what had happened. After I told them, Mrs. O. and Mrs. Sarena exchanged glances. I remember sitting by myself for what seemed like an hour. One thing I knew for sure was that I never wanted to go around Pookie anymore. What was supposed to be a happy time in my life as a child had been tainted by molestation.

"Oba, come with me," said Mrs. O. She picked up a big, black binder off the desk. As Mrs. O. and I walked outside, I was nearly blinded by the extreme incandescence of the noon sun.

"Oba, we're going to the grocery store," said Mrs. O. as she opened the van door.

I noticed that we were not riding in Big Dookie, the brown van. The present van had one seat in the back and appeared to be a van used for maintenance work. As Mrs. O. and I headed to the grocery store, I remember her jamming to Rick James's song "Mary Jane." As we pulled up to the massive supermarket, Fiesta, I remember peering out the window excitedly. I could not wait to go inside the supermarket!

"All right, T. Oba! Let's go," said Mrs. O. excitedly.

As Mrs. O. shopped, I remember riding underneath the grocery cart's basket. As she shopped for groceries, her long skirt swept against her shoes. "Here, eat this," she said, reaching down to hand me a pickle. By the time I got done nibbling on it, Mrs. O. had finished her grocery shopping. Before I knew it, we were back at the facility. As Mrs. O. and I pulled into the large parking lot of the orphanage, so did Mr. Mac and all of the other children.

"Y'all come get these bags out of the van," said Mrs. O. loudly.

Some of the residents helped get the groceries, and the other residents poured into the facility loudly and obnoxiously.

"Quiet down, or everyone is going to their rooms!" said Mrs. Sarena over the racket.

I excitedly ran inside to be with the other children. As I ran to find the boys in my unit, I could hear Mr. Mac yelling, "Everyone go into the big boys' side for group!" Group was a time in which the staff members tried to tell us about listening and paying attention in school. I remember everyone sitting in a circle and talking for an extremely long time. I hated group because I never wanted to hear anything the staff had to say. In my young mind, all I wanted to be was a child, not a patient.

After group, everyone piled into the cafeteria and ate hot dogs for lunch. Because I was so small, the staff members always brought my plate to me. Sitting at the table to eat was uncomfortable because the chairs did not have any backs to them. I put my plate down on my lap so I could eat my food more easily, instead of having to reach to the top of the table. As usual, the cafeteria was loud because everyone was talking.

In general, the big boys would talk about the latest rap artists, while the big girls would talk about the cutest guy in the facility. The boys would talk about the food and how nasty it was. Sometimes the boys would even talk about other staff members.

There was one particular boy in my unit. His name was Jamail, and he would often crack jokes and make everyone laugh. For instance, one day, Jamail blurted, "Man, somebody needs to tell Mrs. Janice to clean her fat ass—she smell like booty butt cheeks." Everyone at the table laughed loudly and started to say "booty butt cheeks" over and over again! As always, a staff member walked in and told us to quiet down or we would all be put to bed early. I was learning more and more that staff members issued ultimatums to control everyone in the orphanage.

Although the staff members gave ultimatums, there was always one young person who would take it way too far. Eduardo, one of the other children at my table, was chubby and loud and known for being a complete riot. When everyone settled down, Eduardo got up on top of the table and blurted as loud as he could, "Booty butt cheeks!" The cafeteria thundered with laughter! Before Eduardo climbed off his perch, someone threw a corn dog at him and hit him in the face. Eduardo, being the wild kid that he was, picked up his corn dog and attempted to throw it back at the person. Before I knew it, the whole cafeteria was in a full-fledged food fight! French fries, corn dogs, broccoli, and ketchup—all were flying all over the place.

Mr. Mac walked in and said, "All right, everybody, get to your rooms now!"

Mrs. Sarena walked in afterward, trying to figure out what all the commotion was. "What's the problem?" she asked, looking as stern as ever.

"They're in here throwing food like hooligans," said Mr. Mac as he looked around the room. "Look at you! You look like hooligans in here, throwing food like you don't have any common sense."

Mrs. Sarena chimed in and said, "Well, since you wanna act like hooligans, everybody is on shutdown!"

When Mrs. Sarena said this, everyone in the cafeteria began to murmur and complain.

"Awww, man," one child said, putting his head down on the table.

One of the big girls blurted, "I can't stand this place!"

Another yelled, "I'm telling my caseworker! Y'all can't put us on shutdown!"

Despite the complaints and the murmuring, Mr. Mac and Mrs. Sarena were not buying it.

"Everyone, go to your rooms now!" said Mrs. Sarena, and she pointed toward the hallway.

All the children jumped up and ran to their rooms. Some threw their plates on the floor, and others yelled more curse words as they walked out. We all went back to our rooms and were commanded to get in our beds. I climbed into my bunk bed and started crying. "I don't wanna s-s-stay in my room!" I said in a high-pitched voice.

"Shut up, stutter box," said Eduardo.

When Eduardo said this, everyone busted out in laughter; however, the laughter was quickly muffled when Mrs. Sarena walked in. She gave us a stern look and walked back out.

As I lay in my bed, I tried to block out what had happened earlier when I was watching cartoons. I closed my eyes, feeling myself drift closer to sleep. Before I was completely under, something hit my head; I turned over and saw that someone had flicked paper on me. I looked up and saw that the boy in the top bunk was leaning down and trying to get my attention.

"What's your name?" he asked.

"My name is T-T-Tyrone," I replied, stuttering.

"Why you talk like that?" he asked with a grin.

"I don't know. It's the way I was b-b-born," I replied.

"Well, my name is James, and I'll be your friend, OK?"

"OK," I replied.

James and I became the best of friends that day, and we talked until the evening staff came and let everyone out of the room. After chastising us for about an hour, the staff informed us that everyone would not be placed on shutdown. When the staff said this, everyone jumped up and down and screamed, "Yes!" However, we were warned that if it happened again, we would be on shutdown for a month. James and I spent the rest of the evening playing with toy cars.

Time seemed to pass slowly while I stayed at Peace Children's Home. At the young age of five, I did not know that other things were going on behind the scenes. My social worker was about to leave me and go to a different agency.

March 9, 1992

    My social worker had a staffing with the CPS supervisor.

    Today, I informed my supervisor that I was leaving the agency. Supervisor stated that I need to do a detailed transfer summary and to be prepared to transfer the case by April 10, 1992, at the latest.

March 24, 1992

    My social worker visited me at Peace Children's Home.

    I told Tyrone that he was getting a new caseworker. He wanted to get the new worker's phone number, and I told him that I didn't know it yet. Tyrone was also worried that the new worker would not have his sister's phone number. I assured Tyrone that I wrote all of the information down for the new worker. Tyrone asked when he could visit, and I told him that Ms. Owunda is supposed to call his sisters' foster mother to arrange a time. I asked Tyrone for a hug, which he gave me. Afterward, he then went to finish his supper.

According to my state records, four days after my birthday, I received a new caseworker.

May 19, 1992

    My new social worker visited me at the orphanage.

    On the marginal date, I visited Tyrone at the Peace Children's Home. Upon arrival, I was greeted at the door by a woman named

Mrs. Sarena, who identified herself as the assistant administrator of the facility. Mrs. Sarena led me to the room where I was to talk with Tyrone. She told me that Tyrone needed a clothing voucher and asked if I could please check on that. I told her that I would and that I would inform her about the voucher when it comes in. When Tyrone came into the room, he appeared a little scared, at the beginning. I introduced myself to Tyrone, who asked me who I was. I told him that I was the new caseworker and that I would be working with him as his new caseworker. Tyrone further explained that he was doing fine, except that he needed some clothes. Tyrone told me he was in kindergarten and that he was six years old. Tyrone stated that he likes toys, money, and bikes. Tyrone also stated that he likes the food Mrs. Sarena cooks and that he likes to play with the other boys on the Nintendo. Tyrone asked me if I had seen his sisters, Trish and Tasha. I told Tyrone that as soon as I received the case and obtained an address, I would visit them to see how they were doing. Everything at Peace Children's Home appeared to be appropriate, and no concerns were noted during the time of the visit. Tyrone appeared to be in good spirits, clean and ready to go back and play. The other children in the facility also appeared to be clean, and no concerns were noted on them.

Meeting my new social worker was boring! In my little head, I felt as if I were meeting a new staff member. I remember Mrs. Sarena leading me to one of the back offices to meet the new social worker.

"Sit down and talk to your caseworker," said Mrs. Sarena sternly.

When I entered the room, I remember seeing a very overweight man with thick, black glasses, a briefcase, and a legal pad.

"Hi there," he said as I wiggled in my seat to get comfortable. "My name is Elijah Almero, and I'm your new social worker." His stared blankly as he spoke.

After he introduced himself, I began to focus my attention on the large object that he had in a brown bag. "W-w-what's that?" I asked, pointing to the right of his knee.

"It's a birthday gift," he said, pushing the bag my way.

I opened the bag and noticed that there was a two-liter bottle of root beer in the bag. "Thanks," I said, setting the bag in my lap.

The caseworker began to ask me questions about living in the orphanage. I answered them to the best of my ability; however, my mind was soon wandering. I wanted to play Nintendo, so I asked to leave and be with the other children.

At the orphanage, playing Nintendo was everyone's favorite thing to do. There was only one Nintendo per unit, so everyone huddled around the TV and took turns playing. In the little boys' unit, everyone loved playing *Duckhunt* and *Street Fighter*.

"Oooh, I got next!" someone would say.

"No, you don't. I got next," someone else would scream.

Being the smallest boy in the unit, I was always overlooked, and the other boys would try to steal my turn. "It's m-m-my t-t-turn!" I would yell, stuttering.

"Man, somebody let this little runt play so he will stop crying," someone would scream.

I never understood what I was doing in *Duckhunt*, but I always wanted to have a turn to see if I could kill the ducks. I would only last a second in the game, so the next person in line to play was always happy. Usually, everyone in the facility played Nintendo on the weekends. Fridays were the best days to play because there was little supervision in the evenings and because everyone could stay up late.

The weekends at the shelter started out very fun. Everyone in the little boys' unit wrestled, played Nintendo, and had pillow fights. However, being able to stay up late had its disadvantages. When the members of the night staff arrived and saw us up late, playing Nintendo, they were not happy.

On one night, Mr. C.J., one member of the night staff, walked in and shouted, "All right, everyone, bedtime. Lights out!"

"Awww, man," everyone whined.

We all went to our bunks.

Mr. C.J. was known to have a mean streak that was worse than Mrs. Sarena's. Because I had little playing time on the Nintendo, I tried to be sneaky and try one more time to kill the ducks. Just as I turned the Nintendo back on, Mr. C.J. yelled in his loud, booming voice, "Tyrone, didn't I just say go to your room?"

I looked at Mr. C.J. stubbornly and yelled, "I w-w-want to play N-N-Nintendo. I only got to play a little b-b-bit!" I stuttered.

"Tyrone, you got five seconds to get your stuttering ass in bed," said Mr. C.J., pointing to my room.

From where I was sitting, I could see that all of the other boys were climbing into their bunks and getting under their covers. "No, I wanna p-p-play!" I said in a loud, high-pitched voice.

Before I could turn my head to look back at the game, Mr. C.J. picked me up and slammed me on the couch. He folded my arms behind my back, pushing them up to my head as far as he could, creating excruciating pain. Tears began to pour down my face uncontrollably as I cried.

"Help! Help!" I screamed. My screams were ineffective. The more I cried, the more Mr. C.J. pressed my face deep into the couch. "Somebody help!" I screamed again, the pain continuing to run through my back and arms.

"Y'all are gone learn not to play with me!" said Mr. C.J., who was still pinning me down.

I could feel my head tingling. My breathing started to become fainter as I continued to scream for help. I remember hearing my heartbeat, and then all of a sudden, all I could see was a white light. I awoke a couple of minutes later.

Mr. C.J. said, "When I say go to bed, I mean go to bed, do you hear me?"

"OK," I said, trying to move my arms. To my surprise, I could not move them on the first try. On the second try, I tried with all of my might to move them, and I was able to rub my eyes. My oversized shirt was covered in stains from my tears. I remember lying in the bed afterward, sniffling and crying for hours. I could not understand why someone would hurt me so bad—all I had wanted was to play Nintendo.

As the tears continued to fall, I began to think about how I missed my two sisters. This, of course, caused me to cry even more.

"You better shut it up right now!" Mr. C.J. yelled. He had come to the doorway.

Out of fear of being restrained again, I stifled my tears as much as I could. When I stopped crying, Mr. C.J. left the room, mumbling to himself. "These damn kids must have lost they mind," he said. His sneakers made a soft thud against the linoleum floor as he walked out of the unit. As the tears dried on my face, my head began to pound with pain, and I tried my best to recover from being body slammed and restrained by a grown man. I could feel my heartbeat through my temples. Eventually, the rhythmic beat of my heart pulled me into a deep sleep.

Looking back on this, I can see I was one of many children who suffered physical abuse in the orphanages. It seemed as if caregivers did not understand that I was a child who needed love and affection. Instead, they physically abused me and submitted documentation to the state of Texas to justify their reasons for putting me on psychotropic medications. Restraints seemed to be the primary mechanism of control in the orphanage, and each time that I was restrained it was a near-death experience.

CHAPTER 5

He Had to Be Restrained

I AWOKE THE NEXT MORNING to the smell of pancakes, maple syrup, sausage, and eggs. I always knew when Mrs. O. was in the building on the weekends because she would have the radio blasting on her favorite radio station when she made pancakes for everyone.

"T. Oba, you hungry, baby?" she would ask, smiling. Mrs. O. had a way of smiling and giggling while she asked people questions.

"Y-y-yes, ma'am! I'm h-h-hungry," I replied. "Mama, y-y-yesterday Mr. C.J. hurt my arms," I said loudly.

To my surprise, Mrs. O. did not say anything at all. She continued to flip pancakes and listen to her music. It was as if she did not care that I had been body slammed the previous night by a grown man.

"C'mon over here. Take this fruit outside, and see if you like it," she said, completely ignoring my comment.

I walked over to Mrs. O., and she handed me a large, round fruit. "W-w-what is it?" I asked in bewilderment.

"It's a cantaloupe," she replied. She took a knife, cut the cantaloupe in slices, and told me to go outside and eat it.

Happy to have something new to spark my curiosity, I ran outside in my oversized shirt and Ninja Turtle underwear and ate the cantaloupe. Afterward, I ran back inside and said, "Ooooh, Mama, I like cantaloupe!"

Mrs. O. smiled and said, "I'm glad you like it, baby. Now go back in your unit and watch cartoons till breakfast."

"Yes, ma'am!" I yelled excitedly.

I ran back to my unit and noticed that some of the other boys were up watching the morning cartoons. Eduardo was sprawled out in his bed, snoring. George, James, Emmanuel, Francis, and Mrs. O.'s sons, Malachi and Troy, were all in the living room, watching *Batman* on the TV.

Emmanuel had a reputation of being very mean. As I walked in, he said, "Watch out y'all—it's the African booty scratcher!"

All of the boys watching TV began to laugh and point at me, saying, "It's the African booty scratcher!"

I hated being teased, so I yelled back, "I'm n-n-not no African booty scratcher!"

"Look at him. He can't even talk right," said Emmanuel, exploding with laughter.

I became so angry that I could feel the tears welling up in my eyes. Looking for a way out, I left my unit and entered the one across the hall. I pushed the door open and noticed that I was in a room full of boys who were four times taller than I. The unit smelled of dirty clothes, starch, and bleach. As I entered the unit and walked around, I noticed some of the boys were throwing dice on the floor and gambling. Four other boys were gathered around a table, rapping to a beat that was being made by a boy banging on the table. When I walked into one of the bedrooms, I saw clothes everywhere, and someone's radio was blasting Bone Thugs-N-Harmony. I walked into the other side of the unit, where a group of boys were doing push-ups.

"Yo, who let little man in our unit?" one of the boys said. He got up from doing push-ups. "How did you get in here, man?" said the boy, breathing profusely.

"Th-th-they were picking on me," I said in a loud voice.

"Who was picking on you?" said McKinley, getting up from his push-ups.

"Emmanuel said I was an African b-b-booty scratcher!" I said angrily.

"It's OK, little man," said McKinley. "In fact, if anybody messes with you, let me know, home slice—I got your back."

As McKinley said this, Pookie—the guy who exposed himself to me—walked in and said, "McKinley, let me borrow some of your grease, man."

McKinley looked up and said, "A'ight, man, but don't touch my Murray's hair grease."

When Pookie walked away, McKinley's friend Dillan said, "Yo, homie, you getting soft? Why you being nice to that weirdo?"

Before McKinley could answer, I yelled out, "That's the d-d-dude that pulled his pants down and told me to suck it!"

When I said this, McKinley bent down, grabbed me by the shoulders, and said, "Little man, he did what?"

I repeated, "That's the guy who pulled his pants down and told me to suck it!"

McKinley's and Dillan's mouths dropped as they exchanged glances with each other. They both appeared to be astounded by the news I had dropped on them. Dillan, who happened to be brushing the back of his head at the time, said, "When did he do this to you, man?"

I shrugged my shoulders and said, "He told me if I s-s-sucked it, he would give me some candy."

Dillan and McKinley exchanged glances again. "That dude is a damn faggot, man! I knew something was up with him!" yelled Dillan. "How the hell does someone do that to a little kid?"

"Yo, I got an idea, man," said McKinley. "A'ight, little man, I got your back. Go back to your side before you get in trouble."

I ran out toward the living room, but before I left the room completely, I noticed a boy off by himself, fidgeting with a small, black, rectangular device. "What's that?" I asked, walking up to the guy. He did not hear me, so I poked him on his leg and said, "What's that on your head?"

The guy looked at me and said, "What the heck? How did you get in here?"

"They were picking on me," I said as I looked to the floor.

The guy looked at me and said, "Yeah, I hate this place too! People get on my nerves all the time."

I continued to look at the guy, hoping he would let me see his Walkman (which is what the rectangular device turned out to be).

Instead, the guy stood up and said, "You should come with me on a little adventure later!"

"W-w-what adventure?" I asked, feeling confused.

"We're going to run away after breakfast!" the guy blurted.

"What's running away?" I asked excitedly.

The guy looked at me and said, "Don't you know anything? Running away is what you do when you are not happy. Just don't tell anybody, and meet me in the front of the building after breakfast."

"OK," I said excitedly.

In my little head, I was happy to go on an adventure. As I ran toward the door to leave, Mrs. O. walked into the unit. "Tyrone, what are you doing in here? Go to the cafeteria and eat breakfast, child," she said, pointing toward the cafeteria.

I ran to the cafeteria and sat at the table with all of the other boys from my unit.

In general, when Mrs. O. came in on the weekends, she cast a happier vibe throughout the cafeteria because she would make great dishes of food. Everyone would be so excited to eat it all. Instead of calling each other names and throwing food, we would focus on eating so that we could have seconds and thirds. Some of the boys would even go back for fourths and fifths! We would mumble our praise for her cooking through mouthfuls of pancakes or other treats.

On the morning in which Mrs. O. caught me in the other boys' unit and sent me scrambling to the cafeteria, I pulled my plate off the table and dived right into devouring my plate of food. Between gulps, I noticed that Eduardo and George were making pancake sandwiches by filling them with eggs. They did not savor their creations; they stuffed them into their mouths. As I got done with my food, I noticed that the boy who had told me to meet him in the front of the building was heading out of the cafeteria. Remembering what he had said, I sneaked out of the cafeteria and ran after him.

"Are we going on the adventure now?" I asked loudly.

"Shut up! Stop talking so loud!" He ducked down to make sure no one was watching. "Go get your clothes and meet me by the couch in the front," he said discreetly, looking back over his shoulder.

I ran to the back, threw some clothes in my "pack-pack," and ran toward the couch in the front of the building. As I knelt beside the couch, I noticed that Mrs. Sarena was heading toward the big boys' unit. To our disadvantage, the phone rang, and Mrs. Sarena ran into the office to answer it. While she was on the phone, the boy who was about to take me on an adventure sneaked past the office door with a small duffel bag on his shoulder. He looked back again to see if anyone was watching; then he opened the front door slowly. To our surprise, the alarm was disabled, so it did not go off! The boy beckoned for me to go first, so I sneaked out of the door, gripping my pack-pack tightly. Immediately after I stepped out, the boy ran out of the building and screamed, "Run! Let's go!" He took off toward the open field, leaving me behind.

"Wait for me!" I said, running after him.

Immediately after I yelled for him to slow down, Mrs. Sarena burst through the door and yelled, "Donald and Tyrone, get back over here right now!" Mrs. Sarena's command did not stop us from running.

"Hurry up!" the boy yelled back at me.

As we continued to run, I noticed that Mrs. Sarena had taken off after us. By then, we were out in the open field and running through the tall grass. As we kept running, I remember thinking, "Wow, I'm really going on an adventure!" But just before we made it to the street, I remember Mrs. Sarena yelling five magical words that stopped me in my tracks.

"Tyrone, come get some cookies!"

When Mrs. Sarena yelled this, I did a double take. I ran back toward her, excited about the opportunity to devour some cookies. I was not going to miss out on eating cookies for anything in the world.

"Where the hell were you going, boy?" yelled Mrs. Sarena.

"He was taking me on an adventure! We were r-r-running away! Can I h-h-have my cookies now?" I said excitedly, looking up at Mrs. Sarena.

"No, you can't have any damn cookies! As a matter of fact, when you get back inside, you go to your room and don't come out! Do you hear me, boy?" she yelled.

As we walked back to the shelter, I remember thinking, "I just wanted to go on an adventure." Mrs. Sarena was using one of her hands to sift through the tall grass and the other to hold my hand. As we approached the door, Mrs. Sarena mumbled, "You got my fat ass chasing you around like you crazy! You go to your room right now, and I better not see you come out!" said Mrs. Sarena. She pointed a finger in my face.

When Mrs. Sarena walked into the shelter, Mrs. O. came out of the kitchen to see what all the commotion was about. "What happened?" she asked as she rubbed her hands on her apron.

"Donald ran away, and Tyrone followed him," said Mrs. Sarena, wheezing in frustration.

I ran to my room in tears, devastated because I had not gotten to go on the adventure and because the promised cookies had been denied.

After drifting asleep, I remember waking up to someone patting me on the head. After I opened my eyes, I saw Dillan kneeling in front of my bed.

"Follow me," he said in a quiet voice.

I jumped out of bed and followed him past the cafeteria and into the laundry room. Upon entering, I noticed that McKinley and Pookie were standing face to face. McKinley's fists were clinched in a ball, and he was flexing his huge muscles as if he had just gotten done working out. I looked back at Dillan and noticed that he was halfway inside the laundry room. From the looks of it, he was keeping watch to make sure no one would enter.

Pookie and McKinley were arguing. Pookie said, "Bro, I don't know what the hell you talking about, man! Get the hell out my face!"

"That's the guy who told me to s-s-suck it!" I yelled, looking up at McKinley. I noticed that Pookie's lips started to quiver when I accused him. Pookie looked as if he was about to say something, but before he could say one word, one of McKinley's huge fists slammed into his right jaw.

"You sick fuck!" said McKinley. He threw another punch.

Pookie tried to come back with a left jab to the head, but McKinley jumped back and struck again with a left jab to the eye. With a swollen eye and loose jaw, Pookie could not defend himself. McKinley, still enraged, grabbed Pookie by the head and slammed it down toward his knee, so hard that I could have sworn I heard his nose break.

"I can't stand faggots that abuse kids!" yelled McKinley.

At this point, I heard other children running into the cafeteria and yelling, "Fight! Fight! Fight!"

Pookie was on the floor, holding his mouth and nose with one hand, and blood was seeping from between his fingers.

"Yo, homie, staff coming! Let's go, fool!" said Dillan as he beckoned for McKinley to come out.

McKinley took off his wifebeater, which was now splattered with blood, threw it in the trash can, and ran out of the room. Scared to be in the room with Pookie by myself, I ran back to my unit. Later that evening, I witnessed Pookie going to the hospital and McKinley being arrested for assault. As time passed, the trauma that I was experiencing at Peace Children's Home continued to intensify. I continued to see things that children should never see. It seemed that the more I spoke about such things, the more they were ignored.

My state records continued to show that every couple of months, I had a new caseworker.

October 23, 1992

A new social worker visited me at the orphanage.

This was my first official meeting with Tyrone. I explained that I was his new CPS caseworker, and he seemed to understand this. Tyrone is a cute six-year-old with an engaging smile. He told me he was in the second grade, when in reality he is in the first grade at Smith Elementary School. He asked when he could see his mother and grandmother and asked if I knew where his mother was. He informed me that it has been over a year since he has seen them. I told him that I did not know where his mother was at this time but that I would try to reach his grandmother and see if she was interested in visiting with him and his sisters. Tyrone has two older sisters, Tasha and Trish. They live in the Morrises' foster home and have been there for five years. Tyrone was very interested in visiting with his sisters, but he did not want to go to the Morrises' foster home because his sister told him that she had been spanked. Tyrone became a little agitated, so I let him go back to play with the other children.

Somehow, my caseworkers always came when I was busy having fun at the orphanage. CPS's lack of protective capabilities and its high turnover rate of social workers caused it to ignore fluctuations in my behavior. According to my records and my recollection, I was a very happy-go-lucky, inquisitive, loquacious child. For me to become frequently agitated all of a sudden should have been a red sign to the agency. As a child, I did not understand why the agency had placed me in a facility that was designed for children with severe behavior problems. I believe that decision was the primary reason why I was exposed to things that children should never be exposed to. As time progressed, I started to recognize that strange things happened at night in the shelter.

One night, I remember turning over in my bed and hearing two boys giggling. I was confused because I could not see anyone at first. I sat up in my bed and then began to scan the room with my eyes. I squinted and finally saw a boy's head pop out of another bed's covers. A couple of seconds later, I saw another boy's foot. The two boys were humping each other under the covers.

I remember whispering and stuttering to the boys, "W-w-what are y'all doing?"

One of the boys turned his head, smiled, and said, "Don't worry about it! Get your stupid ass back to sleep!"

Baffled and scared, I turned over and did just as I was told. As my eyes became heavy again with sleep, the giggles continued; they sounded like two children playing on a playground. At the time, I was too young to understand that these two boys were having anal sex and playing with each other's genitals.

Another night, I woke up to a loud bang. It seemed as if two or three people were wrestling. I continued to listen and heard another loud bang on the wall.

"Watch her head!" said one of the staff members.

Sneakers screeched on the marble floor, and then a loud thud was accompanied by the most horrifying scream that I have ever heard. The scream, belonging to a girl, was so loud that I thought she was being killed. "Let me go! My arm! I can't breathe!" she cried.

As I lay in my bed, I remember two other staff members yelling, "Calm down, Ashley, and count for your body parts."

The girl kept screaming so loudly that some of the other boys in my unit were waking up. After seeing some of the other boys put their pillows over their heads and go back to bed, I did the same. The more the girl screamed, the harder I pressed the pillow to my ears. At the time, I was just a child trying to get some sleep. It did not occur to me that another child was in the other room fighting for her life. I was too young to understand that some children who were restrained in the above manner died from asphyxiation.

On some nights, when everyone in the unit was not on punishment, everyone in the facility would watch movies together in the cafeteria. The cafeteria would be filled with blankets, pillows, and sleeping bags; the smell of popcorn would fill the air. Although there were staff members in the room, somehow I would always see something weird.

On one particular movie night, we were all sitting and watching *Tales from the Hood*, and I looked over and saw that one of the guys had his hands in one girl's pants. An hour and a half later, the movie ended, and everyone lined up at the serving window to get a snack. I remember looking up at the guy who had fondled the girl. "Why is he sniffing his finger?" I thought. At the time, I was just a child trying to get a snack. I did not know that the guy was smelling his finger because he had inserted it into the girl's vagina.

To offset some of the traumatic things at the orphanage, I looked forward to school, as did many other children. It was the part of my day in which I felt like a normal child.

Sometimes during the week, Mrs. Sonya would work in the mornings and run the whole shelter as if it were a boot camp. Mrs. Sonya was a tall and fat lady; she had large eyes, a booming voice, and a quick temper. Everyone hated the sight of her because of her negative demeanor. "Get up and get moving!" she would scream in the mornings, as she banged on the doors. On these days, we really missed Mrs. O.'s morning song! Some of the boys would wake up, throw the covers off their heads, and say something similar to "Damn, Mrs. Sonya's fat ass is working today."

At this point in the narrative, there were more six- and seven-year-old children, which was my age group. One of the new boys, Marcus, would always wake up crying and rubbing his eyes. To this very day, no one ever figured out why he woke up crying.

Waking up to go to school was fun because there was so much movement. Children ran around to find their backpacks, competed to get into the bathroom, and played pranks on each other—the gamut of activities created an excited and eager atmosphere. For the most part, we spent so much time in a structured environment at the orphanage that school was a way for all of us to be free. In 1992, I was in the first grade at Smith Elementary School. Although I was full of energy and taking psychotropic drugs to control my behavior, my teacher, Mrs. Ann McClelland, had a calm way of dealing with me. In short, she was fantastic! Often, I would see her wearing a school shirt with a black Scottish terrier, which was our school mascot. Mrs. McClelland's classroom was filled with vibrant colors, pictures, and stuffed animals. Our days were filled with creative assignments, stories, and recess (of course). Story time was my favorite because Mrs. McClelland would sit in her rocking chair and read great books, such as *Charlotte's Web* and *Sideways Stories from Wayside School*.

Unlike the other children, I would leave the classroom midmorning to go take psychotropic drugs. When the nurse handed me Ritalin and imipramine, I would yell, "I don't w-w-wanna t-t-take it!" My defiance toward the medication never stopped the nurse from making sure the medication was in my mouth.

"Drink your water," the nurse would say, offering no other encouragement.

On some days, I would walk out of the nurse's office and spit out the medication. When I would actually consume the medication, it would severely affect my appetite, so I would end up not eating. It seemed as if the medication was having a weird effect on my body. Sometimes I would shake, feel tired, and have hot flashes. During the lunches in which I was being affected by my medication, Mrs. McClelland would encourage me to eat my food. "You have to eat, Tyrone," she would say, pushing the plates of food toward me. Her attempts to make me eat never succeeded, though.

As the year progressed, I would soon learn that Mrs. McClelland really cared for me. Starting out, I had difficulty reading, especially because of my stuttering problem. I lagged behind the kids in reading, so Mrs. McClelland would keep me after school and help me with my reading skills.

One day, when all the children were leaving, Mrs. McClelland knelt by my desk and said, "Tyrone, I talked to Mrs. O. today, and guess what!"

When she said this, my eyebrows rose in excitement, and I said, "What?"

"You're going to stay after school with me today, and afterward we are having dinner at my house!" she responded excitedly.

"Yayyy!" I said, leaping for joy. I jumped in her arms and gave her a big hug.

Mrs. McClelland guided me over to her rocking chair and pulled out a book. "What do you think the title of this book is?" she said as she reached to the side of the rocking chair and pulled out a blanket.

"I d-d-don't kn-kn-know," I said, feeling confused.

"Well, let's see what it says." She pulled me up on her lap. I could feel her chest rise up and down behind my back as she pointed to the large black words on the cover of the book. "Sound the word out, Tyrone," she said, hiding a portion of the long words with her finger.

"C-c-cloudy w-w-with a ch-ch-chance of m-m-meatballs?" I said hesitantly. As I pronounced each word, Mrs. McClelland used her finger and pointed to it.

"Great job," she said as she looked down, leaning her head to the side and smiling at me.

As I looked up at her, I remember thinking, "Hey, this isn't hard after all!" As we continued to read, Mrs. McClelland rocked in her chair. Reading became fun for me that day, and I read a riveting tale of how food fell from the sky. After we finished the book, Mrs. McClelland and I walked outside and hopped into her forest-green Lexus.

"Where are we going now?" I asked anxiously as I crawled into the backseat.

"We're going to the store first, and then we are going to my house for dinner," said Mrs. McClelland.

"Yaaay! I'm excited!" I said, bouncing up and down in the seat. As Mrs. McClelland pulled into a Randalls, I noticed that I could read some of the words on the signs. As I tried to sound out some of the words, Mrs. McClelland looked at me in the rearview mirror. "G-g-grocery?" I said hesitantly.

"Great job!" Mrs. McClelland said, smiling. "Let's go in the store and get some things for dinner."

We got out of the car. I remember walking around with Mrs. McClelland while holding hands. All I could do was look. This was really the first time in my life that I was with an adult by myself, without twenty-five or so other children with me. There was so much to see—so many colors, people, and words that I could read. Within no time, Mrs. McClelland and I were back in the car and headed to her house.

As we pulled into her driveway, Mrs. McClelland said, "We're here!" I could see her bright smile as she looked at me in the rearview mirror. As we entered the house, I was greeted by a tall guy with short brown hair and a big smile.

"Tyrone, this is my son, Mike," said Mrs. McClelland happily.

As Mrs. McClelland went to the kitchen with the bags from the grocery store, Mike led me into the living room. "Do you like airplanes, Tyrone?" asked Mike.

"I l-l-love airplanes!" I stuttered.

In the living room was a variety of toys, such as GI Joes, Tonka trucks, marbles, airplanes, and race cars. Within no time, Mike and I were playing and making airplane and shotgun noises, and he taught me how to play cowboys and Indians.

"Dinner is ready," said Mrs. McClelland as she stepped into the living room, wiping her hands on her apron.

"Yay!" I said excitedly as I ran into the kitchen. Entering the kitchen, I noticed that a man with gray hair was sitting at the head of the table.

"Hi, Tyrone," he said with a big smile, raising his eyebrows.

"Hello," I said as I looked around to see where the scrumptious smell was coming from.

As I walked toward the table, I continued to focus on the food and not on the man at the head of the table. As Mrs. McClelland brought the food out, I thought, "I wonder if I can stay here forever?" While I was deep in thought, Mrs. McClelland placed a plate of food in front of me—it smelled like heaven! As we sat and ate, I remember smiles and conversations taking place, and I devoured my food happily. I saw that a large, golden dog was sitting by the laundry room. "Oooh! I wanna play with the dog!" I said excitedly.

"Looks like you have found Max," said Mr. McClelland. He leaned back in his chair, smiling.

Max was a young golden retriever with deep-brown eyes and foul breath. I played catch with Max in the house for a while until Mrs. McClelland announced that we were going to watch a movie. While Mrs. McClelland tidied up the kitchen, I managed to walk into the living room, where I noticed a piano. I started to play with the keys. Before I knew it, Mike was sitting next to me and showing me some chords on the piano.

"You boys sound pretty good together," said Mrs. McClelland, leaning against the doorway.

"M-m-movie time!" I yelled, jumping off the piano's chair.

That evening, Mrs. McClelland's family and I watched *Beauty and the Beast*. By the end of the movie, I had fallen asleep on Mr. and Mrs. McClelland's laps. "Time to go, Tyrone," said Mrs. McClelland, her voice causing me to spring up. "We better get you back to Peace Children's Home before nightfall."

I hugged Mr. McClelland and Mike before I walked out. As I walked toward the car, I wondered, "Why can't I stay?" I rode home with Mrs. McClelland, feeling a deep sense of melancholy.

"Tyrone, I am so proud of you for reading today!" said Mrs. McClelland as she looked at me in the rearview mirror. I looked to the floor.

"Tyrone, I left you a surprise! It's on the seat right next to you," said Mrs. McClelland, smiling happily.

"Th-th-thank you," I said in a somber tone.

The rest of the car ride was silent. Mrs. McClelland's attempt to cheer me up was not working. I was sad because I had had a great time with people I felt cared for me but was being forced to return to a harsh environment. As Mrs. McClelland made a right turn on River Valley Drive and entered the parking lot of the orphanage, I could see that the kitchen light was on. Ms. Janice appeared to be working the evening shift, which was unusual because she usually worked on the weekends. As Mrs. McClelland and I walked toward the door, Ms. Janice yelled, "You brought back our favorite child!"

Mrs. McClelland looked down, smiled at me, and said, "He's such an adorable kiddo."

I continued to look down at the floor. While Mrs. McClelland and Ms. Janice continued to talk, I noticed that some of the boys in the shelter were peeking out the door to see who had arrived.

Mrs. McClelland knelt down and said, "I'll see you at school tomorrow, kiddo." She gave me a hug and waved bye; then Ms. Janice walked me to my unit to be with the other boys.

When I walked into the unit, I noticed that a lady was sitting on the couch. "What's your name, boy?" she asked as I tried to walk to my room.

"T-T-Tyrone," I stuttered.

"I'm Mrs. Shaun. Have you had a snack yet?"

"No, ma'am," I said. I sat on the couch.

Mrs. Shaun gave me a napkin full of animal crackers, along with my nighttime medication. After eating my snack, I crawled into bed, feeling sad because I wanted to be with Mrs. McClelland. In her family's company, I had felt like a normal child for the first time, but I was back in a painful place. I opened the bag that Mrs. McClelland had given me, the one with the surprise in it, and realized that it was the book that she had helped me to read: *Cloudy with a Chance of Meatballs.*

As I drifted off to sleep, my mind wandered back to the events that had happened that day. I could still feel Mrs. McClelland's chest against my back as she rocked me in her rocking chair and taught me how to read. Mrs. McClelland had taught me by being involved, and her consistent compassion had overridden my traumatic memories. Now, looking back on this, I feel that I was also being taught that love transcends race, class, and socioeconomic status.

As the school year progressed, Mrs. McClelland and I spent more time together. Special times—such as Christmas, Halloween, and even my birthday—began to take on new meaning. I will never forget that for my birthday, Mrs. McClelland bought me a Buzz Lightyear toy, made popular by the movie *Toy Story*, and a magnifying glass.

Sadly, Peace Children's Home stopped Mrs. McClelland from coming to see me. Everyone looked over the fact that my behavior stabilized while I was spending time with her. Unfortunately, my behavior at school and at home took a turn for the worse after Mrs. McClelland was prevented from picking me up at the orphanage.

My state records show that while in the second grade, I was repeatedly written up and removed from school.

My behavior began to reflect that there was severe emotional, or "tornadic," activity going on inside me. Essentially, I was screaming for a safe and loving environment, yet no one understood that. Instead of getting what I needed, the agency proceeded to further institutionalize me. My state records show that on November 8, 1994, I was removed from Peace Children's Home and placed at Forest Springs Hospital. My case file contains the following:

November 8, 1994
    Placement: Forest Springs Hospital
    Tyrone was placed in Forest Springs Hospital for observation.

The day I was placed at Forest Springs Psychiatric Hospital seemed no different than any other day. I remember waking up, getting dressed, eating breakfast, and returning to my unit to watch cartoons before school. Before I could fully engage in the cartoons, Mrs. Sarena yelled, "Tyrone, let's go!"

Happy just to go somewhere, I jumped up and walked into the hallway. As I looked outside, I could see that Mrs. Sarena had her big Cadillac in the front, and its doors were wide open. Apparently, Mrs. Sarena had packed my stuff; she had placed everything in large black trash bags.

"Where are we g-g-going?" I asked, stuttering.

"Get your misbehaving ass in the car! Had you acted right, you wouldn't have this problem!" said Mrs. Sarena.

I jumped into the car and buckled my seat belt. As I looked out the window, I noticed that the big boys were piling my clothes into the car. As Mrs. Sarena exited the parking lot, I wondered where we were going. Within twenty minutes, Mrs. Sarena pulled into the hospital. Within forty-five minutes, I was registered and upstairs with other children. Upstairs, in the children's unit, I saw several other children in what was called the dayroom. Some children were playing video games or cards; on the other side of the room, others were watching a movie. I remember thinking, "Wow! This looks like fun!"

For the most part, engaging with the young people was no hassle at all. I jumped right in and waited for my turn to play the video games. Over to the right, in a corner, there were crackers and punch. "This is the life!" I thought as I played with the other children. My fun was interrupted when one of the staff members came and yelled my name with a booming voice. I looked to the door and saw a light-skinned black man with dark-blue scrubs.

"My name is Mr. Carl. Come on over here so I can show you your room," said the staff member, still using a booming voice. I left the dayroom and followed Mr. Carl to a room with two wooden beds and a big window. "This is your room, buddy, so start putting your stuff away, and then you can do some art later."

"I like art!" I yelled excitedly. I hurried and placed my things in my drawers and proceeded to go back to the dayroom. As I walked toward it, I noticed that everyone was lining up to go downstairs.

"Just in time!" said Mr. Carl. He guided us onto the elevator, and we all went downstairs. Once we got off, Mr. Carl led us around the corner and into a room filled with chairs and toys. I did not know it at the time, but I was about to engage in art therapy.

"All right, you guys, I want full participation in group today, or you can't watch a movie later," said Mr. Carl.

The other children gave halfhearted responses.

As I looked around, I saw rays of sunlight peering through the big windows. The windows framed tall pine trees and large fixtures of a wooden obstacle course. Before I could move closer to the window, I was interrupted by the counselor.

"Hello, children! My name is Mrs. Jay. Go ahead and take a seat, and we will get started on today's project!"

I took a seat in one of the chairs.

Mrs. Jay brought out boxes of soap and plastic knives. "All right, children, I want you each to take a bar of soap and turn it into your favorite animal," she said cheerily. She grabbed a plastic knife and demonstrated the best ways to carve the soap. While we children were attempting our own carvings, Mrs. Jay turned on a little stereo that was on her desk. The combination of the music and the feel of slippery soap in my hands was relaxing. I was fully engaged in the moment, trying my best to turn my bar of soap into a duck.

"What do you have there?" asked Mrs. Jay. She knelt down and patted me on the shoulder.

Immediately, my focus was broken, and all I could think about was Mrs. Jay's gigantic breasts! "Boobies!" I thought, my jaw dropping in awe.

"Tyrone? What do you have there?" repeated Mrs. Jay.

"Oh, sorry!" I said, focusing my attention back on my bar of soap. "I'm m-m-making a d-d-duck," I stuttered.

Mrs. Jay patted me on the head and said, "Great job."

Before I knew it, our art-therapy session was over, and Mr. Carl escorted us back upstairs to the unit. My stay at Forest Springs Hospital was turning out to be OK! Later that night, we stayed up and watched a movie about a hockey team—*The Mighty Ducks*.

As the days passed, I engaged in more activities, such as swimming, navigating obstacle courses, and having water-gun fights. For a time, I thought I could relax and enjoy myself. I would soon learn that Forest Springs Hospital was very similar to Peace Children's Home in one horrifying way: physical abuse was used as a mechanism of control.

After I had been at the hospital for a couple of days, the nurses started to give me medication after breakfast, lunch, and dinner. At first, I took the medication without any problems. As time passed, I recognized that the medication was causing me to vomit, shake, and feel sluggish. Once again, I found myself void of an appetite. It seemed as if the more I told the nurses how I felt, the more medication they forced into me. Scared of how the medication made me feel, I made the decision to refuse it.

One day, Mr. Carl came through the unit, passing out the midday medication. Once he came to my door, I yelled, "I'm not taking the m-m-medication!" I yanked the pills from his hand, ran into the bathroom, and locked the door. I could hear Mr. Carl murmur on his walkie-talkie; he spoke in some type of hospital language. Shortly after that, I heard two other nurses walk into my bedroom. I knew I had to act fast; they were going to pry open my bathroom door. I looked at the two long capsules in my hands, and as I peered into the capsules, I noticed that there were tiny orange balls in the middle of them. I broke the capsules open and washed them down the sink. Before I could turn around, the bathroom door flew open, and three nurses quickly surrounded me.

"Tyrone, come out here. You need to take your medication!" one of the nurses said, handing me a cup of water and some more medication.

"I don't w-w-want it," I responded, stuttering. "It m-m-makes me feel f-f-funny!"

One of the female nurses knelt down and looked me square in the eyes. She said, "Honey, I know it's scary, but it's for your own good."

Another nurse repeated, "Yes, Tyrone, it's for your own good."

Mr. Carl knelt down next to me and said, "Don't you wanna take the medication so you can go back in the dayroom and watch movies with the other children?"

All of them were attempting to cajole me into taking the pills, and their calm encouragement made me contemplate whether I should or not. I took a large sip of the water, but then I remembered how the pills made me feel. Maddened, I spit the water out on the female nurse's face and tried to shut the bathroom door. Mr. Carl prevented it from closing with his big arms; then he grabbed me by my arms.

"Let me go!" I screamed loudly. I tried to yank my way out of Mr. Carl's grip, but one of the other nurses grabbed my legs. They carried me by my arms and legs into a room in which the walls were covered with white padding. I noticed that in the middle of the room, there was a large board with a white jacket and belt straps. Not knowing what was about to happen next, I screamed more loudly. "Let me go!" I yelled frantically. My screams were futile.

The nurses placed me in the jacket and tied me down on the board. "Stay in here until you are ready to take your medication," said Mr. Carl, and he left with the other nurses. As they walked out, the thick white door closed behind them heavily, making a loud thud.

I was scared for my life! The anxiety from not being able to move consumed me, so I wiggled and yelled for help as much as I could. "Somebody h-h-help me! Anybody!" I stuttered. Eventually, I wiggled and screamed myself to a point of exhaustion. Yelling became pointless because I could no longer verbalize my words without stuttering heavily. My arms started to hurt, so I stopped wiggling. Broken and scared, mentally subdued, I lay there sobbing. As the tears poured down my face, I began to feel myself drifting asleep.

Later, I awoke to a loud buzzer-like noise and two staff members (one of which was Mr. Carl) coming through the door. They were wearing white outfits. My head was pounding from all the crying.

Mr. Carl knelt down and said, "Tyrone, we need you to take your medication. Open your mouth."

I opened my mouth and allowed him to insert the two capsules. At this point, I would do anything to get away from being restrained as I was. Mr. Carl took a cup of water from the other nurse and proceeded to pour it in my mouth. After I took the medication, Mr. Carl unstrapped the belts and took me off the restraint board. "You can go in there with the other children," he said, and he walked out with the other nurse.

Consumed with sadness, I no longer felt like engaging with the other children. I peered into the dayroom and noticed that the other children were watching *The Mighty Ducks* again and eating popcorn. I walked past the dayroom, entered my bedroom, and sat on my bed; I then gazed mutely out the large window. I could feel the tears welling up in my eyes again. The happy thoughts of spending time with the McClellands began to flood my mind. I remembered playing with Max in the living room, learning how to play cowboys and Indians with Mike, and going to the rodeo. All of these memories made me cry even more. The tears fell because the normalcy that I was longing for was nowhere in sight—yet seemingly close at the same time, at the McClellands' home. So many questions filled my head. Why am I taking little pills? Why was I forced into a white jacket and tied to a board? Does anybody love me enough to protect me? I remember going to sleep with hundreds of such questions floating in my head.

According to my state records, my caseworker came out to visit me around this time.

On November 28, 1994, I was discharged from Forest Springs Hospital and placed back at Peace Children's Home. Although I continued to feel discombobulated from the medication, I was happy to leave that place, which had the authority to place me in a room and tie me to a board. As a child, I did not understand why psychiatric medication and physical abuse were being utilized as tools for behavior modification. As an adult, I can finally make sense of these experiences, and I hope that social workers understand that a pill will never replace genuine mothers and fathers—or human compassion.

CHAPTER 6

Champions Treatment Center

When I returned to Peace Children's Home, I was surprised to find out that CPS had placed my sister Trish at the shelter. When I walked through the door, Trish picked me up and gave me a big hug. "Little biscuit head!" she said, hugging me tightly. "Why have you been cutting up in school?" she asked with a stern voice, which turned from happy and high-pitched to firm and motherly.

"I don't know," I replied. "Where's T-T-Tasha?"

Trish looked from side to side and said, "They sent her to someplace called DePelchin."

Trish and I sat and talked for a minute. We were just happy to see each other. Sadly, our happy moment came to a screeching halt, thanks to one of the staff members.

"Y'all get those clothes from the van and go back to your units!"

Trish was known to have an attitude, and this was a moment for it to come out. She yelled back, "This is my brother I'm talking to—damn! Can't we have five minutes?"

"Trish, you know the drill! Go back to your unit!"

My sister rolled her eyes, but she helped me get the big, black trash bags full of clothes out of the van. She gave me a hug before we went back to our units.

Having my sister live at the shelter with me had its perks. No other kids bullied me because they knew my older sister would beat them up. One of my peers thought he could get away with harassing me, but my sister shoved his food in his face during lunch. Of course, she was restricted to her room for a week, but the point was made: "Don't touch my baby brother."

During the first week of my sister's being in the shelter, I noticed that she had become very outspoken and blunt. She was notorious for saying things that other children were afraid to say. I remember everyone from the shelter piling into Big Dookie, the big, brown Ford Econoline, to go see the movie *Dumb and Dumber*. Once we got into the theater and sat down, my sister became disgusted at the fact that we could not get any popcorn. Of course, food for twenty young people would be expensive at a movie theater. To cut the cost, staff members packed pretzels and Cheez-Its and passed them out during the movie. When my sister received a napkin full of the small orange crackers, she became offended, rolled her eyes, and blurted, "I don't want this crap! Why the hell we got to eat Cheez-Its when everyone else is eating popcorn?" Trish was adamant about getting popcorn. She caused such a big scene that every one of us ended up sharing her sentiments and complaining. Needless to say, we did not finish the movie; everyone was forced to pile back into the van, and we were taken back to the shelter.

My sister had no shame in her game. I remember another instance of everyone being in the cafeteria for a meal. Mrs. Janice was the lead supervisor that day, and for some reason, she was monitoring the noise in the cafeteria. "Quiet down and eat your food in silence!" she yelled as she walked in and out of the aisles. I remember Mrs. Janice's beady eyes glaring down on us as she walked past us. I noticed that as Mrs. Janice walked by, some of the children would give a little smirk and hold their heads down. "I wonder why they're laughing," I thought. Shortly thereafter, I found out! When Mrs. Janice walked past Trish, it was all over!

My sister looked from side to side and started laughing hysterically! In fact, she laughed so hard that she spit her food out of her mouth! Between bursts of laughter, Trish blurted, "Damn, Mrs. Janice, you stank! Did you clean your ass this morning? How can you preach to us about hygiene when you smell like ass?"

When my sister said this, the whole cafeteria thundered with laughter and started calling Mrs. Janice "Stank Butt"! Needless to say, we were all sent to our rooms and put to bed early. Although we had been disciplined, from that day forward, everyone would silently call Mrs. Janice "Stank Butt" and giggle when she walked by.

As more days passed, I noticed that my sister's bluntness and humorous candor toward staff members started to catch up with her. Both of us began to get into big trouble. One night, while everyone was lining up for snack time, my sister got into it with a staff member because she was upset about having to eat pretzels for the third day in a row. Rolling her eyes and crossing her arms, she said, "Man, this is some bullshit! We can't have nothing better to eat than these crusty-ass pretzels?"

Saying this caused a lot of the other children to agree and say the same thing. One by one, we began to smack our lips and throw the pretzels away. A lot of the older boys blurted profanities as well, mocking the shelter's poor choices in snacks. As the staff members tried their best to quiet everybody down and to direct us back to our units, my sister continued to go off on the staff members. While all the others went back to their rooms, my sister refused to go and demanded a peanut-butter-and-jelly sandwich. Of course, being her younger brother, I refused to go back to my room too. With our arms crossed, the both of us refused to move. After a couple of minutes, one of the staff members picked me up, threw me over his shoulder, and proceeded to take me into my unit.

My sister, upset at how hard the staff member had thrown me over his shoulder, ran toward him and screamed, "You better put my damn brother down before you hurt him!"

Before my sister could pull me down, one of the other staff members pulled her away, wrestled her to the ground, and forced her face against the linoleum floor. It was happening again! Seeing this happen to my sister jolted me; I felt as if I had seen a ghost. My heart began to beat faster and faster as

I witnessed my sister being restrained. Her face twisted in agony. Her weave had fallen out when she was forced to the floor.

The staff member tossed me into the room with the other boys; however, I ran back into the hallway and into the cafeteria. Panting frantically, I hid in one of the utility closets and tried to gather my thoughts. While I was hiding, I could hear the high-pitched screams of my sister getting louder and louder.

"I can't breathe! Let go of my arm!" screamed Trish, the tone of her cries clearly portraying her anguish.

Adrenaline surged through my veins, and I became certain that I needed to do something! I grabbed one of the brooms in the utility closet and ran out to attack the staff member. "G-g-get off my sister!" I stuttered.

Before I could get much closer to help Trish, the staff member who had thrown me into my unit only moments ago grabbed me, tossed the broom aside, and forced me facedown on the floor, pressing my arms so far up toward my head that I could hardly breathe. What is more, the fall to the floor knocked out one of my front teeth. As I screamed in agony, blood gushed from my mouth and started to puddle around my cheeks and eyes. In the hallway, I could still hear my sister's screams. Her cries wavered back and forth between "You're hurting my arm!" and "Don't hurt my brother!" The staff member who was restraining me felt I was subdued enough, so he instructed me to go to bed.

I did as I was told. As I lay in bed, I heard the staff members instruct my sister to count for her body parts. My sister's cries began to show that she, too, had become subdued. I heard the staff members tell my sister that after she had counted to ten, they would release one of her arms. My sister's cries had subsided to faint attempts to count to ten. As my eyes became heavy with sleep, I could still see the image of my sister's face twisted in agony. Witnessing my sister being restrained in such a violent manner that her hair weave came out had pushed me to a point of fear. As I drifted off to sleep, I thought, "Who will protect me now?"

My sister continued to be the sarcastic class clown of the orphanage; thus, she was restrained repeatedly. Instead of sitting down with someone who could help us process our feelings, my sister and I were isolated in rooms and given more psychiatric drugs. On some days, my sister and I would try to run. There were numerous days when my sister and I ran through the tall grass at the shelter, pretending that we would find our family members and be happy. During these runs, we would tell ourselves that we were escaping the shelter, fleeing to some faraway place where we would be happy. Sadly, we were always unsuccessful at erasing reality in such flights; we only ended up being restricted repeatedly to our rooms after them. Seeing my sister getting restrained always caused me great pain—pain that I did not know how to express to anyone verbally.

There were days when I found myself climbing trees and staying up in the branches for long periods of time. One day, when I was perched high up on a branch, I looked off into the evening sunset and dreamed of a better place. Something in me knew there was more to life than the pain I was experiencing.

According to my CPS records, my behavior began to spiral out of control, and the orphanage sought to have me committed to another psychiatric hospital. On December 22, 1994—less than a month after I was released from Forest Springs Hospital—I was committed to Champions Psychiatric Hospital.

Chaotic activity continued to take place inside me, and no one seemed to truly understand what I needed. The psychiatrists, social workers, and staff members of Peace Children's Home continued to treat me as if I were a patient needing some sort of treatment rather than a child who needed intellectual stimulation, love, and affection. It seemed as if no one cared. On the inside,

I was folding up mentally and emotionally because of the constant physical, sexual, and psychiatric abuse that I was enduring in an environment that was not conducive to my growth and development.

My arrival at Champions Treatment Center was very memorable. I remember walking with my social worker down a long pathway that led to three cottages and a huge, expansive field. As we approached the field, I noticed that the entire field was covered in snow. Off in the distance, I saw a large truck. "Maybe that's where all the snow came from," I thought. The field was full of children my age, and they were running, making snowmen, and throwing snowballs. "Wow, I can't wait to make a snowman!" I thought. Just the thought of making one made me happy and brought a big smile to my face. Full of excitement, I took off running toward the kids playing in the snow.

"Get back over here!" my caseworker yelled. Her high-pitched voice was enough to halt anyone in his or her tracks. We turned the corner, and I noticed that the three cottages had a lush flower garden before them. As we entered the middle cottage, I saw a little wooden sign that read "Brookside Unit" on the door.

"Mrs. McClain, w-w-what does Brookside mean?" I asked.

Mrs. McClain looked down and said, "It's the name of your specific unit now. Be quiet and sit down."

I remember sitting for what seemed like hours. As I sat in the office, I noticed that there were file folders, colorful paintings, and a big copy machine in the office. My mind soon began to wander. "I wonder if the food will be good. Are we going to go on outings or field trips?" My daydreaming was interrupted by my social worker and a nurse walking into the room.

"I'm sure he will be just fine here," said the staff member, smiling down at me with a big grin.

"The Brookside Unit is different than all the others," said the nurse, who continued to talk to the social worker for a while. Once they finished talking, the nurse said, "Hi, Tyrone. I'm Mr. Allen."

I noticed that this man had on dark-blue scrubs and black shoes. After my social worker left the building, Mr. Allen showed me around the facility. I noticed that this hospital had a dayroom just like the last hospital. The dayroom was filled with several sofas, pictures, and even a pet bird. Everything looked so colorful! I remember thinking, "How bad can this place be?" I continued to walk throughout the hospital with Mr. Allen. When I first walked into the unit, I noticed that there was a room with a tiny window at the top. Straight ahead and behind a glass window was the nurses' station. To the left and right of the nurses' station were two long hallways with rooms on both sides. One hallway was for the girls; the other was for the boys.

"This is your room, Tyrone," Mr. Allen said.

I saw that there were two wooden beds and a large window, which provided a view of the open field with all the snow. "This whole room is for me?" I asked excitedly, as I looked up to Mr. Allen.

"No, you have a roommate who will be here shortly," he replied. "Stay in here while I get your stuff." He then left the room.

I continued to investigate my room and noticed that there was a bathroom with two sinks and another door. I opened the door to the other side and found another room with two wooden beds. Back in my room, Mr. Allen had already begun to place the big, black trash bags containing my clothes on my bed. The trash bags reminded me of trash. The idea of trash reminded me of how I had been treated at the last hospital. I walked over to the window and watched the other kids play in the snow, but I suddenly felt a feeling of fear hit me like a ton of bricks. The memories of being strapped to a board and left in a room played back in my mind. "I wonder if they will treat me like trash here," I thought.

My thoughts were interrupted by the staff member's voice: "Tyrone! Put your clothes up and come in the dayroom for group."

"OK," I said. I waited until the staff member left my room, and then I threw my clothes under the bed. As I ran from my room and toward the dayroom, I heard the roaring voices of children and teenagers. Just knowing that I was about to meet new people brought a big smile to my face. I entered the dayroom and plopped on the couch, next to two arguing teenagers.

"Dude, seriously? The best artist around is 2 Live Crew, but you're stuck on Hootie and the Blowfish? What the heck is wrong with you?"

"Hi, I'm T-T-Tyrone," I blurted, interrupting their conversation.

"Hey, twerp, this seat is taken," one of the boys said. He shoved me out of the seat.

After I picked myself up off the floor, I heard someone say, "Hey, over here." I looked around but did not see anyone. "Over here, retard," the person said a little more loudly.

I glanced to my left. A girl my height was waving her hands. She was sitting on a couch, so I climbed up next to her and excitedly sat down. Before I could tell her my name, she put her fingers on her lips and said, "Shhh, don't talk." I stared at her, feeling confused because all of the other kids were talking. "Look over at the window! We're on yellow," she said, pointing across the room.

Still confused, I looked over at the window and noticed that there was a traffic light behind the nurses' station. "W-w-what's that for?" I asked.

"If it goes to red, then we are put on shutdown," the girl replied.

After a moment, a boy with red hair and freckles stood and yelled, "Hey, everyone, shut up! I'm not going on shutdown for all of you busters."

Someone else blurted, "Troy, you're going on shutdown because you and Becky won't stop kissing." Everyone in the room started to laugh at the comment. Troy and Becky were sitting next to each other and blushing deeply.

"All right, everyone, settle down!" said a staff member, who came in with a stern face. "You guys know the drill! Should I cancel tonight's activity and put you on shutdown?"

All of the kids shuffled in their seats and murmured no.

"Well, I suggest that all of you settle down and get ready for group counseling."

The staff member then left, and an older woman with gray hair walked in, holding a big box. She plopped it down and excitedly said, "All right, everyone, today's group activity is called music therapy!"

The woman instructed everyone to get a blanket and to lie on the floor. While lying on my blanket, I heard the sound of waves crashing against the beach. The soft sound of the music caused me to slowly drift asleep. Later, I awoke to someone slapping me on my head—the girl I had sat by earlier.

"It's time to go!" she said. "We're going skating."

I jumped up, tucked my shirt in, and headed toward the door with all of the other children. Before I could get out of the door, a staff member yelled, "Tyrone, come back in the dayroom."

After talking with the staff member, I ran to my room, angry tears falling down my cheeks. The staff member had told me that I had to stay in my room because the doctor was placing me on a one-to-one. To top it off, I did not even have a roommate anymore! Apparently, I could not leave my room, and I had to have a staff member watch me at all times.

Many days passed in which I just sat and looked out the window, merely watching the other kids play in the snow. A tall white guy with a clipboard often sat at the entrance to my bedroom; he periodically would glance my way and write a note. My thoughts were interrupted three times a day—when a staff member brought my breakfast, lunch, and dinner. Each meal came with pills. Some of the pills were fat and yellow; others were little and white. "Open your mouth and lift up your tongue," the staff member would request, always making sure that I swallowed my medication. I would often feel like a lab rat when I was in my room. On most days, the medication would bludgeon me into a deep sleep. "When will I ever get a chance to be a normal kid?" I often asked myself.

Christmas came quickly, and I remember waking up to a remote-control car. Happy to have something that could hold my attention, I played with the car constantly—until it broke. A couple of days after Christmas, a new staff member, Mr. Newman, took over watching me in my room. He was a heavyset man with a bald head and no neck. When he was around, I found myself getting happier and happier each day. For once, things started to get a little better.

Mr. Newman would come into my room each day and try to cheer me up by cracking jokes. He always had something exciting for me to do. There were days when he and I played baseball with paper balls and broken hangers. We would do anything just to prevent boredom.

On some days, he and I would have a dance contest. In one particular dance session, the radio was blasting the song "Slam," by Onyx.

"All right, I'm about to show you how to break it down," said Mr. Newman as he tried to dance. His big belly and bald, round head really made me laugh as he spun around. To me, he looked like a big and fat California raisin, just like the cartoon. What was so funny was that he actually had the nerve to try to dance. After ten seconds, Mr. Newman said, "All right, boy, your turn! Hell, you got my big behind in here sweating and farting." He turned up the radio, and I tried my best to dance and sing the lyrics to the song.

"S-s-slam! Duh duh duh! Let the b-b-boys be boys!" I said, stuttering and smiling. Both of us laughed hysterically because neither of us could dance.

Mr. Newman and I continued to do fun things until my last day on the one-to-one.

"Bubba, I got good news! The doctor took you off the one-to-one!"

I could not believe it! After weeks of thinking that I would never leave the four walls of the bedroom, the day had actually come! I looked up at Mr. Newman and grinned, but he had tears in his eyes.

"I'm proud of you, bubba," he said, patting me on the head. I gave him a hug and ran to find the other children.

My stay at Champions turned from horrible to somewhat fun overnight! I started to go on fun activities with the other kids and made friends by attending the on-campus school. I was having a blast! In class, we learned about the Amazon rain forest, baked cookies, and took turns feeding the classroom's pet hamster. Just when I thought it could not get any better, I received the best news a child could hear at the hospital.

"Tyrone, a visitor is here to see you," said a staff member, who then led me outside.

As the staff member walked with me to the playground, the smell of pine trees filled the air, and the sun shined brightly through the trees. "I wonder who came to visit me," I thought. As we turned the corner, I saw that my visitors were Mrs. McClelland and Amy, her daughter.

"Mrs. McClelland! Amy!" I yelled as I ran into their arms. Since Mrs. McClelland had shown up, I knew we were going to have fun, because she never came empty-handed. On that day, Mrs. McClelland and Amy brought a bag full of colorful plastic eggs, which they hid all over the playground to create an Easter egg hunt. I smiled from ear to ear and never stopped to breathe as I searched for the Easter eggs.

After the Easter egg hunt, Mrs. McClelland handed me a Goosebumps book, by R. L. Stine, and said, "Now, Tyrone, I want you to continue your reading, OK?"

"Yes, ma'am," I said, stuffing myself full of jelly beans and milk-chocolate candy bars.

Mrs. McClelland and Amy hugged me before taking me back to the cottage. When Mrs. McClelland left, it was as if she had taken a part of me with her. For some strange reason, I felt as if I would never see her again. When I walked back into the shelter, I was instructed to go to my room for quiet time.

The walk down the long hallway to my room seemed to take a little longer that day. Suddenly, the salty taste of my tears blotted out the taste of the candy from the Easter egg hunt. As I lay on my bed and stared out the window, I became consumed by sadness. I did not want to be at Champions anymore. Just that quickly, I missed how special Mrs. McClelland made me feel. "Why can't I feel special like this every day?" I thought.

After Mrs. McClelland left, I no longer wanted to be around the other children. I halfheartedly participated in school and picked over my food. I noticed that the nurse at the hospital started to give me different pills. As the days passed, I began to feel as if something bad was about to happen. I would soon recognize that my intuition proved to be correct.

A couple of weeks after Mrs. McClelland left, it happened again! It was movie day at the hospital. All of the children had gathered in the dayroom to eat ice cream and watch *The Goonies*.

"All right, everyone, go to your rooms for quiet time," said a staff member as he pressed the eject button on the VCR.

"Ahhh, man, can't we finish the movie?" begged one kid.

"You know the drill, guys. You all need to stay in your rooms until the shift change is over!"

All the kids in the room began to leave the dayroom and walk toward their bedrooms. As I walked down the long hallway toward my room, I noticed that there was a lady painting the wall. The thick smell of the paint made me cough. As I walked past the lady, we exchanged glances, and I continued to walk into my room and to lie on my bed. Before I could shut my eyes, the lady came to my door with two male staff members. "That's him right there!" she said, pointing.

Confused, I sat up in my bed and blurted, "W-w-what's going on?"

"You know what you did, Tyrone! You know better than to slap people on the butt! Let's go!" said one of the staff members.

"I d-d-didn't do nothing," I replied, walking toward the door. I became so angry that I started to cry.

The staff members and I walked down the long hallway, and I could see some of the other children peeking their heads out of their rooms. Suddenly, I found myself standing in front of a white door with a window at the top. When one of the staff members opened the door, I saw that the room's walls had white padding, and there was a small cot in the corner. When I recognized where the staff was trying to put me, I took off running down the hall. Tears welled up in my eyes; everything became a blur. My eyes locked on the door at the end of the hallway, and with every step I took, I felt my heart increase its hammering in my chest!

"Hey, get back here!" one of the staff members yelled, and they both chased after me.

Just the thought of going into that quiet room gave me chills. "I have to run for my life!" I repeated to myself frantically. As I approached the door at the end of the hallway, I noticed that there was a sign with red letters that read "Exit." I pressed my hands hard against the metal door, gave it a hard push, and found myself on the playground. The sound of the alarm going off added haste to my tiny legs.

Bam!

Before I knew it, I had been tackled to the floor. "Let me go!" I screamed as the staff members grabbed me by the arms and legs. I tried with all my might to break free from their grip, but I was no match for their combined strength—my kicks and punches were futile. They carried me back inside and down the long hallway, and other kids laughed and pointed.

"Watch his head," one of the staff members said. They plopped me on the mat in the quiet room.

"Calm down, Tyrone, and stay in the room," said the other staff member. "Calm down...Calm down!"

The more the staff member told me to relax, the more I began to yell uncontrollably. I tried to force my way out of the door, but then a nurse walked in with a large needle. "Tyrone, honey, we need you to calm down, OK?" she said, and she motioned for the staff members to hold me down.

I wrestled for my life.

I fought, kicked, and squirmed to prevent the nurse from giving me a shot. Eventually, the nurse and staff members gave up. "It's pointless," said the nurse. She and the staff members then left, slamming the door behind them with a loud thud.

"S-s-somebody help me! Mrs. McClelland! Anybody!" I screamed. My T-shirt was saturated with tears. The cold air combined with my wet T-shirt and caused me to shiver. I cried and screamed relentlessly, eventually curling up into a ball on the floor, where I lay feeling lonely, rejected, and sad.

After this incident, I remember waking up in my bedroom with a crushing headache. My stay at Champions became dull. My mornings, afternoons, and evenings were filled with pills, group-therapy sessions, and team-building activities, all the way up until the day I left. Once I left Champions, I was placed back at Peace Children's Home. I did not know what to think. In a way, my emotions had become numb.

"Tyrone!" screamed Trish as I walked through the door. "Boy, you are so bad!" she said, wiping tear-stained crud from my eyes. "Y'all come see my brother!" yelled my sister, smiling from cheek to cheek.

To my surprise, there were more children at the shelter. When she beckoned them, all of the girls from her unit came out of the back room. Most of the girls were new to the shelter; however, there was one who caught my eye.

"Ugh! Oh, y'all, look at how he looking at Kiesha! Tyrone, do you like her?" said Trish, smiling.

I did not answer; I just looked at the ground.

"Come here, Kiesha," my sister said. Before I knew it, my sister had pushed our heads together to make us kiss.

All of the kids laughed and ran back into their units, saying, "Tyrone and Kiesha sitting in a tree—K-I-S-S-I-N-G!" They sang loudly, taking their time with each letter of the word *kissing*.

Making the transition back into Peace Children's Home was easy, primarily because Kiesha, a light-skinned girl with long hair, swam through my head continuously, smothering all other thoughts. I volunteered to do chores around the facility just so I could see her. We passed letters back and forth, sat by each other during mealtimes, and even played outside during recreation time. When the recreation periods were over, Kiesha and I always found a way to sneak away from the other children and kiss behind the building. Things were going well until we got caught by one of the staff members. Both of us were restricted to our rooms for what seemed like forever.

During the restriction, I sat in my room, unable to think about anything else but her. I wrote letters to her, but without a way to give them to her, I found myself just lying in bed. I did nothing from sunup to sundown, except wait…and wait…and wait. Eventually, I tried to find things to occupy my attention, and I found myself paying attention to a small creature that was moving on the other side of the room. I squinted—it was a cockroach. Having nothing else to do, I ran over and picked it up. "Where are you going?" I asked, imagining that the roach could talk. "I think I will name you 'Bertha,'" I said. I played with Bertha the roach as often as I could that day. Occasionally, I would see ants in my room, and I would catch and play with them.

Eventually, I got tired of searching for little things to occupy my attention. I wanted to get out of the room and be with the other kids. I tried to escape my prison.

"Tyrone, you got five seconds to get back to your room!" yelled a staff member.

During the time of my restriction, my older sister was transferred to another shelter. Before she left, a staff member let her come to my room and sit with me.

"It's gone be OK, Tyrone," said my sister, laying my head on her chest. "One day, you will get out of here, and you won't have to worry about all this bullcrap."

"One day, we will we see M-M-Mamma and our family, right?" I stuttered.

My sister pushed me off her chest and said, "Boy, don't you get it? We don't have a family! They don't care about our asses; that's why we're in child protective services!"

We sat in the room and cried together until a social worker took her away.

Life at Peace Children's Home took a turn for the worse after my sister left. I guess the staff felt sorry for me, because they let me out of my room after Trish's departure. But little good my freedom did; my first girlfriend, Kiesha, had started to hang out with another boy, I was picked on more frequently, and I felt increasingly lonely. I started seeing the orphanage's in-house counselor, and it felt good to talk to someone to let things out.

I would go on relentless tirades, demanding to live like a normal kid, asking why I had to live there and be picked on, insisting that I be given a mom, dad, and friends, and so forth. For the most part, the counselor would sit there and reassure me, repeating that everything would be OK. My counseling sessions lasted only a couple of weeks. Just when I thought I could finally open up and trust her, I was hurt to my core all over again.

While I was explaining to the counselor my desire for a normal life and real family, the counselor felt the need to tell me that I was mentally retarded. When she said this, I felt as if I had been punched in the chest.

"Tyrone, you're retarded; that's why you are here," she repeated.

When she said this, I ran to my room in tears, the words "*You're retarded*" running through my head repeatedly, causing me to cry myself to sleep. I could not take living at Peace Children's Home anymore. I was tired of the ups and downs and feeling like a throwaway. I remember leaving a voice mail on my caseworker's phone, begging her to take me away from the orphanage.

To my surprise, it worked!

One of the staff members told me during breakfast that I would be going to a foster home. Although I tried to wait patiently to leave, traumatic things continued to happen at Peace Children's Home. On some days, I was forced to rub a staff member's feet after school. "Since you're so hyperactive, come rub my feet until your medication starts working," the staff member would say. I would have to pull off the staff member's socks and rub her feet for what seemed like hours, while she would snooze on the couch. On some days, the children would laugh and tease me about my forced chore. "African foot-rubber," they would chortle. Regardless of their taunts, I feared what would happen if I did not rub the staff member's feet.

While I was waiting to go to the new foster home, new staff came in and out of the shelter. Some staff members were nice; however, there was one new staff member named Mrs. Lisa, and she was meaner than a junkyard dog. I remember several evenings in which she would lock me in a room and turn off the lights or others in which she would wake me up and throw me outside in my underwear. "Mrs. O. may like you, but I don't," she would say. I would beg her to not throw me outside by myself, but Mrs. Lisa was stronger than I was, so my resistance only caused my hands to get caught in the big metal door.

I remember crying my eyes out as I sat outside in the back of the building. The back of the building often had a lot of water, so I would become soaked in old rainwater and dirt. I was only ten years old at the time. I was still afraid of the dark, so when I was thrust into the darkness outside, I would feel as if I were about to die. In each of these temporary exiles, Mrs. Lisa would let me in after about fifteen minutes; then she would make me face a wall for what seemed like hours. I never understood why she treated me this way. All I knew was that when she let me go to bed, I was too tired to cry.

One of the last traumatic memories I experienced turned out to be a positive situation for me. As the medications increased, I found myself becoming more sluggish and irritable. All I wanted to do was sleep. One of the staff members became upset because I refused to get out of bed.

"You think just because you're going to a foster home that you can do whatever you want," said the staff member, and he proceeded to drag me from my bed.

Everything in me wanted to resist the staff member, but I could not because I was too weak. Once again, I found myself lying on the cold floor with my arms folded behind my back. As the staff member pressed my arms higher and higher toward my head, I could feel myself growing more lightheaded. The very fact that I could not resist made this all the more painful. After the restraint was over, I remembered just lying there. As I lay on the floor, I felt broken, subdued, and worn out. With the little strength I had left, I got up and pulled myself together. I sat on the couch and tried to watch TV, but my body kept aching from the excruciating pain of being restrained. Since the other children were playing board games, watching TV, and wrestling, I found it hard to drift asleep with all the noise.

When the shift change took place, one of the staff members took one look at me and asked, "Baby, what's wrong with you? You don't look good. Go to bed and lie down."

I did as I was told. After collapsing on my bed, I slept until late that night, and later I woke to a pounding headache. As I lay in bed, I felt myself becoming lightheaded again. My mouth was dry; I felt a sharp pain in my chest. I closed my eyes and then felt myself floating aimlessly high above my bed. Right before my body floated out of the building, I saw an angel. His skin was flawless and whiter than snow; he was clothed in a long, white tunic. He came floating toward me, and as he looked at me with his serious eyes, he made a loud soprano noise, causing me to wake up. This was one of the last memories I had before leaving Peace Children's Home.

CHAPTER 7

The Thibodauxs

―⁂―

SEPTEMBER 4, 1997, WAS THE day that my dream came true! God had heard my prayers for a real mom and dad! Leaving Peace Children's Home ended up being easy for me. I had become excessively tired from being abused and from feeling abnormal. I just wanted a real family, just like those of the children at Smith Elementary School.

I was so happy to leave that I could not pack my bags fast enough. I threw all my clothes into my big, black trash bags. The other children were at quiet time when I packed and left. As my caseworker and I sped off in her blue Camaro, I could not stop wondering about where we were going. I could not stop asking questions. "How long w-w-will it take for us t-t-to get there?" I stuttered excitedly. "Are they w-w-white or b-b-black? What if they—"

"Relax, Tyrone, and sit back in your seat," said my caseworker, interrupting me.

"Well, can you at l-l-least tell me where we are g-g-going?"

"You're going to a foster home in Alief, Texas, Tyrone. I told you that already. Now sit back and hush!"

Too excited to sit back, I gazed out the window and imagined a mother greeting me at the door with freshly baked chocolate-chip cookies and a glass of warm milk. I envisioned a dad who took me fishing and hunting and a big brother who gave me noogies. I imagined having an annoying little sister who got into my things and broke my action figures.

I thought, "What if they have an attic with a treasure map, and I travel off with my neighborhood friends in search of hidden treasure—like in *The*

Goonies! Wait a second. What if my caseworker is trying to surprise me? Maybe I'm really going to Mrs. McClelland's house!" I grinned from ear to ear. I continued to daydream up until the very moment we pulled into the driveway. I noticed that there were a blue Plymouth Voyager and a silver Volkswagen Rabbit in the driveway of a small, one-story house. Excited and impatient, I burst out of the car door and rang the doorbell. At last, I was about to meet the parents of my dreams.

"Stan, he not gone make it! Call the agency back, and tell them to come get this nigga!" said my foster mother angrily.

"Give the boy a chance, Dana! He hasn't been here three weeks, and you're already itching and scratching to put him out!" replied my foster dad.

"Stan, the boy is retarded and throwed off. Can't you see that? The boy is on six different medications and still can't function, not to mention this fool sat up and ate all the Little Debbie cakes in the house! Oh, and wait! The little nigga is eleven years old and still don't know how to wash his face and brush his teeth! I promise if he get in my car one more time and I get a whiff of that booboo smellin' breath, I'm putting him out the car!" yelled my foster mother.

"Dilly, will you calm down? I have a good feeling about him and—"

"Stan, no! We're not doing this! I told you that I didn't want developmentally delayed or retarded children in our home! I don't have the time or patience to deal with this. Stan, the only butt I'm washing is mine! I'm not washing that nigga's butt again. Have you walked through the hallway? This throwed-off nigga hasn't bathed in five days!"

"Dilly, we gone give this boy a chance, and that's the end of it," my foster father concluded.

After one month at my new foster home, I quickly recognized that my new parents were far from the status quo. In fact, Stan and Dana Thibodaux were the complete opposite of what I had envisioned. Stan was an African-American pastor; he had a medium build, curly black hair, a big belly, and phenomenal cooking skills. Unfortunately, the closest I ever got to going fishing with my foster dad was when we all piled into the van and went to a grocery store called Fiesta and bought catfish ourselves! As for Dana, my foster mother, let us just say that she was far from the "tuck you in bed at night" or "Son, I made you some cookies" kind of mother. Mrs. Thibodaux was a heavyset black woman with curly hair, full breasts, and extremely short nerves. She was the kind of mother who was sweet, innocent, and rule abiding when the social workers were at the house, but she would not hesitate to throw something at me if I did something out of line after the social workers left. Dana was notorious for throwing shoes, spatulas, sausages, and even jars of peanut butter, and she was always willing to hit me in the head with such objects if I "worked her nerves," as she would say. Dana wore the pants in the house, and everyone knew to stay out of her way. It took me a while to understand, but just like most black women, Mrs. Thibodaux was a stern Christian woman who did not play. I quickly learned that I had to ask Stan for anything that I needed or wanted. Most of the time—that is, 99.9 percent of the time—Dana would answer a curt "No!" to my questions, even if they were innocent questions.

"M-M-Mama, can I sit by the fireplace and read my book?" I would ask excitedly.

"Naw, nigga. Anything that's set aside for my relaxation you want! Get your narrow behind over there and sit down somewhere."

"M-M-Mamma, c-c-can I have a c-c-chemistry set?"

"Naw, nigga. You not gone blow up my house with that foolishness! Get yo' behind to your room, and stop bugging me! I'm not here to entertain you!"

My new mother, Mrs. Thibodaux, was from the old school and extremely unpredictable.

I had two foster brothers: Eric, who was only four, and Tray, who was older than me. Eric knew to stay out of Dana's way too. Most of the time, he was mute and spent his days playing in the corner with his toys. Tray tried to give me the scoop on how things ran in the home. To my surprise, every rule that he advised me to follow was a rule that he broke!

For instance, he said, "Don't go to the refrigerator and take food because that's stealing, and Mama gets mad."

This took me by surprise because I thought normal children could go in their refrigerators and get snacks if they were hungry. I thought, "How is it stealing if this is my home and I'm hungry?"

Apparently, Tray felt the same way. One night, I rolled over and saw him eating chips and dip in our bedroom. The next morning, I woke up to my foster mother having a loud conversation with Tray.

"I didn't do it! Tyrone stole the food!" yelled Tray repeatedly.

After hearing this, I jumped out of bed and ran into the kitchen to defend myself. "He's l-l-lying! I saw him eating the f-f-food last n-n-night!" I cried, my stuttering impairing my claims of innocence.

"He can't even get his words out, Mama. He's lying!" Tray fired back.

As tears welled up in my eyes, I asked myself, "Why would he lie to me?"

Before I could make another claim, my foster mother yelled, "I accepted both of you trifflin' niggas into my home, and this is how you repay me? I'm doing what your own black mothers and fathers chose not to do, and you have the audacity to steal from me?"

Her vehemence forced me to plead my case. "I p-p-promise I—"

"Shut up, nigga!" said my foster mother, cutting me off. "When I speak, you don't say a word. Do you hear me?" Her booming voice seemed to be causing a mild earthquake.

"OK," I said, looking at the floor.

"Nigga, you got your people confused! When you reply to me, you say, 'Yes, ma'am.'"

"Yes, ma'am," I replied.

"Both of you are on room restriction, and I better not see you come out of that room at all!"

Devastated and in tears, I ran back to the room and slammed the door. Wham! The door slammed so hard that the wall shook. I locked the door and threw myself on the bed, yelling, "It's not fair! I didn't do anything!"

I guess I slammed the door so hard that it startled my foster dad. "What's going on here?" he said as he joined my foster mother outside my door.

"This fool has locked himself up in the room!" said Mrs. Thibodaux.

Before I knew it, the door flew open.

"I can close the door if I—"

Wham!

Before I could say anything else, Mrs. Thibodaux had me by my throat and up against the wall. "Boy, you got yo' people confused! Nigga, this my house!" she said, her hands wrapped around my neck. "When I say, 'Go to your room,' you go to your room, and don't you ever lock my door!"

Pinned between the wall and her hands, all I could do was nod my head and mumble, "Yes, ma'am."

As her eyes beamed down at me, she yelled, "Nigga, since you got a funky attitude, pack yo' mess and get out my house! Stan, I want this nigga out my house!" She released me and slammed the door closed on her way out.

Devastated, I ran after her, crying. "P-p-please! I don't wanna go back to that place!" I screamed. Snot and tears streamed down my face as I followed Mrs. Thibodaux around the house, begging her to let me stay.

"Naw, nigga, you can forget it! I'm calling the agency so that big black cow who brought you can take you back!" she said, laughing and smiling.

When I heard these words, I cried more vehemently. As I cried, Mr. and Mrs. Thibodaux walked around the house and mocked me by making crying noises. "Dilly, you a mess!" said my foster dad, chortling.

Left with no other choice, I ran back to my room. I lay on my bed, crying heavily, and I saw that Tray had the hugest grin on his face. He retrieved the chips from where he had hidden them—between his mattresses—and laughed out loud. "Dummy! You thought she would believe your stuttering ass?"

I was too angry to say anything; I did nothing but wait in silent anger for sleep to come.

The next morning, Mr. and Mrs. Thibodaux acted as if nothing had happened the day before.

"A'ight, niggas, rise and shine!" This was a frequent command used in the mornings. Waking up at the Thibodauxs' residence for school was like waking up at boot camp. If I did not wake up quickly, I got a belt across my face. My fantasy of waking up to a smiling mother wearing an apron and to a breakfast of fresh chocolate-chip pancakes, steaming eggs, and orange juice had become null and void. Breakfast was served at school.

I could not wait to get to school—at first. I was so happy to finally be back in a public school that I could not get there fast enough! I remember walking up to Albright Middle School and saying to myself, "Wow, I'm going to a real school—just like normal kids!" To my surprise, my attending Albright Middle School brought on culture shock! Nearly all of the school's students were black, and let us just say that being the new kid on the block and having a stuttering problem merited unfair treatment.

"Look at this nigga with the high-water pants! He must be waiting on a flood," said one student.

"This nigga so skinny that he can hula-hoop through a Cheerio!" another said.

As I walked through the hallways one day, someone yelled, "Look at that retarded nigga with the white stuff around his mouth!"

Essentially, I found myself the butt of every joke, in class or out of class. I felt horrible and out of place. This was the first time in my life when I started to recognize that I was socially delayed. I did not fit in at school, and I could not wait to get home.

"Hi, Mom!" I would say when I walked into the house after school. On good days, I was met with "Hey, Son, how was your day?" On bad days, I was greeted with "Go to your room, nigga. I've been dealing with kids all day long, and I don't feel like talking."

After school, my foster father would be either on the couch watching TV or in the kitchen frying catfish for dinner. Eric would always be in his own little world, in some corner, playing with his toys. As for Tray and me, wrestling and fighting about something petty usually occupied our time until dinner. When dinner was ready, Mrs. Thibodaux would yell, "A'ight, niggas—wash your hands!" I quickly learned that what I did not eat for dinner on one evening I would have to eat for dinner on the following day.

After supper, I would take my psychotropic medications, do my chores, and then head to bed. When everyone went to bed, I always knew not to go all the way to sleep. Without fail, right before I would be completely asleep, Mrs. Thibodaux would wake me up.

"Get up, and come rub my feet, boy," she would say as she walked into my room, wearing her pink robe.

Although I dreaded this particular chore, there was something about making her happy that made me feel happy in return. Mrs. Thibodaux was diabetic, and the neuropathy affected the circulation in her ankles. A bottle of Jergens almond-scented lotion was always waiting for me in front of the couch.

"Rub the lotion in your hands so it's warm before you rub it on my feet, chile," my foster mother would always remind me.

For hours, I would rub her feet and slide my fingers between her toes and up and down her calf muscles.

"Bend 'n' flex my ankle, boy," she would say, flipping through the TV stations. "Oooh yeah, baby, that's good—right there, boy! Chile, you gone be a massage therapist one day, and you gone be a good husband!"

On some nights, my foster mother was not concerned with TV, so she would wake me up and put a pallet on the floor in the middle of the living room. "Rub my lower back, chile," she would say, lying down on the pallet. Just about every other night, I rubbed her lower back for hours, working my way up toward her neck and shoulders and then back down to her lower back. I was extra careful not to spend extended amounts of time gazing at the TV, or my foster mother would say, "Nigga, you supposed to be focusing on my back!" It seemed as if I had to rub her back for hours! Every night when she would finally say, "Go to bed, chile," a huge burden would lift from my shoulders.

Living with the Thibodauxs was so monotonous through the week that I looked forward to the weekends. The first couple of weekends were somewhat fun. On Saturdays, my foster father would cook a big breakfast. I remember waking up to Kirk Franklin and the Winans playing on the radio. The aromatic scent of grits, eggs, pan sausages, and big and fluffy buttermilk biscuits would fill the house. Saturday mornings were the happiest times at the Thibodauxs. Sometimes my foster parents would play fight and dance in the kitchen. Seeing this always made my foster brothers and me laugh. After they got done play fighting, our foster mother would yell, "Fat nigga!" Everyone would laugh at her comment.

On many Saturdays, we would pile into the old Plymouth minivan and go to the Celebration Station to play miniature golf. Such golf-related outings would exhaust us (but in a good way). On most Saturday evenings, my foster brothers and I would play *Mortal Kombat* on the Sega Genesis.

"I'm S-S-Scorpion!" I would say as we prepared to battle. We would spend the rest of the evening being normal eleven-year-olds, having fun until our foster mother found chores for us to do.

"Come here, triflin'...mo nasty and pitiful...mo sorry," Mrs. Thibodaux would scream. She had a knack for adjectives. She always said Tray was more "triflin'" than he was nasty, and I was more "pitiful" than I was sorry.

On one of these Saturday evenings, we were playing our Sega as usual, but our foster mother became frustrated with our dirty room. "Why haven't you niggas cleaned your room?" she demanded with a serious expression. She had a large leather belt around her neck. Tray just stood there silently, rendered speechless. Of course, I could not get my words out.

"W-w-we was g-g-gone c-c-clean—"

"Both of you niggas drop them draw's right now—lay them down!" said our foster mother, cutting me off.

No place on my body was left untouched by the belt. As Tray and I rolled around on the floor crying, our foster mother yelled and screamed as her belt landed on our legs, butts, backs, faces, and necks. After the spanking, I cried as I lay in my bed. In my mind, I continued to see the images of her swinging the belt. Tray and I continued to sniffle and cry for a long while. That day, we learned to keep our room clean.

Sundays were full of excitement. On some weekends, we would have church at the house, and other weekends, we would attend Willing Workers Baptist Church. Church at the house was a time when some of Mr. and Mrs. Thibodaux's relatives would get together and pray and sing. My foster father would preach long and hard about a sermon titled "The Year of the Open Door." When he preached, he preached with passion, and sometimes I got this weird feeling that one day, God would use me in a miraculous way. In some of these sermons, my foster father could not preach at all because my foster mother would get up and start preaching the rest of the sermon for him! After such hijackings, my foster mother would say, "Sorry, y'all, that thang registered in my spirit, and I couldn't help it."

Mrs. Thibodaux's sisters, Vernice and Loretta, would call her by her nickname and say, "Dilly, you something else." My foster mother was a character, and most of the time, everyone just laughed off her religious episodes.

Mrs. Thibodaux was an awesome cook, so after church, everyone sat around the house and ate the best soul-food dinner in Texas. I'm talking collard greens, neck bones, cornbread, candy yams, smothered ham hocks, corn on the cob, broccoli and cheese casserole, and peach cobbler to top it all off. After everyone ate, some of the relatives left, and some of them stayed. Most of the time, the relatives who stayed had what we called "the itis." Mama would always say, "When niggas get good 'n' full, they get the itis." According to Mrs. Thibodaux, the itis was that drowsy feeling that came after eating soul food.

Without fail, when everyone was done eating and picking their teeth after the Sunday dinners, "Uncle Fat Nasty" would come bursting through the door, late and drunk, as always.

"You ole, sorry nigga! Church let out an hour and a half ago, but here you come galloping through the door!" my foster mother would say.

"Aww, Dilly, don't be like that!" Uncle Fat Nasty would say, grinning from ear to ear. Mrs. Thibodaux would give him a plate; she always had a plate for everyone.

The Sunday dinners would not be complete until the family did the electric slide. On one of these nights, Kirk Franklin's song "Stomp" played on the radio (it was a new song at the time), and everyone danced happily, smiled, and felt full (in a spiritual sense). As Tray and I ran around the house and played with the other kids, the grown folk would be in the living room, either dancing or talking.

Sometimes, though, I would come inside for water and hear the adults saying things like "Dilly, what's wrong with that new youngster you got?"

Mrs. Thibodaux would always respond in a dismissive and disrespectful vein: "I don't know, y'all. The boy is retarded. The psychiatrist got him on six medications."

Church at the house was mostly fun, despite the guests' harsh, confused comments regarding me. Tray and I, however, loved to go to Willing Workers Baptist Church. On every Sunday spent at the church, a big and fat lady named Mrs. Gerline would catch the Holy Ghost. Tray and I got kicked out once for looking at her facial expressions and her jiggling body as she danced to the music at church. Tray would lean over and whisper the letters "J-E-L-L-O," and I would finish the joke by saying, "It's alive!" Essentially, we were mimicking a Jell-O commercial.

Our time after church was always hilarious because Mrs. Thibodaux always had something to say about the people at the church service. "Stan, did you see that big-tittied cow up there singing and leading the praise team?" she once asked. "She ought to be ashamed of herself for runnin' around the church with them big, ole titties flopping around the sanctuary."

Tray and I tried our best not to laugh.

"Will you hush? You just don't know what to say," our foster father said.

"Whatever, fat nigga," Mom said sharply.

Tray and I could not hold it in any longer; our laughter roared throughout the car.

Life began to change at the Thibodauxs' home. I remember walking home from school on a cold November day. My breath was smoke before my eyes; the cold air was nipping my face. "I must get home so I can read my new library book," I thought, trying to walk briskly. When our house came into view, I was taken by surprise at what I saw; two cop cars were in the driveway. Mrs. Thibodaux was leaning against one of the cop cars with her arms folded, and she was talking to the officers. "His full name is Trayvion Green."

One of the officers scribbled down her words on a notepad.

"W-w-what's going on?" I asked, walking up to the house, feeling confused.

"Go in the house, baby, and sit down," my foster mother replied.

Again, her tone was sweet and affectionate, as it always was when some sort of official person was around.

"Wait a second, chile," she said. "Do you remember what Tray had on when he walked to school with you this morning?"

"N-n-no, ma'am," I said, looking down. I had been so excited about reading my book that I failed to notice that Tray had not walked back with me. I thought, "Tray can't be gone!" I ran to our room, opened the closet, and looked in the drawers. I thought, "His clothes are still here! He can't be gone!"

Out loud, I said, "S-s-stop playing, Tray!" Smiling, thinking this was all a game, I looked under the bed. Tray was not there. No matter how much I wanted to believe that Tray was hiding somewhere, the truth would turn out to be that Tray had run away from school.

As I sat on my bed, I began to remember how we used to fight and argue but, somehow, always found a way to play *Mortal Kombat*. Of course, Tray was often mean and got on my nerves, but I was sad to know that he was gone. After the police left, Mrs. Thibodaux came into my room; she had a big, black trash bag and instructed me to pack his clothes.

School seemed a bit odd the next day, now that Tray was gone. When I got back from school, I noticed Mrs. Thibodaux was sitting in the living room. "Come here, boy," she said sternly as I closed the door. "Tray ran away and told the agency that I whoop y'all. I suggest that if you want to stay here, you better lie when they ask you if I spank you."

All I could think about was being placed back at the orphanage and being restrained. The next day, a white man in a suit came to the house to talk to me, just as my foster mother had predicted. After making small talk, the social worker finally asked the big question, "Do Mr. and Mrs. Thibodaux spank you?"

"N-n-no," I said. "Mr. and Mrs. Thibodaux are very nice people, and I enjoy staying with them." Although Mr. and Mrs. Thibodaux spanked us, she was the only mother I had. Living with the Thibodauxs was better than any other placement I had been in, so I said whatever I could to stay in their home.

I will never forget that before Thanksgiving in 1997, Mrs. Thibodaux took me to see a psychiatrist because she felt I was too sad about Tray leaving. "You not gone sit here and slip into a state of depression because Tray run away. I'm taking you to see Dr. Haggs!" yelled Mrs. Thibodaux.

Once we got to the lobby, it seemed as if we had to wait forever just to see the psychiatrist. Just before I dozed off in my chair, the receptionist called Mrs. Thibodaux over the PA system.

"Wait here," said my foster mother.

After ten minutes, she stormed out of the office and said, "Let's go!" Once we got in the car, she slammed her door shut and sat in her seat without saying a word. "Open your mouth and tell me your name, chile," she said.

Confused, I looked at her and said, "My name is T-T-T—"

"Spit it out, chile!" she said, cutting me off. "Your name is Tyrone Obaseki, and don't you forget that! Just because you got a stuttering problem and may be a little throwed off doesn't mean that you're crazy and retarded!" she yelled.

"I've looked at some of your records, boy, and regardless of what that psychiatrist said, you're very smart for your age!"

There was silence in the car for the longest moment.

"But the c-c-counselor at my l-l-last shelter said I was r-r-retarded and—"

"I don't care what the counselor said at the shelter! The Bible says that you have the mind of Christ and that you can do whatever you set your mind to. Look at me, boy."

I looked at her.

"You go out there and get an education. You hear me? And don't let no one tell you that you can't do it! Always remember that no one can ever take your education from you."

Mrs. Thibodaux told me that Dr. Hagg explained that because my mom was mentally ill, I would be dependent on psychiatric medication all my life; according to the doctor, I had a genetic predisposition to mental illness. Mrs. Thibodaux continued to talk to me about moving past sorrow in life and the importance of getting an education until we pulled up in the driveway. After this talk, I felt as if I could be and do anything. At dinner later that night, my foster parents talked about the argument that took place in the psychiatrist's office.

"Stan, I had to pray because if that psychiatrist had said one more word, I was gonna ram his bald head through the window! I tried my best not to stomp a mud puddle in his behind! I'm taking him off all the medications, Stan."

"So my boy can stay after all?" asked Mr. Thibodaux jokingly.

"Stan, seriously, he may be a little thrown off, but the boy is making almost all A's in school. I just don't believe he needs all those pills and labels. Let's see how he fairs off the medications, and if he becomes increasingly depressed, angry, or defiant, I'll just commence to whooping his behind. You and I both know the Bible says that if you spare the rod, you spoil the child. Sounds like a plan to me."

(Mrs. Thibodaux always said a hard head makes a soft behind.)

Mr. Thibodaux said, "We can't stop being hard on him now. If we don't teach this boy some sense, then the cops will end up beating him. The Bible says spare the rod and spoil the child, and we're not raising spoiled niggas."

Time continued to pass at the Thibodauxs. My little foster brother, Eric, started talking! In fact, he talked too much. Now that I was off my medications, the Thibodauxs did not let up one bit. I did not get away with anything.

"Boy, you too old to not follow simple instructions," Mrs. Thibodaux would say.

"Use your head for more than a hat rack, boy," Mr. Thibodaux would repeat endlessly.

It seemed as if my foster parents worked extra hard to teach me life's lessons. Without the psychiatric medications, I had more energy and found myself able to think more clearly.

When the holidays rolled around, all of us had energy galore. For Christmas and Thanksgiving, everyone met at the house of Mrs. Thibodaux's father, whom we called "Paw Paw." According to Mrs. Thibodaux, Paw Paw stayed in the hood on the north side. Eric and I loved going to Paw Paw's house on Sundays because of all the food he would cook. We knew that if we went to his house for the holidays, we would get to drink a lot of soda and eat a lot of tasty food.

"Hey, it's Paw Paw's boys," he would say upon seeing us, and we always ran up to him to give him hugs.

As we entered Paw Paw's house after church on Sunday, the smell of the soul food filled our noses. I had never seen so many black people get together and eat and dance in my life! Mrs. Thibodaux was the center of attention, reminiscing and telling stories that made everyone laugh. She told a story about how her great-grandmother would throw household items at all of the children when she was upset. Sometimes she would tell stories about her experiences in college. The house would roar with laughter as everyone spent time reminiscing and telling stories about all the fun they had behind the courthouse in Thibodeax, Louisiana. Sunday and holiday dinners were happy times, filled with people laughing, eating, and dancing.

The holiday cheer and fun shifted when Leroy started coming around. Everyone knew Leroy as LA around the house. The word around the family was that LA went to jail for robbing some lady. Back when the cops arrested him, Mrs. Thibodaux showed no mercy for him and encouraged the cops to take him to jail.

"I taught him better than that, so y'all take him, and do whatever you need to. Teach him a lesson!" she said.

Now that LA was out of jail, my foster mother believed that he wanted revenge. He would pop up at the house, park his car in the driveway late at night, and turn his headlights off. Sometimes, I would see him through the blinds while I was restricted and grounded in my room. The day my foster mother got fed up with LA was a day I will never forget.

One night while Mr. Thibodaux was at work, Eric and I were rubbing Mrs. Thibodaux's feet. All of a sudden, we heard a knock on the door and car engines revving up.

"This nigga got his people confused," my foster mother said as she ran to her bedroom. She came back into the living room with a long, silver Smith and Wesson Magnum 500. "Y'all get over there by the front door, and don't open it for nobody!" she said, holding the gun toward the ceiling.

"Yes, ma'am," we said together, crying and feeling scared.

Mrs. Thibodaux was the only mother we had, so we did not want anything bad to happen to her. She held the gun up toward the air, leaned her back up against the door, and waited a couple of seconds before opening the door. When she opened it, LA took off in his car, and Mrs. Thibodaux went chasing after him.

"I thought I told yo' retarded butt to stay in the house!" our foster mother said when she found out I had followed her. "Get yo' butt back in that house, and shut the door."

As I ran back to the house, I saw Mrs. Thibodaux hiding in the bushes, waiting to see if LA was going to come back around the corner. Her pink bathrobe was filled with grass, and the strap of one of her slippers had come undone.

I found Eric on the floor crying when I went back into the house. Shortly thereafter, Mrs. Thibodaux came back into the house, looking upset. "That low-down nigga got his people confused!" she yelled angrily. She sat on the couch. She explained the situation to my foster dad when he came in, and the police were notified.

As time progressed, LA continued to creep around the neighborhood. His petty attempts to taunt us eventually encouraged us to relocate to Sugarland, Texas.

Moving to Sugarland meant I would have to make new friends and that I would have to be the new kid on the block again, which was what I dreaded the most. Although I was fourteen at the time and in the ninth grade, it seemed as if life had an insatiable desire to whoop my ass. I felt as if life thoroughly enjoyed seeing me sad and upset.

"All right, class, listen up! Make sure your book reviews are complete and ready to be turned in on Tuesday! No exceptions!" yelled my teacher as the bell rang.

The sound of twenty teenagers rushing out of the classroom filled the air. I packed my books as quickly as I could, hoping that I could slip out of class without being noticed. Right before I reached the door, the bullying started again without fail.

"Yo', special ed, where you going, nigga?" yelled a student.

"Bring yo' Tyrone Biggum–looking ass back over here!" yelled another.

As they walked past me in the hallway, one of them pushed me into a locker and said, "Go buy you some food, hobo!"

Being the new kid on the block again came with its own set of problems. Apparently, my being in special education and the way I looked and talked merited teasing. Once again, that old foe of mine—that is, bullying—had come back for an encore.

I hated Dulles High School, I hated the new neighborhood, and I just hated moving—period! Going to school made me angry because I did not fit in and was always picked on. All of the other boys made me the laughingstock of the class because of the clothes that I wore. To top it off, no one sat by me at lunch!

"Eww, it's the weirdo!" the girls would say, moving away from me.

"This seat is taken! Move the fuck around!" others would say.

"Why are his pants so high?" asked another, pointing at my shoes.

To escape the embarrassment of having to sit by myself, I did what I thought anyone else would do. I would quickly throw my backpack over my shoulder, pick up my food, and leave the cafeteria. When walking toward the hallway, I could feel the eyes of hundreds of students looking at me. I would think, "It'll all be over in a second if I keep walking." I would pick up the pace whenever I felt tears filling my eyes. Once I reached the bathroom, I would walk to the stall closest to the window, set my tray on the floor, bury my head in my hands, and let the tears fall. "People are mean," I would tell myself, crying heavily.

I can recall numerous days of eating in the bathroom. All I knew was that in the bathroom, at least I was free from the scornful eyes and ridicule of my peers, which caused me so much pain.

"Nigga, did you speak?" my foster mother said as I walked through the door.

"Oh, hey, sorry," I said in a soft voice as I headed toward my room.

"Nigga, I've had it with your funky attitude! If you can't speak to me when you step into my house, then stay yo' black butt outside!"

I shook my head, walked to my room, closed my door, and collapsed on my bed. "Life sucks," I thought as I closed my eyes. Seconds later, I grabbed the back of my head in pain; as I turned over, pain shot through my right eye. My foster mother had flung the door open and was ferociously swinging her belt. I wiggled and jumped, attempting to dodge the blows, but I was mostly unsuccessful.

"No!" I yelled, and I attempted to grab the belt from her.

Worst mistake...ever!

I nearly fell backward when Mrs. Thibodaux punched me hard in my chest. "Nigga, you better check yo'self before you wreck yo'self. This my house! You don't have any privacy in here! You turned fourteen, and now you smelling yourself! I tell you what; since you don't wanna speak and rather slam doors, get out of my house, nigga! Get to steppin'," she said, violently guiding me out the front door, using her belt.

I heard the dead bolt lock after she slammed the door shut. As I sat outside, tears streamed down my face, and I clenched my hands in anger. I cried, feeling like a rejected dog. All of the emotional turmoil throughout the years had a tendency to bubble up in such moments of intense anger, and it always made me cry and clench my fists. It seemed as if no one understood that instead of being beaten, isolated, and laughed at, all I needed was attention, validation, and positive reinforcement, coupled with more exposure to a church-like family.

Twenty minutes later, my foster mother opened the door and told me to come back inside. After she let me back in, we talked about my day at school. After I told her what happened, Mrs. Thibodaux started to teach me how to fight.

"Now don't be no punk, chile," she said, hitting me hard in the chest. "You better not start a fight, but you better finish it."

I honestly did not know what to expect with the Thibodauxs, especially with my foster mother. One moment, she was kicking me out; the next, she was teaching me how to stand up for myself.

As I progressed through my ninth-grade year in high school, I noticed that there was something about the Thibodauxs that never made any sense to me: they were devout Christians who sang in the choir and ministered on Sundays, yet their harsh behavior and words in day-to-day interactions contrasted sharply with their faith. Mrs. Thibodaux kept my foster brother and me in church, prayed for us weekly, and even sang gospel songs around the house; however, I could not understand why they sometimes felt as if I needed psychiatric medication. At one point, my foster father told me that I was chemically imbalanced. This switch in viewpoints regarding my mental health was confusing and hurtful at times. At night as I rubbed Mrs. Thibodaux's feet and back, she would say, "Some people need medication, Tyrone, just like I need medication for my diabetes."

"Yes, ma'am," I would say, rubbing the lotion on her ankles.

Some nights, Mrs. Thibodaux would talk to me about slavery and the importance of knowing my history. "I know I'm hard on you, but you gotta remember you're a black man in this world! If I don't teach you, the cops won't hesitate to pop a bullet in your butt. Your daddy and I are working hard to teach you how to be a strong man of God in this world."

Mrs. Thibodaux would often remind me of a little black boy named Emmitt Till, who was murdered for whistling at a white woman. She also talked about a man named James Byrd, who was killed in 1998 after he was tied to a truck and dragged for three miles. "They dragged him until his head popped off, and this just happened two years ago! Chile, you need to wake up, pay attention, and understand that this world is no joke," she said fervently.

She also educated me about seventeen-year-old Jessie Washington, who was brutally killed in Waco. "They called it the 'Waco Horror' when he was killed, and I believe it was around 1916 or 1917. If my memory serves me correct, they accused that boy of raping and killing some white lady. The people in Waco banned together, and people from all over northern Texas came to watch this boy die. They beat him, gouged out his eyes, threw gas on him, and barbecued him like a pig," said my foster mother, looking down at me over her thick glasses.

"Why would they do that, Mama?" I asked with wide eyes.

"It's the spirit of hate, chile, and don't ever let that infect your heart. The same spirit that filled those ten thousand people is the same demonic spirit that filled the mob of people that crucified Jesus Christ."

Although the Thibodauxs were stern and sometimes very strict, it seemed as if they were trying to get me ready to operate in a world that I had yet to fully understand. After I got done rubbing Mrs. Thibodaux's feet one night, I lay in bed, feeling frustrated and angry. I was old enough to understand racism and its effects on blacks, but I could not understand why my people, those who were black like me, were so condescending and cruel to me. As I lay in bed that night, I thought about how all of my pain thus far involved people with black skin like mine. Tears began to fall, and I thought about how I was physically and sexually abused at the orphanage by my own people. I remembered that it was my own black mother who left me in an apartment when I was two months old. "If black people endured so much pain and racism from white folks, then why are we so damn mean to each other?" I thought angrily. All I could think about was the fact that people with black skin were the ones who talked about my stuttering and laughed at me. "Why does my own foster mother beat the hell out of me every chance she gets?" I thought. I curled my fists and punched my pillow over and over. I hated racism, and I hated the cruel behavior of my people. Exhausted, I went to sleep, feeling confused and angry.

As the school year progressed, I found myself fighting left and right. I stopped running from my bullies and started facing them head-on. One day during my American history class, the teacher gave us an assignment to watch a movie and answer questions. I tried my best to focus on the movie, but I could not because of a student named D'ante and his three groupies. Apparently, they found it funny to make wisecracks about my haircut.

"Have you ever seen a crackhead with a chili bowl?" one of the groupies blurted, and the classroom boomed with laughter.

"I know you hear us, hobo," another one said.

My efforts to focus on the movie were futile. I sat there with clenched fists, my body filling up with rage as the students laughed. Suddenly, I felt a sharp pain on the back of my head. D'ante had thrown a textbook at me! I could no longer take the abuse. Before I knew it, I had picked up a chair and started to beat D'ante over and over with it. As everyone ran out of the classroom, I kicked and punched D'ante countless times. Blood gushed from his nose, and the sight of it inspired a sense of accomplishment in me. I kept hitting and punching him until the teacher from across the hall pulled me off him. Luckily, because I had not started this incident, I was only given in-school suspension. Despite the fight with D'ante, students continued to poke fun of me. School became a living hell.

During this long, drawn-out period of confusion and frustration, my anger was slipping out at home. I found myself restricted to my room daily for refusing to do my chores. The only thing that I found enjoyable was going to our new church, the Rejoice Family Worship Center. Attending that church was amazing. The warm, fuzzy feeling that I got during praise and worship was phenomenal. As I looked around during the services, I saw rows and rows of people praising God loudly. On some Sundays, the power of Jesus would be so heavily present that the pastor would drop to the floor and cry. During those moments, it seemed as if the pastor was very repetitive. "Change your way of thinking!" she would exclaim. "Don't miss your hour of visitation!"

After the sermons, Mrs. Thibodaux would sometimes get up and sing a song titled "Change" by Tramaine Hawkins. When my mother first sang this song, I told God that I believed in him. Although I had accepted Christ at Peace Children's Home, reading from the back of a Gideon Bible, I felt the need to reassert my devotion to him. On some days, I did not know if I was an atheist or a Christian because I had experienced so much pain. In my head, I felt as if life had dealt me so many blows, I needed a change. If accepting Jesus again and with a sincere heart was the change that would make things better in my life, then I was ready for it. As I walked to the altar to accept Jesus, people clapped and gave me big hugs. "What's happening to me?" I wondered. My mind was trying to figure out how I could feel so much joy in a time when life seemed so brutal. At the time, all I knew was that I felt clean, excited, and loved.

I did not know it at the time, but my life was about to change in an unimaginable way.

It was a Sunday evening, and the house still smelled like mustard greens, smothered chicken, okra, and corn bread from Sunday dinner. As Mr. and Mrs. Thibodaux were taking a nap before the night service, I practiced my algebra at the kitchen table. After one hour of studying and practicing, I still could not figure out how to solve for x. I slammed my textbook closed and thought, "I hate algebra!"

Looking for something new to occupy my attention, I left the kitchen and started to read my foster father's King James Bible in the living room. As I sat on the floor with my back up against the couch, I started to skip through the pages of the Bible. I remembered my foster father's sermon "The Year of the Open Door" from the book of Deuteronomy, so I spent some time there. I continued to flip through the pages and found myself captivated by the book of Revelation. I stumbled upon a scripture that stated there is a blessing in store for those who read that book. "Wow, I get a blessing for reading this book!" I thought.

The imagery was amazing. It was as if the words popped off the page. The stories of dragons coming out of the sea, Jesus arriving to earth with horses, and the moon turning red fascinated me. Another thing that stood out to me the most was that in heaven, there are creatures worshipping God day and night, repeating the phrase "Holy, holy, holy is the Lord God Almighty, who was, and is, and is to come." Although I could not understand all the passages, I believed that if I repeated this phrase, then God would bless me right then and there. I started walking around the house while repeating, "Holy, holy, holy is the Lord God Almighty, who was, and is, and is to come."

After ten minutes of chanting, I sat down by the couch, closed my eyes, and started to pray to God. To my surprise, I started to feel a warm sensation come over my body, even before I finished praying, and the most amazing thing happened to me. First, I saw its feet, which were white as snow. I noticed that it was wearing a long white tunic with a golden sash across its waist. As I continued to look up from the floor, I saw that it had shoulder-length hair that was curly and brown. I looked into its eyes and beheld its face, and I recognized what I was looking at. It was the angel from my dreams, the one who had brought me back to life when I was at the orphanage. Excited and amazed, I stopped breathing and just stared. Awe forced my eyes and mouth wide open, and I slowly began to get up from the floor. I noticed that his eyes were serious and dark like coal. Before I could figure out what the colorful markings were on the angel's chest, it disappeared into thin air.

"Wait, come back!" I said.

I could not believe what had just happened. Suddenly, I remembered what the pastor had said at church: "Don't miss your hour of visitation."

When Mr. and Mrs. Thibodaux woke up, I jumped up and down, telling them I had seen an angel. I was quickly told to go put my church clothes on for the evening service. Not fazed by their lack of interest, I later told everyone at church about the angel. That night during the altar call, I looked up at the pastor and told her every last detail of what I had seen. Gracefully, she put her hands on my head and prayed for me. She then smiled. It was almost as if she had already known.

That was the day in which I learned that there is something more beyond the corporeal world, something that our physical senses cannot immediately detect. Yes, this was the day that I recognized that there is more to this world than what is seen with the natural eye.

One would think that after seeing an angel, everything would become smooth sailing from there. To my surprise, things began to spin out of control at such a fast pace that I could not keep up. It was as if I were in a vortex. Shortly after I saw the angel, Mr. and Mrs. Thibodaux took me to a psychiatrist and said that I was behaving strangely and fighting at school. Once again, I was placed on psychiatric medications. I started writing letters to Jesus and my foster parents turned the letters in to the psychiatrist as if my behavior was abnormal.

"Sometimes, people have to take psychiatric medications because they have chemical imbalances in their heads," Mr. Thibodaux reiterated as we rode home from the psychiatrist's office.

As time passed, there were many days of feeling drained and numb. I felt as if the psychiatric medications were controlling me and making me feel down. Sometimes, I wanted to laugh but could not. Sometimes, I tried to talk, but the words just would not come out of my mouth. My attempts to convince the Thibodauxs to take me off the medications were futile.

One night, I took my medications after dinner, and as I lay down for bed, my heart started to race so loudly that I could hear it through my pillow. I felt as if I were about to die. Scared, I ran into the living room and told Mr. and Mrs. Thibodaux about my racing heart. They were unconcerned. They rushed me back to bed and instructed me not to leave my room. As I lay back down, my heart started to beat fast again, and I found myself unable to move. I tried to yell but could not; it was as if my body had shut down, and although I was awake, I had no control. I remember praying to Jesus and asking him to help me move again, and doing so worked. From that day forward, I made a vow and decree that I would never take the psychiatric drugs again.

As time passed, Mr. and Mrs. Thibodaux acted even harder on me because I would not take the psychiatric medications. My spirit was being crushed, and I found myself becoming increasingly angry because the bullying continued at school, I did not have any friends, girls thought I was weird, I felt as if I were about to die from all the psychiatric drugs, and—most important—an angel had appeared before me but vanished without saying one word.

"Life stinks," I thought.

Soon, I found myself being restricted to my room and getting beaten with belts for not doing chores. The Thibodauxs kept repeating the same phrase: "Be responsible." To be honest, I was trying to ignore those words. I was trying my best to make sense of a world that was proving itself to be confusing and hateful, and I felt abnormal.

I did not know it at the time, but the Thibodauxs were keeping progress notes of my behavior and submitting them to the agency. Mrs. Thibodaux kept telling me that if I did not change my behavior, they were going to send me away from their home. I was not concerned about being sent away because I was so restricted and sedated; I felt as if leaving her home would be just the break I needed.

During this time of ups and downs, I did find moments of joy. Mr. and Mrs. Thibodaux took in a sibling group of four kids. Jerome, the youngest, was a four-month-old baby; Michael was a two-year-old toddler; Candace was a four-year-old; and Monica was a ten-year-old. I became less occupied with my problems and focused more on trying to help my new little brothers and sisters. Having a house full of younger siblings seemed to bring a new ambience to the Thibodaux residence. I remember feeling so much excitement as the big brother.

After church, I sometimes would group them together and tell them stories. Everything was going well until I took it into my own hands to reprimand the children for getting into my things. When Monica told Mrs. Thibodaux that I beat her and the kids with a belt, I was restricted to my room for what seemed like a month. Once again, I felt as if everything I did was misconstrued.

I did not know it, but the foster-care agency was already making plans to move me because of my behavior. What should have been considered normal sibling play was interpreted as me touching one of my foster sisters inappropriately. After that incident, the agency decided to move me from the home.

The day before the agency took me away from the Thibodauxs, I was caught with a dirty magazine in my room, and boy was Mrs. Thibodaux mad.

"You nasty, low-down nigga," Mrs. Thibodaux said. "Lie down on the bed like you were lying in your room while you were reading that magazine, nigga!"

Scared, I lay down on the bed. Before I knew it, Mrs. Thibodaux was beating me with a belt and yelling, "You nasty nigga! I'm about to beat you for the old and the new!" She then forced me into her bedroom. Once I got into her closet, I was forced to take all of my clothes off, and she proceeded to beat me with her belt for about thirty minutes, but it felt as if it lasted forever. I remember crying and screaming so hard that my temples hurt. I tried to squeeze my butt cheeks together, but the blows of the belt forced them apart. As I wiggled and squirmed, the belt struck my balls, causing me to collapse into a fetal position; it felt as if someone had stomped hard on my genitals.

Lying in the fetal position was a horrible mistake—the blows of the belt then struck me upside my head.

"I want CPS!" I yelled amid a flurry of blows.

"Nigga, say what?" said Mrs. Thibodaux. "You want CPS? I got yo' CPS right here!" She whipped me faster and harder.

I remember just giving up. I lay there crying loudly, bracing myself for each blow, feeling like a subdued dog.

On November 14, 2001, a caseworker came and removed me from the Thibodaux home. I begged my caseworker to let me stay with them, frantically repeating that I had not abused my foster sister sexually or in any other way. My caseworker was adamant: I was to leave the Thibodauxs'. After I packed all of my trash bags and put them in the car, Mrs. Thibodaux gave me a hug. I thought, "Why is she hugging me?" As my caseworker sped off with me in the backseat, I did my best to navigate my confusion.

Part of me was sad to leave because the Thibodauxs were the only family I had known; another part of me was glad because the home had been so confusingly restrictive. Living with the Thibodauxs had become monotonous, and I was hoping for an environment that would provide intellectual stimulation that could occupy my attention.

CHAPTER 8

Troubled Years

"Do it or get punched in the mouth," one of my new foster brothers said.

They were huddling around a dresser.

Looking down at the powdered substance gathered in a straight line, I put my finger over my left nostril and inhaled as hard as I could, and I nearly fell over backward. My eyes began to water; my nose began to burn. "All right, I did it!" I said, rubbing my nose. "A deal is a deal—now let me have the top bunk!" My foster brothers were now on the floor and laughing maniacally. "W-w-what's so funny?"

"I can't believe your bitch ass thought we were serious!" said Deshawn. "Thanks for letting us know how stupid you are!"

My foster brothers, still laughing, got up and walked out of the room. Snorting my psychiatric medication, trazadone, proved to be a painful mistake.

My attempt to please my foster brothers by striking up a successful deal had backfired. I was tiny compared to my new foster brothers, Deshawn and Armondo, and I had worked hard to gain their acceptance, hoping their friendship would dissuade others from picking on me at school. After a week in my new foster home, I learned that I was in for a rude awakening. Deshawn and Armondo were not only bullies at the house but also the most aggressive bullies at Anahuac High School!

After being removed from the strict environment at the Thibodauxs' home, I was placed two hours outside the city of Houston, in a small country town called Anahuac. When my caseworker pulled up to the residence, I blurted, "What is this? This place looks like it belongs in *Little House on the Prairie!*"

My caseworker looked back at me and said, "Just make sure you don't get put out of this placement too!"

Everything in me wanted to scream, "Well, stop placing me with foster parents who get paid to beat my ass!"

I must admit that the change of scenery was nice, and the best part was that Mr. and Mrs. Raymond (my new foster parents) had horses, chickens, pigs, and goats on the ranch. I remember many days of getting off the school bus and running to the stable to play with the horses. Although I found happiness in playing with the animals, it seemed as if I could not smile for five minutes before life had to knock me down. I remember countless days of wrestling and fighting with my new foster brothers, Deshawn and Armondo. I remember days when we would be waiting at our bus stop, and I would become enraged because of my foster brothers' constant ridicule, which they perpetuated in front the other high school kids waiting at our stop. Each insult would make my hands clinch more tightly.

"Pop off, bitch. I dare you to say something!" Deshawn would say, towering above me.

What made such harassment worse was that there were three fine girls who were always present when I was being ridiculed.

"Ain't no sense in you looking over there. They not giving yo' bitch ass no pussy," Armondo would say.

The insults would continue on the bus rides. I remember countless rides in which I merely laid my head against the bus's windows. On those ridicule-filled bus rides, I could not get off the bus quickly enough.

At school, I felt like a reject. Nobody respected me because my foster brothers did not. As the days passed, I found myself eating in the bathrooms to escape from having to deal with my foster brothers' insults. In the evenings, I found that trying to talk to Mr. or Mrs. Raymond was futile. Mr. Raymond would blatantly ignore me; he would only sit on the couch in his underwear, scratching his balls and chewing tobacco. I would try to talk to

Mrs. Raymond as she talked on the phone and prepared dinner. She would say something similar to "Boy, get out my face with all that foolishness!" Then she would continue to talk on the phone.

"Great," I thought, "one foster family was too stern, but this foster family could practically care less."

My life became a blur at this home, and I felt myself becoming more and more emotionally numb. Thanksgiving and Christmas zipped by, and both days seemed as if they were just ordinary days. My life was moving swiftly before my eyes, and I felt as if I were being forced to watch from the sidelines. Right after Christmas, given no explanation, I was shipped to another foster home. As I threw all of my big black trash bags into the car and hopped in the front seat, I thought, "There's got to be more to life than this shitty-ass life I'm living in CPS."

"We're here!" my caseworker yelled, and I woke up, squinting my eyes and rubbing the side of my jaw. Apparently, I had slept deeply; drool was pooled right where the window met the car door. I looked off to the distance, and I saw an old water tower with big letters that said "Rosenberg, Texas." As I removed all of my clothes-filled trash bags and placed them in the house, I looked around and thought, "Wow, this house is huge! Staying here might not be so bad."

Mr. and Mrs. Egans had two biological children, Weslie and Melonie. Weslie was into sports, and Melonie was a cheerleader for B. F. Terry High School. Mr. and Mrs. Egans also had two foster kids, Tracy and Jason, who were both in their teenage years. Jason was a tall white dude who wore all black and was heavily into gothic stuff. As for Tracy, well, let us just say that he was Mrs. Egans's special boy. Tracy never said much of anything, and he walked with a limp. After a couple of days, I found out Tracy was mentally challenged.

Everything started out great at the Egans' foster home. I remember everyone going out for pizza on the first night and playing dominoes on the first weekend. I remember thinking, "Finally, a normal home." We attended a Baptist church in Wharton, Texas, which was similar to the Thibodauxs' church.

However, once the honeymoon phase was over, I started to recognize that something was not right at that home; there was a difference in the way my foster brothers and I were treated when compared with Mr. and Mrs. Egans' real children. I could not go outside and walk around the block, make private calls, or go to the movies by myself. (Her own children could, however.) Thus, life with the Egans became mundane. My entertainment and leisure were limited to watching TV, while the biological children went to parties and did practically whatever they wanted.

On one morning, before I rushed out the door to catch the bus, I remember telling Mrs. Egans that I did not want to take my medications anymore because they caused headaches. Her expression changed dramatically; she looked as if the world were coming to an end.

"You've been doing well in my home, Tyrone. I suggest you stay on the right path," she said with a serious look.

I explained to her once again that I was not going to take the medications anymore, and I quickly ran out the door to catch the bus. I thought the conversation was over until Mr. Egans, screaming and hollering, woke me up that night.

"Wake your ass up, and take these pills," he said, pulling my covers off me. The rank smell of alcohol and cigarettes emanated from his breath.

"I d-d-don't have to take these p-p-pills!" I said, stuttering.

Mr. Egans would not hear me. He dragged me downstairs into the garage and hit me hard on the right side of my head, I keeled over in pain and grabbed my head. My ears were ringing, and I could see little white stars. As the tears welled up in my eyes, I remembered what Mrs. Thibodaux had told me about finishing a fight. After my eyes readjusted from the blow, I lunged at Mr. Egans, but he merely pushed me hard to the floor.

"That's enough, boy!" Mrs. Egans said as she walked into the garage. She had her robe on. "You think you better than everybody? Well, guess what, nigga—you not special! Everyone in my house takes their medications!" She and her husband walked around me in circles.

I felt intense adrenaline because I could not tell which one of them was going to hit me next. Out of fear of being beaten again, I caved in and took the psychiatric drugs. As I lay in bed later that night, I stared at the ceiling, asking myself, "Why in the world was I even born?" I was so consumed with anger that my throat hurt. I wanted to scream, but I couldn't. Life, up to that point, seemed as if it would never be satisfied unless someone or something was whooping my black ass or causing me to shed blood and tears. It seemed as if life were working extra hard to prevent me from smiling and experiencing any form of happiness. Something then snapped in me. "I'm not taking this shit anymore!" I thought.

I grabbed whatever clothes I could find and fled the house. Everything in me was telling me to run to protect my sanity and dignity. As I ran aimlessly into the night, I failed to recognize that I had no home to run to. I remember roaming the country streets of Rosenberg for hours like a vagabond.

My only hope of leaving the Egans' foster home was talking to someone about what happened. I remember telling a cashier at a gas station about everything that happened. Shortly thereafter, a cop arrived, and I found myself giving a detailed account of what had happened at the foster home, begging him to believe me. I showed the officer my bruises and told him where my foster parents lived. Moments later, I was in front of the foster home, watching the officer talk to Mr. and Mrs. Egans. I could not wait to see the look on Mr. Egans's face when he would realize he was about to be arrested. Unfortunately, I became confused. I wondered, "Why the heck are you looking at me?" I thought this because the officer nodded his head and looked back at me in an odd way. When the officer got back in the car, I nearly fell over in my seat at his words.

"You're lucky they didn't press charges on you," he said.

Mr. and Mrs. Egans told the officer that I had tried to jump on Tracy, my foster brother, who was mentally retarded. As I rode in the cop car's backseat to the Chimney Rock Center, I could feel the frustration pulsating in my veins. Life was becoming a nightmare with no way to escape.

"You can stay here until morning," the social worker said as she set snacks on the table next to the sofa.

"Where am I going next?" I asked. I guess it was too late at night to ask such questions; the social worker only walked back to her desk without saying a word.

As I lay down that night, I found comfort in knowing that I was out of the Egans' foster home. The next morning, I awoke to a social worker telling me to grab my things. Within no time, I was off to a new place; however, to my surprise, I was not going to a foster home. As we drove up the center's driveway, I noticed that there was a two-story building attached to an enormous church.

"You've got to be kidding me," I said angrily. "You're making me live at a church?"

"No, you're at a residential treatment facility. Grab your bags," the social worker said, opening the door before walking toward the facility.

As I unloaded my trash bags filled with my clothes, fear began to run through my veins. All I could think about was all the pain I had endured while at Peace Children's Home. As I sat in the car, I could see other boys my age peeking out of a large window upstairs. "Here we go again," I thought.

"All right, everybody, get up and move!" a staff member said as she flicked the lights on.

All of us in the room smacked our lips and pulled our covers over our heads, being temporarily sensitive to the light.

"Clean your asses, make your beds, and be in the cafeteria in ten minutes!" said Mrs. Xena, the staff member, and she walked out of the room.

I could not stand Mrs. Xena's fat ass. Every time she came into my room, she acted as if she were an overseer policing slaves. Life at this orphanage could be compared to living in a boot camp. Everything was scheduled on a rigid schedule. There was a certain amount of time for breakfast, lunch, dinner, recreation, church, and phone calls.

Great Life Beginnings was an emergency shelter; however, it reminded me of Peace Children's Home. There were different staff members who came in around the clock. The primary method of transportation was two big white Ford Econoline vans, and to top it off, I shared a room with five other dudes. My first impressions were similar to my other placements, and so was the outcome. I thought that everything would go well, but then everything gradually went downhill.

Once Mrs. Xena left that morning, I rushed to the bathroom so I could shower first and use the hot water. I quickly undressed, jumped into the shower, worked up a lather, and jumped out. "I hope we're having biscuits this morning," I thought happily, reaching for a towel. As I was putting my clothes on, I heard the door to the bathroom shut and lock.

I quickly tied my shoes and walked to the door. "Why the heck are you blocking the door?" I blurted angrily to the guy standing there.

"My name is Alex," he said, stepping closer to me. "I just wanted you to know that if you ever want to release yourself, you can come to me."

Baffled and confused, I yelled, "Dude, what are you t-t-talking about?"

He and I just stood there and regarded each other for a few moments. All of a sudden, he blurted, "If you ever want your dick sucked, I'll be in room three," he said before walking out of the bathroom.

I quickly became the laughingstock of the cafeteria that morning after telling everyone what had happened. Shortly after this incident, I got into a fight with another teenager who tried to pull my shorts off while I was sleeping.

While staying at this orphanage, I often felt confused. I did not understand why I was not safe at a place that a church supposedly ran. At night, I would wish to be placed back with the Thibodauxs—anything would be better than being at a place where sexual abuse was rampant. As time progressed, I found myself growing fearful by the day. At night, I would see boys engage in sexual behavior that did not look right. I began to have nightmares about the horrifying event when I was sexually abused at Peace Children's Home. I wanted to get as far away from this new place as possible.

After church on one Sunday, I finally met Mr. Reed, the director of the orphanage. I remember thinking, "If I tell him what's going on, then perhaps he can change things." Once again, I was wrong. Before I could say two words, Mr. Reed instructed me to go back over with my other peers, who were forming a single-file line to go back to the shelter. After being dismissed by the director, I quickly recognized that nothing was going to change.

I attended Forest Brook High School while living at this emergency shelter. Each morning, I found myself growing desperate to leave the uncomfortable environment of the orphanage and to enter the school's doors. While at school, I found myself drifting through each class, feeling emotionally unresolved to the extent that I was not retaining any of my coursework. Also, it seemed as if other students did not know that I existed. When I walked through the hallways each day, the students' smiling faces always intrigued me. I wanted to know what made them so happy. Something in me wanted to smile, but life would not permit me to do so.

Back at the orphanage, things began to spiral out of control. It was as if the staff members did not care what my peers did. On the weekends, all of my peers would run around and do whatever they wanted. Fights would break out sporadically, and no one was there to stop them. One of the things I hated most about Great Life Beginnings was the constant bullying directed toward the younger children. There was one particular guy called "Big Red," and he was taller than everyone else. Big Red made it the highlight of his day to sit and "rank" anyone that he could get a response from. To rank someone means that a person sits and talks about someone until he or she makes the targeted person mad. I remember seeing one guy run to his room and punch a wall because he had become so angry from Big Red's ranking.

One morning, I could not take Big Red's antics. While he was ranking on one of the other boys, I stood up and yelled, "Man, you're a c-c-coward! You need to pick on someone your own size and to stop messing with these little kids!" I said angrily.

Within moments, I was in a full-fledged fight with someone twice my size—both in height *and* in mass. He hit me hard in my chest and face, while my swings and punches accomplished nothing. Big Red landed a right punch to my left eye and added a quick jab to my stomach—I found myself kneeling on the floor, holding my face. The cafeteria became loud with random shouts and comments like "Damn, that nigga got his ass kicked!" Everyone in the cafeteria—even the younger boys I was standing up for—were laughing.

Enraged from shame and embarrassment, I ran out of the cafeteria and to my room. "Why is this happening to me?" I wondered, frantically throwing clothes into my backpack. My left eye was still pounding with pain, and I could barely see because of the tears blurring my vision. "I can't stay here," I thought. "All I was trying to do was help someone, and I get an ass whooping!"

After fleeing, I walked aimlessly, roaming the streets with nowhere to go. As each car passed by, it was as if I could hear the rhythm of the city, a rhythm that was oblivious to the tornadic activity brewing inside my soul. All I knew was that I could not go back to the emergency shelter. I remember walking miles upon miles and ending up at a fire station. Shortly thereafter, I found myself riding in the passenger side of a cop car, while a million thoughts ran through my head.

I thought about how special Mrs. McClelland made me feel, which contrasted sharply with the way I had been treated for the past six years. I thought about how I had been beaten by Mrs. Thibodaux and constantly bullied at school. I thought about my having to take psychotropic medications to smother my emotions. In that very moment, I felt as if something was seriously wrong with me. "It's your fault you were sexually abused!" I told myself.

As I stared out the window and watched the other cars zip by, I felt nonexistent in a world that was moving at an incredibly fast pace. I felt as if life itself were constantly trying to break my spirit.

According to my case file, on June 14, 2002, I was placed at the Chimney Rock Center Emergency Shelter (CRC) again. Shortly after being placed there, I had a family visit with my sister Tasha at the CPS office next to the Eastex Freeway.

Once the elevator opened on the sixth floor, I ran to the visitation room, feeling excited. I noticed that she had put on weight and had long braids. My sister and I did not say much during that visit. We just sat together, my sister resting her head on my chest. In a way, I sensed that Tasha wanted to tell me something. Although she spoke no words, I heard every word. My instincts were telling me that something horrible had happened to her. Although Tasha was mentally challenged, I knew when something was bothering her. After numerous attempts of asking her what was wrong, I just patted her head and let her cry against me. I remember that my lap became drenched with tears.

Years would pass before I would learn that my sister had been raped by a staff member at a group home.

At the family visit, Tasha gave me a crumpled piece of paper. When I opened the letter, I could not make out the words, except for three that said, "I love you." After the visit was over, my sister rode away in one car and I in another. As I rode back to CRC, I wondered what would become of my sister. My social worker told me that Tasha was about to age out of CPS. My other sister, Trish, had already aged out and was on her own.

My social worker then proceeded to lecture me about how I should change my behavior. As he talked, I just stared out the window, trying my best to ignore him; after all, he was just another person who did not understand what I was going through.

While living at CRC, I found myself with other transient teenage boys and girls; many of them were just like me: they either had been removed from their foster homes or had run away.

CRC was a vibrant place, filled with social workers and ringing phones. The living area for the youths had a large dayroom that was equipped with a big-screen TV; the living room also had two hallways, one for the boys and one for the girls. What I liked most about staying at CRC was that I had my own room and shower. It felt good to know that I did not have to worry about anyone trying to pull down my pants at night. Staying at CRC allowed me to experience a new part of life. Though I was an angry and scared sixteen-year-old, I found myself smiling more because I connected with some of the other youths, with those who understood me. Instead of talking about each other, I found that most of my peers talked about how crappy CPS was. Before lunch on several occasions, all of the kids in the shelter sat in the dayroom and discussed random things about CPS. Somehow, we found it funny that it took eight months for our caseworkers to bring us clothing vouchers, only to find out that we could only shop at Weiner's stores.

Staying at CRC allowed me to breathe a little. It seemed as if every other day, we were traveling and going somewhere exciting. I remember trips to Moody Gardens, the Houston Zoo, all-you-can-eat buffets, and countless trips to the movies. Just when I thought things could not get any better, I met Alicia—a beautiful girl at the shelter—and we became more than friends. Alicia was a biracial girl with long, curly hair and a big butt. Outside of her nice physique, I found out that she had been abused by her father and had spent her life moving from foster home to foster home. If Alicia and I were not talking about growing up in foster care, we were watching the staff so we could find a time to sneak around and kiss.

My best memory with Alicia was when everyone in the shelter piled into two big Ford Econoline vans and went swimming in Galveston, Texas. When her bikini top fell off, I became a deer caught in headlights. Let us just say that the rest of the time at the beach was the best time of my life up until that point. Unfortunately, my time with Alicia was cut short; she was sent to another group home. Shortly thereafter, I found myself feeling empty because my best friend had been taken from me. Luckily, I did not have too much free time to feel lovesick; within a week, I was removed and placed in another group home. I left CRC feeling as if a weight had been lifted off me. It had felt good to have genuine fun for once.

When the social worker pulled up at Stanshire Village and told me to grab my things, I refused to get out of the car. "I'm not staying here!" I told the social worker, folding my arms and reclining back in my seat.

Stanshire Village comprised three trailers sitting on about four acres of land. Everything about the shelter screamed, "Ghetto!" Eventually, I had to get out of the car and put my trash bags in a room. Shortly after my caseworker left, I got into an argument with one of the staff members, who was yelling at me because I had given away my food. Refusing to stay in a place where I was going to be yelled at, I grabbed my bags and walked out of the shelter. "I'm tired of people treating me like shit," I said to myself as I walked down Farm to Market Road 1960. My bags began to get heavy, so I tossed my clothes aside the highway and kept walking and walking with nowhere to go.

Instead of being placed back at CRC, I was placed across the street at a facility called the Exceptional Care Program (ECP), which was a gated facility that had five large cottages and a cafeteria in the middle. When the social workers pulled up, I noticed that a large gate closed behind us. I yelled, "Come on! Are you serious? Why are you putting me in jail?" I was furious and refused to get out of the car.

The social worker looked at me and said, "This is a place for system abusers like you." Later, I would find out that ECP was a place for all of the bad children in CPS.

After a month of staying at the shelter, I found out there were children who had severe behavior issues. During my first weekend at ECP, I witnessed a horrific fight between two boys who were playing basketball. The fight was so bad that one boy's face became unrecognizable. As he was being carried away in an ambulance, the other boy was being restrained on the concrete. It took three staff members to take the boy down. Although all of the onlookers were rushed off to their rooms, the boy's screams could be heard throughout the building.

While staying at ECP, I had to talk Francisco, one of my roommates, out of hanging himself. Just about every morning, I would find Francisco sitting in a corner, crying, and saying, "Fuck life, man—I'm gonna do it!" His frequent tears told me that the life he had faced was breaking him down. Somehow, after spending several minutes talking with him, I would calm him down, and he would go back to bed. There were other times in which Francisco would try to slice his neck with a knife. One day, he scared everyone in the cottage by closing himself in a room and threatening to kill himself with another knife. Once again, I had to talk him out of killing himself.

While staying there, I had my own issues to face as well. I often found myself face to face with bullying again. Although I was seventeen, I still stuttered, and to many of my peers, that was funny. My efforts to talk back and defend myself were pointless because the angrier I got, the harder it was for me to let out my words. My persecutors would say things like "Bitch, shut the fuck up. You can't even talk right." Somewhat compassionate people would say things like "Leave that retarded-ass nigga alone, man." I remember getting into a full-fledged fight with one guy who was talking about my mother. Although I did not know where she was, I was not going to let anyone talk about her.

I dealt with bullying not only from my peers but also from Mr. Cory, who was one of the staff members. Mr. Cory never had anything nice to say to me, and when I finally stood up to him to defend myself, I was tossed into a dark room. I guess I was in the shelter's quiet room, because I noticed the door had a little window just like the one at Champions Psychiatric Hospital. I remember banging on the door to get out. Without any warning, the door flew open, and someone grabbed me by the arm. I was thrown high in the air and body slammed hard on the floor, my head taking the brunt of the fall. As Mr. Cory forced my hands behind my back, warm blood poured from my nose. Once again, I found myself being restrained and crying loudly. The louder I yelled for him to let go of my arms, the higher he pushed them toward my head. I literally thought I was going to die from the intense pain. I lay broken, angry, and abused.

Throughout my stay at ECP, I found myself becoming more and more perplexed at the bullying and poor intervention of the staff members. Mr.

Cory continued to restrain me repeatedly, and I often found myself in the quiet room for refusing to go to my room, where my roommates would bully me whenever I was present.

One day, I was placed in the quiet room, and I simply balled up on the floor and cried loudly because I could not understand why life was so cruel. I was having an emotional meltdown. The frustration I felt was excruciating. For the life of me, I could not understand why I was suffering so much pain, especially because I had seen an angel. Although Mrs. Thibodaux used to whoop my ass, I began to think about all the lessons she had tried to teach me about being a black man in this world. I remembered her raising her hands in church with tears streaming down her face. Suddenly, I remembered the many times Mrs. Thibodaux tore the church up by singing "Changed" by Tramaine Hawkins. I remembered the happy feeling I got when I was at church, clapping my hands to the rhythmic hymns. I could not contain the strange emotion coming over me; I began to blurt out these lyrics, singing uncontrollably:

> I will sing Hallelujah, I will sing, oh Lord!
> I will sing Hallelujah, oh Lord!
> For you are the source of my supply, Lord,
> I praise and I lift you high!
> I will sing Hallelujah, oh Lord!

When I opened my eyes, I remember seeing a lady in the doorway; she was wearing a pantsuit and carrying a briefcase. Glaring at me with her piercing eyes, she just stood there as we exchanged glances. I thought, "Maybe she will pray with me and tell me everything will be OK." I continued to look at her, confused as to what would happen next.

Without warning, the lady in the suit said, "Go to your room." Her voice was soft.

As time passed at ECP, I continued to feel as if life was trying to break me. After getting into another fight, I ran away from ECP, searching for a place where I could breathe. Once again, I found myself running with nowhere to go.

Throughout the next year in CPS, I ran from every foster home and group home in which I was placed. After visiting with my sister again, I was able to get a telephone number for Meme, our grandmother. After I had stayed with my biological relatives for three days, they turned me in to CPS because they were afraid they would go to jail for harboring a runaway. After my grandmother turned me in, I again ran from every placement CPS put me in. I was running from the psychotropic medications, sexual abuse, and emotional trauma. Life was trying its best to choke me to death; however, I was determined to persevere.

Vagrant Teen

Off I ran with nowhere to go!
Searching for love yet nothing to show!
The days were hot, and my stomach did ache.
Yet, all I wanted was for someone to pat me on my back,
Look me in the eyes, and say, "Son, it will be OK."
I didn't understand why life was hurting me so
So I wandered aimlessly, like a vagrant, with no place to go.

CHAPTER 9

Running Back

"Promise me you aren't running away," said Principal Miller as he handed me a manila folder with my school records.

Tears began to fill my eyes. He and I were standing face to face and silently. Breaking our stare, I shoved my records into my backpack and then ran outside to the yellow taxi that was waiting for me. I wanted to get as far away from Tomball, Texas, as possible. As the taxi gained momentum and sped away from Tomball High School, I reached into my pocket and pulled out the four psychiatric pills that I had spit up at school. After throwing them out the window, I leaned back in the seat and sighed in relief. I began to think about how my eleventh-grade year at Tomball High School had been pure hell! The foster home that I was running from was filled with loud arguments, bullying, and fighting with my foster brothers. Keeping three teenagers with anger-management issues cooped up in a house proved to be a bad combination. We fought over everything: who sat in the front seat, who controlled the television's remote control, who got to shower first, and so forth.

Over the past year, I felt abnormal because it was against the rules for me to go to any of my friends' houses. After befriending a few people, I found myself constantly telling them lies as to why I could not hang out with them after school. What made things the most difficult during eleventh grade was the constant visits to the Red Oak Psychiatric Clinic and the psychotropic drugs I was forced to take. Once again, I found myself taking a pill to get up in the morning and a pill to sleep at night. While on these pills, I started to hear voices, to lose my appetite, and to lose sleep. On some nights, my heart would beat so rapidly that I could hear it through my pillow. It seemed as if the psychotropic medications that were supposed to help me were having the reverse effect—that is, they were triggering the psychosis they were meant to prevent. While taking the psychotropic medications, I became more violent; one day, I almost stabbed my foster brother after he pushed me down some stairs. The medication gave me erections that hurt and made me feel as if my body were being torn apart internally. After experiencing such pain and anger, I knew that I had to stop taking the medications. "I'm not a murderer," I thought.

I can recall several days in which I was restricted to my room for refusing to take my medication. After getting into a fight with my foster brother on the last day of school, I knew I had to leave to keep my sanity. I ran back to the one place that I felt was safer than being in group homes and in the system: the Thibodauxs' home.

"Nigga, you need a job! You can stay here, but you aren't going to sit up and mooch off me and your daddy. One thing I can't stand is a shiftless nigga. After church, you make sure you walk up there to HEB and put in an application," said Mrs. Thibodaux.

After my three-year absence, Mr. and Mrs. Thibodaux were still as stern as they were in 2001, back when I was taken from them.

As my senior year got underway in the fall of 2004, I had to acclimate to Alief Hastings High School. It turned out that a lot of the students I went to school with during my freshman year were still there. Some of the people who remembered me would ask, "Dude, where were you all these years?"

Embarrassed, I would reply, "My family moved out of town for a while."

Throughout my senior year, I was faced with many obstacles. For example, I found it difficult to fit into an environment of students who had already formed bonds and friendships. I can recall several days in which I waited in the free-lunch line at school without having anybody to talk to, and I remember other days in which I was blatantly ignored when I tried to strike up conversations with other students. After a while, I stopped trying to fit in and just focused on my coursework. For the most part, I was a loner, day in and day out.

I had my work cut out for me; although I was a senior in high school, I still wrestled with the idea of whether or not I was smart enough to graduate high school. There was always that little voice in the back of my head that said, "Nigga, you're retarded!" That voice was especially loud when I failed my algebra tests. Having been in special-education classes since elementary school, I found myself struggling to get through special-ed algebra. I remember countless days of staying after school to practice solving for x and to practice slope intercepts but to no avail. For some reason, algebra just would not click. On some days, I did not want to stay after school and study because I was worried that the Thibodauxs would never come pick me up.

One day, I called Mrs. Thibodaux to come pick me up because I was hungry and did not feel like walking.

"Nigga, I've been fighting traffic all evening! Walk your narrow butt to the house," she snapped back before hanging up the phone. After walking the four-mile walk, which took one hour and twenty minutes to complete, I was even hungrier and more irritated. What made things worse was walking up to the house and seeing several cars in the driveway. When I walked into the house, I became livid. In the house, Mr. Thibodaux was frying catfish, hush puppies, and green tomatoes. Mrs. Thibodaux and her sisters were in the living room, sipping red Kool-Aid and laughing about some childhood memory. I was so angry that I could not stop myself from yelling, "There are three cars outside! Someone could have picked me up!" My frustration was evident in my body language and facial expressions.

Seconds later, I found myself ducking to avoid being hit by a shoe. I was now face to face with Mrs. Thibodaux. "Nigga, do you have gas to put in my car?" she asked.

"No," I replied angrily.

"I suggest you check your attitude before I put you out of my damn house! Better yet, since you wanna have an attitude, make a bologna sandwich and go to your room."

As I lay in my bed after eating the sandwich, I began to worry about whether or not I would ever pass algebra.

Life at the Thibodauxs' home became a nightmare overnight. When Mrs. Thibodaux told me to clean the other rooms in the house because she was getting five more guys, my heart started to race. Mrs. Thibodaux had received a license from Texas MENTOR to house sex offenders. When the five other boys came to the house, I was scared and angry. After being sexually abused twice already, I did not know whether I would be safe in the Thibodauxs' house with five sex offenders.

As time passed, I found myself dealing with the same stress I had dealt with at the other group homes and foster homes during the previous three years. One of the guys was three times as big as I was and made it his business every day to tell me that I was a "dumb square." Perhaps he was intimidated because I was about to graduate high school and he had spent the past three years in juvenile detention. Whatever his malfunction was, I knew that I hated his repetitive, hateful remarks.

At the house, I found it difficult to study. The house was filled with arguments. Mrs. Thibodaux yelled uncontrollably because the kitchen always looked as if it had been rummaged. To top it off, the second story of the house smelled horrible. I remember waking up several mornings and feeling as if I were in boot camp.

On many mornings, our bedroom doors would fly open and slam into the doorstop, and Mrs. Thibodaux would yell, "Rise and shine, niggas! I want my house cleaned! Since you niggas can't be responsible and clean my house like grown men, I'll treat you like children."

Mrs. Thibodaux put everyone on a schedule. In the mornings, we each had three minutes to brush our teeth, five minutes to eat, twenty minutes to relax after school, and three minutes to bathe at night. Before we went to bed, one thing we did not want to do was fail inspection. For example, there was dust on Mrs. Thibodaux's finger after she checked the furniture, which I was supposed to have cleaned. I was forced to stay in a push-up position for thirty minutes.

"You niggas gone learn to be responsible men, one way or another!" Mrs. Thibodaux would yell.

To escape the bullying and boot-camp experience at the house, I tried to pick up extra shifts at HEB in the evenings. As I sacked groceries, I would think, "I ran away from the group homes so I could have peace, but now I'm living in one!" As the year progressed, I became increasingly frustrated. I started to participate in volunteer activities at school because I did not want to go back to the house.

In addition to the household stress, I had to deal with a bully in my aquatic-science class. John, the bully, would often call me an "anorexic Bill Cosby," causing everyone in the class to laugh. John had to be at least six foot three and 250 pounds. His dark-black skin and enlarged gut made him resemble a grizzly bear.

I remember being the focal point of the class whenever he picked out my every flaw—from the shape of my head to the clothes on my back. "Look at Tyrone's mama," he said while the class was watching a documentary about humpback whales. I remember getting so angry that I walked out of the classroom. As I sat in the stall closest to the window in the nearest bathroom, I could feel the anger bubbling up in my face, and I clenched my fists. I was so angry, causing tears to form in my eyes. "Why the heck do I always have to be bullied?" I wondered. I kicked the stall door. "Today is the last day! I'm not going to let people pick on me any longer!"

I pulled myself together and walked back into the classroom. As I sat in my seat, I noticed that everyone was oddly quiet and focusing on the video. Surprisingly, John blurted, "I'm sorry for picking on you." I remember looking into his beady eyes. For a second, I thought it was over; I thought he was being genuine.

"I just got one question," he said, leaning forward in his seat. "Are you related to Jay Z, because you got them big ole pussy-eating lips!" The class roared in laughter. John continued to make wisecracks throughout the duration of the class. "This nigga's lips look like he just got done sucking on a sea elephant's titties!" As the class continued to laugh, I zoned out and simply sat there, having no recourse to prevent him from taunting me.

Because of the bullying, household stress, and educational insecurities, I became fearful as to what would happen to me after I reached my eighteenth birthday and aged out of foster care. The word in the group homes was that when someone turned eighteen, he or she would get booted out. On many nights, my heart would beat rapidly as my thoughts shaped themselves around this new fear: "What if I don't graduate and become homeless? What if I fail to save up enough money and don't have enough to get an apartment?"

I attended the preparation for adult living classes (PAL) and listened to the instructor stress the importance of saving for the future. I knew that when I turned eighteen, I would not have enough money to move out on my own. Deep within, I felt as if I were supposed to become somebody important; however, I did not know how my life would unfold. My mind was trying to figure out how I was going to make it out of high school and be a man. On most nights, I lay in my bed, cried, and prayed to Jesus, asking him to help me make it in life.

As the year progressed, I found myself shutting down. The stress of work, the bullying, and the extra studying for algebra was becoming too much to handle. There was one thought that stood out the most: "Where the hell did my childhood go?" Life had sped by, and now I was a senior in high school and about to graduate. Life up to that point seemed nothing more than a combination of unfortunate and confusing events. At a time when I was supposed to be nurtured and validated, I was being physically abused constantly and given psychotropic pills to mask the pain. All my life, people had made decisions about me and for me, yet no one had stopped and asked me what I wanted. All I could think about was that one word: *Why?* Day in and day out, my senior year in high school became repetitive and mundane. I remember seeing other seniors who were happy or in love. I saw seniors who had countless friends. I remember being fascinated as to why they were so happy. "I was given this shitty-ass childhood of abuse, but all of a sudden, I am supposed to act like a man!" I could not understand why I had to spend my childhood in an environment where people told me I was bipolar, crazy, and chemically imbalanced, rather than in an environment filled with love and compassion. I found myself slipping into an abyss of sadness. I stopped talking and engaging with the other boys around the house. I felt as if I just needed to be alone and to be by myself to think.

During that time, Mrs. Thibodaux would yell, "I'm not entertaining that spirit of depression! I'm sick of your arrogant and entitled ass! I've bent over backward to help you and welcome you back into my home, but here you are sulking and feeling sorry for yourself!"

I felt as if the Thibodaux family had decided a long time ago that they would not be nurturers. During that period, Mr. Thibodaux's response to everything was "Make a decision." As I sat at the breakfast table on the weekends, Mr. Thibodaux constantly repeated that simple imperative sentence. I also became irritated at his snide remarks. I thought, "Everyone has made decisions for and about me all my life, but now I'm supposed to just automatically become a self-sufficient adult?"

"Life stinks!" I thought. I can recall several nights of staring at the ceiling fan, wishing I could turn back the hands of time. Right before I would drift off to sleep, I would be aggravated further. Just about every night, Mrs. Thibodaux would bumble through my door and state the command that I had come to dread: "Come rub my feet, nigga!"

When I rubbed her feet, my overall frustration would be visible on my face.

"I know you're not poppin' an attitude about rubbing my feet after I let you back into my house!" she would yell. She often lectured me about my depressed demeanor when I rubbed her feet.

"I'm sick of you sulking around my house! What's wrong with you?" she would yell. Often, Mrs. Thibodaux would make several such attempts to draw me out, but I would not respond in any meaningful way, only continue to rub her feet. She would then dismiss me to my room with more bouts of yelling. Here's an example of one rebuke: "I'm not entertaining you and your attention-seeking behavior! If you don't wanna talk, I don't wanna look at you! Get out my face, nigga."

After being banished, I would lie in bed and try to make sense of her. There I was at a major turning point in my life, but that woman was focused on having me rub her feet.

Mr. and Mrs. Thibodaux became so concerned about my reticence that they threatened to take me to a psychiatric hospital. I was terrified of going back to such a place, so I opened up. I remember explaining my apprehensiveness about graduating high school to the Thibodauxs after dinner one evening. I talked about how I felt that my life had moved too fast thus far. Before I could finish sharing my thoughts, Mr. Thibodaux yelled, "Make a decision!" Once again, I found myself in a conversation in which the Thibodauxs chose to be hard on me rather than listen to me and show compassion. Once again, their approach was harsh and nonnurturing.

"Tyrone, God has given you more than most, and you choose to sit here and wallow in self-pity?" Mrs. Thibodaux said. "You will either walk in destiny or wander in the wilderness, delaying what God has for you! You want people to plop you in their laps and titty-feed you! Nigga, you a grown man now! I have—"

"Dilly, you need to calm down," said Mr. Thibodaux.

"Shut up, fat nigga!" Mrs. Thibodaux said. She continued her tirade. "I've poured the word of God into you and kept you in church! You better act like you know God is real and pull yourself out of this slump." When she finished, she walked out of the kitchen, ending the "conversation."

Later that night, I thought about how harsh the Thibodauxs were. "They did not even let me explain to them what happened!" I thought. More than anything else, the comment "God has given you more than most" rang through my head over and over again. I thought, "How did God give me more than anybody else when my childhood was ripped away from me?"

All of a sudden, a particular thought hit me: "Maybe God gave me more than most because of the angel I saw." Life had become so twisted, and a great deal of time had passed since I had seen the angel—it is no wonder that I forgot about seeing him.

That night, I started to dream for the first time in a long time. I thought about my future wife and kids. I began to dream about having a fulfilling job and about possibly mentoring other youths who had troubled childhoods. "Life has kicked my ass enough!" I thought. In that very moment, I knew that I wanted to become someone. "If Jesus blessed me to see an angel, then I must be special!" I thought. I made up my mind that night to graduate high school and not let anything stop me from going to college.

Though I had a bit of an epiphany, all of my concerns did not simply disappear.

As the school year progressed, I still struggled with inadequacy, low self-esteem, and the fear of whether or not I would graduate high school. John continued to bully me throughout the day; however, he did not affect me as he did before. As he and his friends sat by me at lunch and made wisecracks, I tuned them out, reminding myself of where I wanted to go in life. I refused to allow someone else's foolishness to prevent me from moving forward. I applied this same principle at home when I found myself being bullied by the five sex offenders in the house. I had a new attitude, and I was on a mission to become someone.

The latter part of my senior year was filled with long hours of studying with teachers after school. I walked from the school to the house countless times because the Thibodauxs refused to pick me up from school. I worked at HEB every other day during the week, and my job took on new meaning and value because I wanted to save money for college.

I continued to work hard during the school year and worked with the special-ed teachers at Alief Hastings High School. When I received the letter in the mail from the registrar stating that I was a candidate for graduation, I was overjoyed! Although I graduated at the bottom of my class, I remember jumping up and down in my room. In that moment, I did not care about being the valedictorian or graduating summa cum laude. All I was concerned about was my dream of simply graduating and moving forward, which was then becoming a serious reality.

On May 15, 2004, I woke up excited, not only because it was graduation day but also because it was my birthday. In the bathroom, I put on my nice shirt and tie, and I could not help but smile at myself in the mirror. "I'm a man now," I thought, feeling confident. It felt good to know that I would walk across the stage and turn eighteen at the same time. I remember riding to the George R. Brown Convention Center; I rode in the backseat of the Thibodauxs' new pickup, and we listened to the sniffles of Mrs. Thibodaux.

"That's why I was hard on you, boy, because I knew you could do it!" said Mrs. Thibodaux, crying aloud and reaching back to grab my hand. I was stunned! I knew that the Thibodauxs cared about me in their own way. All I could think about in that moment was all of the times I had to walk home, only to find her and Mr. Thibodaux stuffing themselves full of catfish and hush puppies. I also thought about how I was beaten butt naked for thirty minutes for looking at a dirty magazine. I also thought about all the times Mr. and Mrs. Thibodaux laid their hands on me and prayed for me.

"Do you hear me, boy?" Mrs. Thibodaux said, interrupting my thoughts.

"Yes, ma'am," I said, oblivious to what she had said.

"The psychiatrist wrote you off as crazy, but here you are about to graduate high school."

Once again, I was confused: I recalled several times in which she and Mr. Thibodaux told me I had a chemical imbalance in my head. I stopped trying to make sense of her hypocrisy and focused on graduating. After we pulled up to the George R. Brown Convention Center, I jumped out and ran through the big red doors. I could not wait to find my seat. I did not have any friends, so I sat by myself with no one to talk to. I sat in the fifth row, swelling with excitement and energy. I saw other high school graduates taking pictures with each other, laughing, and signing each other's graduation programs. As the graduation ceremony progressed, I sat in my chair, thinking about how crazy my life had been up to that point. Many things flashed through my mind—all the pills I had had to take, the group homes, the sexual abuse, being forced to smell another boy's smelly penis, and the constant beatings. On one hand, I was happy to be graduating; on the other hand, I was nervous about what would happen next in my life. I wondered, "What if my adult years are worse than my horrible childhood?" That thought immediately caused my head to throb with pain; I broke out in a cold sweat. However, I remembered my promise not to let anything stop me from graduating college. I recognized that if I wanted to go somewhere in life, I had to stop entertaining the what-if thoughts and just focus on setting and reaching new goals. After all, I had focused on graduating high school, and despite numerous obstacles, I was about to realize that goal.

Families cheered and blew horns for their graduates. The excitement in the room was increasing by the minute. When the principal called my name to walk across the stage, I tried to hold back my smile, to seem cool. My attempt not to smile was unsuccessful—a huge grin spread across my face. When I walked across the stage, it was silent enough to hear a pin drop, should one have fallen. The shouts and loud cheers subsided. Regardless, I raised my arms in excitement, posed for the picture, and sat back in my seat, feeling excited. In that moment, all that mattered was that I had reached my goal.

After graduation, I met the Thibodauxs in the lobby. "My baby! My baby!" Mrs. Thibodaux yelled, giving me a big bear-hug. Afterward, I found myself wondering what road I should take as an aspiring college student. As I lay down that night, I found myself fighting back nervousness and the fears of moving forward.

CHAPTER 10

Nightmare on Lovett Street

ALMOST A YEAR HAD PASSED since I graduated high school, and my life had taken a nosedive for the worst. It all started when the Thibodauxs started to lecture me about getting a disability check, or supplemental security income (SSI). Since I had been on psychotropic medications for the majority of my life, they felt as if I should collect a check and pay them the money to stay in their home. I remember Mrs. Thibodaux dropping me off at the SSI office and giving me money to catch the metro bus back to the house. I played crazy throughout the interview, as Mr. and Mrs. Thibodaux had instructed, in an attempt to get the check. Shortly after the interview, I was notified via mail that I did not meet the criteria to be placed on disability.

During that period, I felt as if the Thibodauxs were trying to manipulate me. When they found out that the state allocated $3,000 to a fund for aged-out foster youths, called Aftercare Room and Board, I was told that I had to pay rent and sign the money over to them or get an apartment. Rather than be lonely in my own apartment, I stayed in their home. The money was released to the Thibodauxs in a monthly stipend of $500. In addition to the money the state was paying the Thibodauxs, I also had to pay $200 out of the money I earned from my job at HEB.

"You need to learn responsibility," they would say. Looking back on this, I know now that Mr. and Mrs. Thibodaux were trying to teach me responsibility.

The Thibodauxs were also trying to persuade me to go to a private school called Mid-America Christian University, which is in Oklahoma. The state of

Texas offered free tuition to every child who had aged out of foster care, and it seemed as if my foster parents did not want me to take advantage of that benefit.

"Why would I pass up free education in Texas to get in debt in Oklahoma?" I asked the Thibodauxs. For some reason, they felt that I would not appreciate the college experience if I did not pay for it like everyone else. Despite their claims, I made preparations to attend Houston Community College. I did not feel smart enough to attend a four-year university, so a community college seemed to be my best shot at starting my college education.

It seemed as if the closer I got toward enrolling in college, the more pressure I felt. The Thibodauxs started to ride my back for everything I did. If I left a piece of paper or trash on the floor in my room, I would have to pay one dollar for every piece of trash. I found myself stressed and heavily burdened by all of the new responsibilities the Thibodauxs thrust upon me. It seemed as if my responsibilities were endless. I had to wash the car, mow the lawn, clean the house, put the chairs out for church on Sunday, iron Mr. Thibodaux's clothes, and (of course) rub Mrs. Thibodaux's feet and lower back—all the while holding down a full-time job. The load was too much to bear!

The day that I had enough should have been a happy day in my life. I was in a rush to catch the bus; I had a meeting with my academic advisor downtown. However, I had forgotten to wash the dishes. When I returned home and entered my bedroom, my mouth hit the floor in shock. Mr. Thibodaux had removed my bed and dresser from my room. He left a note that said, "Welcome to boot camp! Since you don't want to be responsible, sleep on the floor!" After reading this note and looking at all my clothes on the floor, I became furious. All I could think about was how the phrase "sleep on the floor" made me feel like a dog. My childhood had taught me a simple lesson thus far. "Just because life constantly tries to relegate me to the status of a dog does not mean that I have to bark!" I thought. I refused to be treated like an animal, so I ran away from the Thibodauxs' house.

I ran to my biological relatives, hoping that they would accept me and help me transition into college. Just as I thought, they were excited about my going to college; however, I felt myself dealing with opposition. Initially, my aunt Shyanne did not want me to have a relationship with her children.

"This nigga look and act like his uncle Gary!" she said.

According to my grandmother, my uncle Gary was a homosexual who had died of AIDS. The actual truth was that Gary endured years of being raped by my grandfather, as did my mother. I thought, "What type of sicko repeatedly rapes his own kids?"

During that time spent with my biological relatives, I remember my aunt telling me, "It's OK to be gay, Tyrone! I just want you to know that we accept you for who you are."

I became deeply saddened by such comments. Even my cousins made fun of me and called me gay. The situation was hurtful to me because I never knew that I was perceived as gay by other people. I found myself wondering which of my traits made everyone think I was gay. While staying with my biological grandmother, I would spend hours trying to walk with a masculine stride and make my voice sound deeper, so that my cousins would not call me gay. I found myself trying to fit in with a family that treated me according to their preconceived notions and faulty assumptions, rather than simply listen to me. At a time when I needed support in embracing my independence, I found myself exasperated and exhausted. I was busy running full speed in an attempt to win my biological relatives' approval instead of focusing on my purpose.

While staying with my biological relatives, I also received a lot of insight into why I was placed in CPS. My grandmother explained that my grandfather had been a brute who beat her and forced her to have sex with other women for his viewing pleasure.

"Baby, your grandfather was a cold man," Grandma would say as she stared off in the distance. "After he raped your mother and uncle, I reported him to the police and ran so that he wouldn't kill us."

As my grandmother told me all the stories of how my grandfather molested his own seed, I burned with anger. I thought, "No wonder my mother couldn't take care of me; she had been repeatedly raped by her own father."

After a month of staying with my relatives, I was happily enrolled at HCC. I was proud of myself for catching the bus and taking the steps toward becoming a college graduate. However, I found myself getting into arguments with my cousins. I was never good at sports, but I tried hard at basketball in the hopes that that my cousins would accept me.

"This faggot-ass nigga can't even play basketball," said one of my cousins' friends.

"Why this nigga's pants so high?" asked another.

After such comments, I quickly became tired of being ridiculed by my cousins' friends, so I started talking back to all of them, including my cousins. That ended up being a big mistake because after my aunts found out that I was talking about their children negatively, they all banded together and ridiculed me.

"My children had a life before you got here, nigga!" my aunt Shyanne yelled.

"We don't owe you a damn thing, and you should be grateful we're giving your fruity ass a place to stay," my other aunt insisted.

Of course, when my cousins picked on me, no one said anything. In fact, it was comical to everyone else when my cousins were picking on me. When I stood up for myself, everyone would become angry and I would become the object of scrutiny.

As time progressed, I figured out that my aunts did not like me or my sisters because of our mother. For hours, I would listen to my aunts and my grandmother talk about my mother, Shana, and her mistakes. It seemed as if they resented her and dreaded her presence. During this time, my aunt Shyanne evoked tension between me and my male cousins. I remember numerous times in which I was forced to fight one of my male cousins with boxing gloves.

"Whoop that nigga's ass!" my aunts would yell as we fought.

After the boxing matches, my cousins and I would often get into verbal altercations. Within one week of the final boxing match, I was forced to give up half of my financial-aid refund check from school, and I was dropped off at a homeless shelter in Texas called Covenant House.

"You're just like your mother! We can't deal with it!" said my grandmother as she opened the car door. I was devastated and felt rejected. My attempts to be accepted by my relatives were unsuccessful and landed me right on my face.

After one day at the homeless shelter, I ran back to the Thibodauxs and begged them to let me stay with them. I pleaded and let them know that I did not mind washing dishes and being responsible. I stayed with them for one month before my time with them came to an end.

What happened was that after receiving a free laptop from CPS, I started to explore the vast world of sexuality on the Internet. I became curious about the world of sex and became addicted to all sorts of pornography. During that time, the memories of my being sexually molested and my relatives' calling me gay fueled my desire to explore. I was confused, lost, and attempted to fill a void that could only be filled with my purpose and destiny in Jesus (which I did not realize at the time). After leaving my computer open one day, I was busted, and my life turned upside down again.

"Stan, get this nigga out my house!" yelled Mrs. Thibodaux as she slapped me across the head. "After all we did, this nigga ran away from our house to stay with people who didn't want him! But then we accept this foolish nigga back into our home, and he disrespects it by looking at illicit sex videos! Get his throwed-off, retarded, demonic ass out of here!" She slammed her room door after she finished.

Mr. Thibodaux and I rode to the homeless shelter in silence. I was too embarrassed to speak. As he parked the minivan in the driveway of Covenant House, he said, "It's not a bad place, Tyrone. You didn't think you were going to stay with us forever, did you?" He popped the lock on the truck. He handed me a package, and before instructing me to get out of the car, he looked me in the eye and said, "Tyrone, one day everything you believe in will be questioned. In those times, trust God."

As he drove out of the parking lot, I stood in one place, unable to move, fearfully wondering what to do next. I thought, "How can he sit here and talk to me about God as he kicks me to the curb? He'll come back! He's just trying to teach me a lesson."

After seeing Mr. Thibodaux's truck turn right on Westheimer toward downtown Houston, the realization hit me like a ton of bricks: Mr. Thibodaux was not coming back. In that moment, I hit rock bottom, realizing that I had no one to turn to. My fear of becoming homeless had become a reality.

"All right, you guys, grab your belongings," a staff member said. He opened the large glass door to the waiting room.

After sleeping on the floor for my first four days back at the shelter, I was relieved to hear those words. "Finally, I can sleep on a bed with my own pillow," I thought.

However, there was something about being cramped in a tiny waiting room with ten other people that was rapidly increasing my frustration. The lack of air conditioning, the hot breath filling the room, and having to eat sack lunches every day were pure torture. It felt good to know that I could eat in the cafeteria with the other youths in the shelter.

As we walked outside of the shelter, I noticed that there were other youths smoking cigarettes and talking loudly. We continued to walk past the courtyard and into the second building, where we were met by security guards. "Empty your pockets and place your bags on the table," an officer instructed loudly.

As the officers checked our belongings, I looked around the facility. To the left, there was a large cafeteria; to the right, there was a long hallway filled with offices. Closer to the cafeteria, there was a door with a staircase, and I assumed that it led to the bedrooms. After the bags were checked, the staff members led us upstairs and showed us our sleeping quarters.

The upstairs area of the shelter consisted of a large living room and eight bedrooms. On the other side of the stairwell was a unit for girls. The staff member instructed us to put our clothes up and join the other youths for dinner. Upon entering the room, I saw that there were four lockers and four bunk beds packed together.

"Damn," I said, "I spent years running away from group homes, and here I am again, back at square one!"

"Welcome to the shanties," said one of my peers as he slammed shut his locker door.

That night, dinner was filled with the loud babble of my peers. As I stood in line to get my food, I felt alone in a cafeteria full of people. "I can't stay here," I thought as I sat down with my plate. As I looked around the cafeteria at the other youths, there was a soft voice in my head telling me to keep moving.

"Hey, what's your name?" one of my peers yelled, interrupting my thoughts. Life had taught me that I should not come off as too friendly whenever I met someone, so I ignored him. "Skip you, then," he said, and he turned around. Looking at the bright side, I was happy to know that I had endured my first altercation without getting into a fight.

After we finished our food, the staff members instructed everyone to help clean up the cafeteria and to sit down in the living room for group. Group was a time when the staff members talked to the youths about chores and any issues that were taking place. In that first group session, an argument broke out between two girls; one of them accused the other of stealing her bus tokens. That was when I found out that the shelter provided the youths with free bus tokens.

As I lay in my bed that night, I began to obsess over what I needed to do differently than all the other youths in the shelter. Something inside me was saying that if I did not keep moving, I was going to die. That night, I reminded myself of the promise I had made in my senior year of high school: "Don't let anything stop you from going to college." As I drifted off to sleep, I prayed to Jesus, asking that he would direct my path.

"Damn, I overslept!" I thought, throwing my covers off. I quickly jumped out of the top bunk, grabbed some clothes out of my locker, and ran into the bathroom.

All of us guys were trying to rush and groom ourselves so we could get downstairs for breakfast before the girls. While I brushed my teeth, I found myself fighting back laughter. In the corner was a guy wearing six-inch heels and a towel around his head, and he was singing Whitney Houston's song "I'm Every Woman." I thought, "This place is wild," and then I ran downstairs. I remember wolfing down my breakfast, grabbing my bus tokens, and hitting the streets with enthusiasm.

Within a week, I was reenrolled in classes at Houston Community College's Holman Campus. I did not have time to congratulate myself because the staff members at the shelter were pressuring me to get a job, which I tried to do but felt was hopeless. However, one day, I received a phone call from the local Kroger, informing me that I had been selected for an interview. I was blown away. On the day of the interview, Mrs. Landry, director of the college's career center, spent an hour preparing me for it. It would be held later that afternoon. I ran out of the college's career center to catch the bus to South Houston, feeling excited and hopeful. "If I get this job, I'll have extra money for food," I thought.

To my disadvantage, it started to rain, and I did not know my way around the city—both of which caused me to arrive late to the interview. The paper Mrs. Landry had given me—that is, a paper with interview instructions—was rendered unreadable. I left the interview drenched in water, seriously doubting that I would get a call back.

The day after the interview was stressful. Hitting the streets of Houston every day was hard because I had to manage my time properly; I was not only searching for a job but also studying for an exam. On days like these, I sat at the bus stop with extreme frustration because of my circumstances. "Life is too hard," I thought. During this time, I would yell in anger or pray out loud at the bus stop—whichever felt more appropriate in a given moment. When people started to lock their car doors and when children started to point in my direction and laugh, I recognized that I had become a crazy homeless guy. I felt unwanted and rejected in a world that was moving at a fast pace. No matter how hard I tried, life kept trying to knock me down. If I took two successful steps toward obtaining a job, I would be knocked back down by rain, the bus being late, or just flat out being denied the job. On days such as these, days in which fate seemed to hound me, I could only place my head in my hands and try to figure out the heart of my plight. "God, why did you have me go through all those changes as a child, only to have me suffer as an adult?" I would ask. On some of the nights of the fruitless days, I had to sleep on the trash-covered Houston streets because I would miss curfew at the shelter. Again, I could only ask, "Why?"

However, I quickly learned that pouting about my circumstances only made things worse.

Shortly after my interview at Kroger, I started having Christian counseling sessions with one of the pastors. Everyone called him "Minister J.," but everyone viewed him as a big brother. Minister J. was a young, fast-walking Hispanic guy. He had a way of talking to you that challenged your way of thinking while also making you feel special. Although he had an ingenious way of making me feel special, I was reluctant to pour out my emotions. After several promptings by Minister J., my emotions, thoughts, and fears poured out like an eruption at Mount St. Helens. At the first outpouring, I spent at least thirty minutes gushing from my heart and rambling about the pain I had endured for the last eighteen years in the foster-care system. I opened up and explained how it felt unfair to be born into a world where no one wants you.

Everything came out: "To hell with life! CPS removed me from my home after my mom neglected me, and instead of protecting me, I got my ass beat repeatedly! I was restrained repeatedly just for being hyperactive or having a bad day at school! Child protective services was supposed to protect me, yet I was sexually abused four times, but not one person asked me if I had been touched! I couldn't even sit down and watch *Looney Toons* as a kid without some staff member trying to poke me in my ass or without some other child asking me to suck his funky-ass dick! Not one person sat me down just to ask me what I wanted. Why?

"I remember being tossed outside in the middle of the night by staff members. I remember feeling like no one in the world cared whether I lived or died!" At this point, I had risen to my feet. "Fuck life, man! It was always 'Take this pill. Take that pill. Get your retarded and stuttering ass to your room. Come rub my feet, nigga. Now rub my lower back. You're bipolar. You have a chemical imbalance. Come suck my dick. I'll suck your dick. Give God praise—now get out my house!' I have all of these memories, but now I'm supposed to pull myself up by the bootstraps and be a man? I don't understand why—"

At that point, Minister J. interrupted me and said, "Tyrone, God has a plan for you. Think about Joseph and how he—"

"Man, I'm not trying to hear that shit! Fuck Joseph! The same foster parent who carried me to church, dancing and shouting when I received prophecy after prophecy, was the same woman who beat the hell out of my ass and made me feel like an indentured servant instead of a son! I don't wanna hear another fucking word about what God is about to do! I don't even have five dollars to get a two piece and a biscuit from Popeye's, but you're sitting here telling me about what God is about to do!"

An awkward silence filled the room as Minister J. and I stared at each other. I continued, "I spent eighteen years being treated like a fucking lab rat and being experimented on! Do you know what it's like to be placed in a straitjacket at seven years old because you refused to take psychiatric medications?

"There were mornings when I woke up as a child and stared out the window, waiting for my family to come get me, but they never came! I would stare out the window, hoping that someone would come and take me away from the pain, but the pain continued! For years, I felt abnormal and out of place! I spent years longing to be around cousins and aunts who looked like me, only to one day age out of the system and find out that no one wanted me! All that my relatives did was look me in my face and say, 'You're just like your crazy-ass mother and gay uncle!'"

After I had spilled out all my pain, Minister J. spent another thirty minutes telling me how God has a plan for all of his children. He reminded me of how Joseph was thrown into a pit by his family and later became a mighty person. "Just because some people abuse their free will and make life unfair for others does not mean that Jesus can't turn the suffering around for his glory," said Minister J., leaning forward. "I'm pretty sure Joseph had to go through a grieving process when he was in the pit that his relatives had prepared for him. He kept his faith!"

Minister J. then went on to talk about how he was engaged for two years, but his fiancée decided not to marry him the day before the wedding. "I had to trust God through my pain," said Minister J. forcefully.

Before we ended our session with a word of prayer, he opened the Bible and instructed me to read Philippians 1:6 aloud. "I'm not reading the Bible anymore," I said obstinately.

Minister J. moved his chair closer, looked me in the eyes, and said, "Read it!" Again, I stubbornly refused.

"The Bible says that the truth shall set you free, Tyrone. Today, you need to come to terms with the truth."

I leaned my chair in and read aloud the particular verse: "Being confident of this, that he who began a good work in you will carry it on to completion until the day of Jesus Christ."

Minister J. looked at me sincerely and said, "Now that you've read it, believe it!" Then he and I prayed, and he gave me one last bit of instruction, telling me to keep my eyes open: "If you want to make it out of this pit, Tyrone, you need to stop focusing on your history and learn from the other youths who are in your current situation. Keep your eyes open, man."

I adhered to Minister J.'s instruction. I started to be watchful while around my peers. I sought to learn from them and noticed that a lot of them were taking the bus tokens and returning to the shelter, where they would discuss how they just hung out with friends across town. I noticed how none of my peers were in college and appeared to have no plans for the future. I saw numerous youths smoking weed, fighting each other, and talking about their sexual escapades with other residents. Some of the girls in the shelter became pregnant from the male residents. I watched, listened, and learned enough to recognize that if I wanted to make it out of this pit, I needed to steer clear of building relationships with any of the girls, stay away from drugs, and—most important—stay in college.

I struggled to keep up my grades while at Houston Community College. After failing test after test in my remedial math class, I almost gave up. If it were not for my friends in the career center, Mrs. Leslie and Mrs. Plunkett, I would have dropped out of HCC. As I kept my eyes opened, as Minister J. had said, I recognized that Jesus placed people in my life to help point me in the right direction during my homeless period.

Keeping my eyes opened, I started to notice how some of the bus drivers were nice and approachable. Every day when I rode the bus, I made sure to ask the bus driver questions. As time passed, I started to collect good advice. Some of the male bus drivers encouraged me to stay in school, even though I was homeless. One of the male bus drivers who drove Westheimer Road would always welcome me on the bus.

"Hey there, bubba," he would say.

"What's up, pops?" I would reply.

Our conversations ranged from the Bible to women to my progress in school. When I reached my stop, I always found myself feeling happier and more enthusiastic than when I got on the bus.

"Bubba, you might need this," he would say whenever I was getting off. He would hand me an envelope that always had a ten-dollar bill and extra money for bus fares. "Keep your nose clean," he would say.

Out of the blue, I finally received a call back from the local Kroger after what seemed like months. I was excited to finally have a job! I remember putting my apron on with pride. "Jesus is honoring my attempts to be a responsible man," I told myself. Things were finally turning around for me! In addition to this, I was accepted into the Rights of Passage Program at Covenant House. This program was for responsible youths who were observed to be making responsible decisions toward becoming self-sufficient and productive adults. I was excited to move into a smaller, dormitory-style room. "I'm finally grown," I thought as I caught the bus to work from school.

Shortly after getting the job at the local Kroger, I was fired after being caught eating some of the deli meat in the freezer room. I remember feeling extreme embarrassment as the manager instructed me to turn in my badge and apron. "You know you could be arrested," said the manager as he crossed his arms. His beady eyes stared at me sternly.

I explained to the manager that I did not have money for food and was simply hungry. After apologizing and begging to keep my job, I was told to leave the premises immediately. As I sat at the bus stop waiting for the number fifty-two to pick me up, I felt an increased sense of anxiety. After losing my job at Kroger, I began to get fearful as to whether I was going to make it in life. It seemed as if things were spiraling back down again and beyond my control.

During this time, I continued to have counseling sessions with Minister J. at the shelter. It seemed as if his words of support became repetitive. "Keep your eyes open and learn from your peers, Tyrone!" he would say, always smiling. Minister J. also encouraged me to take advantage of opportunities to engage in church activities.

I attended the street church at Covenant House. Street church was when everyone in the shelter met outside and listened to different pastors preach. Afterward, everyone would enjoy a meal. Youths from all different backgrounds would come to those gatherings. Some of the youths would break out in fights during street church, while some of the youths sat with their heads hung low. During this time, I was earnestly looking for a way to support myself and was searching for answers to my problems.

As I kept my eyes open, I noticed that Armondo, my new roommate, had grown up in the system just as I did. Some nights, Armondo and I would smoke weed and talk about life in the system, sometimes listening to the Jay Z song "Song Cry." As the song played on the CD player, we talked about how the system was set up to prevent black people from "making it."

One night, Armondo said, "We gotta stay on our grind." Then he took a hit of weed. By the time we rolled up the last blunt, Armondo had switched the song to the rap artist Bun B's song "Pushin." Before I rolled over to get some shut-eye, I had made up my mind to keep moving, no matter what.

Armondo later introduced me to a place called the Houston Alumni and Youth Center (or the HAY Center). "You should come up there, bro! It's a cool spot to chill!" he told me excitedly. Between classes, he and I started to hang out at the HAY Center, which was a one-stop shop for former foster youths to receive resources to aid them as they set out toward attaining success. To some, it was just a hangout spot where they could get a meal and sleep. During my time visiting the HAY Center, I befriended several social workers, and they took the time to listen to my struggles as a homeless youth. As I kept my eyes open, I started to recognize that a lot of the youths who hung out at the HAY Center were floating aimlessly in life—that is, they had no apparent direction. When I walked in on Armondo having sex with a girl in a bathroom, I knew it was time for me to step up my game. I started to recognize that Armondo talked a good game but did not walk the walk. All I could think about was Minister J.'s advice to learn from my peers.

As time progressed, strange things began to happen, leading me to believe that it was time for me to move on. I began to get this eerie feeling at the shelter after I witnessed a guy use heroin late one night at the bus stop. Shortly thereafter, I noticed that I was being pursued by two homosexual youths, so I started to fear for my safety. There was something on the inside that was beckoning me to take a leap of faith and find a change of scenery. The day I was pushed over the edge and ultimately decided to leave the shelter was when I returned from class one evening and saw that all of my clothes had been stolen. Armondo swore up and down that he did not have a clue about what happened, and there were no cameras that could have caught the culprits.

"I can't win for losing," I thought.

I poured and poured my frustrations out to Minister J. "What am I supposed to do? My clothes are gone! Gay guys keep hitting on me, and some old guy was shooting drugs in his arm at the bus stop!" We then prayed for direction, and together we came up with a plan for me to leave Houston and attend a junior college.

"Have you ever thought about a place where you can eat, sleep, and study all at the same time?" asked Minister J. "I found this college in the middle of nowhere, and I think it would be good for you. How about going to Navarro College in Corsicana?" He had a huge smile on his face; he was confident in his suggestion.

While we were sitting in the chapel and looking at the website, I knew that this was my way out of this hellhole. I remember looking at the school's website and being amazed at how everyone was so happy. There was something on the inside of me that wanted to feel that happiness, to feel what those smiling faces were experiencing.

I decided to give Mrs. Thibodaux a call and let her know of my new decision to go to college. To my surprise, I was not met with a happy response. Mrs. Thibodaux was still upset about my poor decisions in the past, and she fussed long and hard about how arrogant I was to run away from her home and stay with my biological relatives. "Nigga, you didn't leave my house on good terms!" she said. "I raised you the best way I could! I taught you to stand up and be a man of God, yet you sat up in my house, watching pornography! I'm sick of your arrogant, selfish, and entitled butt!"

My attempts to get Mrs. Thibodaux to drop me off at the college were unsuccessful. Although I had made mistakes in the past, there was something in me that wanted her acceptance. I wanted her to be proud of me now that I had grown to be more responsible. After several unsuccessful calls to try to explain to her that I had changed, I stopped calling. Her brother, whom I knew as Uncle Reynard, agreed to take me to the college. I will never forget the day he picked me up from Covenant House. As I packed what was left of my belongings into his truck, Armondo was being arrested for trying to rob the Kroger across the street.

"You know that guy?" asked Uncle Reynard.

"Yeah," I replied. "I learned from him." We watched the cop car leave the shelter. "He taught me to keep on pushing."

As Uncle Reynard's truck trudged along the highway, leaving Houston, I felt both extreme joy and nervousness. Part of me was excited about making a fresh start in a new city; however, there was this slight trepidation about whether I was smart enough to succeed. "I've come too far to give up now," I thought. As I stared out the passenger window, I noticed how the broken white lines on the road became a blur. "That's how my life has been so far—a blur," I thought. As I stared out the window, it was if I was having a flashback. I began to recall memories of myself trying to run away from the orphanages. I recalled Mrs. Thibodaux telling me about being a black man in America while beating me with a belt. I recalled images of sitting at a CPS office with my two sisters, who were crying because Mama did not come see us. My mind was flooded with all of these memories. As I leaned up against the cold car window, I remembered what it felt like to be restrained up against the cold floors of the orphanages. All of my trauma slowly passed before my eyes. Regardless of how hard life had become, I had come to terms with reality. I had two choices: die on the streets of Houston, Texas, or bring my dream of graduating college into reality. Failure was not an option.

CHAPTER 11

Leap of Faith

~~

"Welcome to Navarro College," the registrar said with a thick accent from eastern Texas. I could not help but flash a big grin. She was smiling at me with such big blue eyes, peering over bright-red glasses.

January 17, 2007, was turning out to be an awesome day.

After registering for all my classes, I was able to get a private room all to myself, and to top it off, I found out that in college, students could eat as much as they wanted in the cafeteria! "You mean to tell me this is an all-you-can-eat buffet?" I asked the cafeteria lady excitedly.

"As much as you like, son! By the way, they call me 'Mama Kay,'" she said, and she handed me a ticket.

I remember eating myself sick on my first day of college. Come to think of it, almost a year had passed since I had had a hearty, southern-style meal. I was thankful just to have good food to eat.

I remember walking around amazed at how nice the campus was. Right outside the cafeteria was a large clock tower on top of a hill. The large trees, wide-open fields, and happy faces made me feel as if I had finally escaped all of my troubles. The mere thought of graduating college one day gave me so much joy as I started my educational journey at Navarro College.

After an eventful first day, I remember unpacking the few bags that I had and organizing my room. I noticed a small package on the floor and remembered that it was the package that my foster dad had handed to me when he dropped me off at the homeless shelter. "A CD?" I thought. I ran down to the computer lab in my dormitory and listened to the song "I'm

Going All the Way," by Sounds of Blackness. The positive lyrics and the catchy, rhythmic beat made me feel as if I could accomplish any goal that I wanted.

Waking up in the mornings became less stressful at Navarro College. It felt good to no longer have to worry about sleeping outside or going hungry. People no longer stole my clothes. My days of waking up to a guy singing Whitney Houston songs had finally come to a screeching halt. I also liked that everything I needed was right here on campus! Although I was twenty-one years old at the time, every morning felt like Christmas Day. Each morning, I would burst through the cafeteria doors with so much energy. Without fail, I was met by Mama Kay and a lady everyone called Mrs. G. For some reason, both of these ladies were filled with joy and had a reputation for being motherly to all the students.

On the first day of class, I remember waking up late and in a panic. I did my morning yawns, threw some clothes on, brushed my teeth, and darted out of my dorm, heading toward the other side of campus for breakfast. I ran so fast that the trees and the buildings became a brownish-green blur. In the cafeteria, Mama Kay said, "You better get to class on time if you wanna graduate, son!" I quickly grabbed some cereal and took off toward class.

"What are they looking at?" I thought upon entering the classroom. I quickly noticed that most of the students were staring at my clothes.

The first day of class was intimidating, not only because I looked homeless, but also because of the large number of students in the classrooms. "You can do this, Tyrone," I told myself as I grabbed my syllabus and made my way toward the back of the classroom. Throughout the day, I found myself constantly fighting negative thoughts, which were relentless: "What makes you think you're smart enough for college? You're a crazy street rat—just like your mentally ill mother, Tyrone. How are you going to graduate college when everyone knows you're retarded?" I countered such thoughts by reminding myself of Philippians 4:13: "I can do all things through Christ that strengthens me." I told myself that even though I had come from the streets, I did not have to live and act like a street rat. Overall, I kept my head up—I had come too far to flop out now.

As the semester trudged along, I felt as if I were in a class all by myself. I sat alone in the cafeteria and literally had no friends. My numerous attempts to get a girlfriend always seemed to backfire in my face. Most of the girls were head over heels for the athletes, and I definitely did not fit the athletic mode. I weighed 160 pounds and sported the same khaki pants and shirt everywhere I went. I kept my hair in a small Afro, and I wore the same old, off-white Nikes. During that time, I did not recognize that most girls considered me a "scrub." Being a scrub meant that I was an unattractive guy who was trying to talk to them. After several rejections, I decided to just focus on school.

Acclimating to college life seemed a little easier when Mama Kay invited me to join a Christian organization named Chosen Ministries. "You don't need to be focused on a girlfriend, boy; you need to be focused on Jesus," said Mama Kay after I agreed to join the ministry. Chosen Ministries was a Christian fellowship of students who met twice a week and ministered in the community through song and mime. Becoming a member of Chosen Ministries afforded me the opportunity to attend Bible study, learn new gospel songs, and meet new friends. At the ministry, I met a girl named Tanae, and she became somewhat of a big sister to me. Tanae was a voluptuous, brown-skinned girl with full lips and a big smile. Every time I saw her, she was always dressed to impress. Tanae had a very mothering spirit about her and was the girl on campus who braided students' hair.

"Ty, don't forget about choir rehearsal tonight!" she would say when we passed each other in the cafeteria. Sometimes she would playfully go for the jugular: "Don't forget to brush that nappy head and stanky breath!" Both of us would laugh at such comments. Although Tanae and I joked in the hallways, we were serious during choir rehearsal and Bible study.

Mama Kay often preached hard about the importance of young people's yielding their bodies to become instruments of worship. It was as if we entered a whole new world when we had choir rehearsal. I remember seeing other students' hands rising toward the ceiling as they sang their love for Jesus. The unison of our voices while singing praises to our King created a sense of peace like none other.

I remember writing about Chosen Ministries in class and, as a result, making friends with a young lady named Tiana, who was friends with several people in Chosen. She was a dark-skinned girl with a big booty, short hair, and braces. She and I became study buddies within no time, and as the semester progressed, I found myself hanging out with her friends as well. Although my social network was growing, I still found myself the subject of ridicule by my peers. For some reason, I was always the butt of people's jokes because of my clothes, my nappy hair, and my speech impediment. For example, one person said, "This nigga stutter like crazy and have the nerve to try to sing."

Gossip traveled quickly around the college, and I found out that students had me pegged as the hobo on campus. After constantly getting into arguments with other students, I left Chosen Ministries and stayed to myself. The rejection from my so-called friends caused me to reach out to my foster parents. I remember borrowing someone's phone to call Mrs. Thibodaux to tell her all about my life in college. After I told Mrs. Thibodaux that it was I who was calling, she said, "Nigga, I told you to stop calling my phone! Leave me alone!" She hung up the phone before I could say anything, leaving me speechless.

I thought my foster mother would be proud of me for going to college—I was wrong. It appeared that Mrs. Thibodaux was still angry with me for watching porn in her house and for running away.

After attempting to speak to Mrs. Thibodaux, I contacted my biological relatives and was met with another disappointing response. After speaking with my grandmother and aunt, I became disgusted at how they compared me with my cousins. Instead of providing positive sentiments and encouragement, they gave me an earful of how I thought I was better than everyone else because I was in college. I hung up the phone, consumed with frustration. I wondered if anyone cared about me on this planet. During that time of separation from my social group and rejection from my family, I became a loner. I decided to spend more time focusing on my grades and praying to God for direction. I remember asking God questions that always had the word *why* in them: "God, why am I a sophomore in college, yet I feel detached and out of place? Why do I keep running after people who treat me like shit?" Although

I never got a response when I prayed, I was learning how refreshing it was to get on my knees and pray. It felt good to get everything out.

By the end of the first semester, I had become tired of the social-life roller coaster in college. I was also wrestling with the rejection of my foster family and biological relatives. Although my social life crashed, my first semester was not a total waste. Somehow, I managed to pass all of my classes, except for remedial math. Math was a constant struggle for me when I was at Houston Community College, so I was not surprised by not passing my remedial math class. I decided to attend summer school since I had nowhere to go home to. During the summer, nearly all the students left, except for the athletes. Of course, I did not fit in with the athletes, so I spent the first part of the summer alone and focusing on schoolwork.

Toward the latter part of the summer, I befriended my computer-science teacher. Mrs. Beal was a quirky, redheaded Caucasian lady with blue glasses and a high-pitched voice. After I offered to wash her car for haircut money, we became the best of friends. I met her husband one evening after mowing their yard.

"Hey there. I'm Steve! You must be Tyrone," said Mr. Beal as he stepped out of a gray car that was quite dirty. The sun was beaming heavily in his eyes, and I noticed that he had his hand above his brow to block out the sun. Mr. Beal was a short, high-energy guy with wispy gray hair and big ears. I turned off the lawn mower, walked over to him, and shook his hand.

"My name is Tyrone," I said excitedly. "Your wife is my computer-science teacher, and I asked her if I can do odd jobs to earn some money." I rubbed the sweat off my forehead.

"Well, if you want, you can wash this dirty old thing here!" he said with a big grin. I noticed that his dirty car was a 1998 Toyota Camry.

As he walked toward the house, he said, "Feel free to stay for dinner! Mrs. Beal makes the best enchilada casserole."

After washing his car and mowing the yard, I sat down to the best enchiladas I had ever had. Mr. and Mrs. Beal seemed very interested in where I grew up and asked questions about my family.

Around mouthfuls of enchilada casserole, I explained the whole story of my parents' abandoning me in an old apartment building and the whole story of my life as a ward of the court. The Beals were not surprised when I told them how after aging out of foster care, I was put out on the streets by my foster family and rejected by my biological relatives. To my surprise, the Beals were court-appointed special advocates, individuals who volunteer to be the legal representatives for children entrusted to the state of Texas. The Beals told me all about their experiences in mentoring youths in foster care. As we sat in the living room and ate dessert, the Beals took it upon themselves to offer encouraging words.

"Tyrone, one thing we stress to all foster youths is to journey beyond," Mr. Beal said.

Over the next twenty minutes, I sat and listened to the Beals. They stressed the importance of taking life one day at a time and journeying beyond the pain of my past. "Your later years will be so much greater if you just trust in the Lord," said Mrs. Beal.

By the end of the evening, the Beals and I had become well acquainted. As we rode back to my dorm, the Beals extended the opportunity for me to stay at their house on the weekends, which they hoped would help me rest from school. Throughout the rest of the summer, the Beals and I continued to hang out. Recognizing my need for decent clothes, the Beals took me shopping and bought me school supplies for the fall semester.

I remember telling Mama Kay all about Mrs. Beal. Afterward, Mama Kay said, "Boy, you need to thank God for all the people he's placing in your life!" After I told Mama Kay about the Beals, she invited me out to her home, saying that I should visit throughout the week. Mama Kay told me that she had horses. I knew visiting her house would go smoothly. To be supported by such generous people really made me feel happy.

By the middle of the fall semester, my primary objective was to get a car. I noticed that all the cool guys on campus with girlfriends had nice clothes and cool rides. "Now that I have nice clothes, all I need is a cool car to help me get all the ladies," I thought. With the help of Mrs. Beal, I was able to get my driver's license. After contacting a social-service organization in Dallas, I received a grant called the Education and Training Voucher, which awarded me $5,000 for the purchase of a vehicle. When the check came in the mail, I remember going to the car lot and picking out a burgundy Buick LeSabre. For the first time in quite a while, I felt like an accomplished man! I was no longer invisible! Some of the girls started asking me for rides to the store and across campus. It felt good to finally be one of the cool students on campus.

A couple of weeks into the fall semester, I decided to join Chosen Ministries again. To my surprise, most of the people I knew in Chosen were nicer than before. I found myself struggling with my desire to be accepted by the people in Chosen and the people outside Chosen. Although I enjoyed the singing and the connectedness, I was curious about experiencing the excitement that people outside Chosen were involved in.

I remembered hearing about a club named Grahams, which was in Waco, Texas. On Friday nights, most of the college students at Navarro got all dressed up and drove there to party and drink alcohol. During Bible study on a Friday evening, I decided that I was going to satisfy my curiosity. I sneaked out of Bible study, ran to my dorm, got dressed, and jumped on the highway, heading toward Waco. The thought of experiencing the club life and the loud music I was playing in my car combined to create a heightened sense of excitement. "Today is the day I will finally be able to see some ass in real life!" I thought, grinning from ear to ear. Unfortunately, my grin was cut short because thick, white smoke started to pour out from under my hood. My destination was only a few exits away, but my car had broken down!

After looking at the engine, I figured the car was broken beyond repair, so I left the car and called the one person I knew would come get me.

"You did *what*?" asked Mrs. Beal.

As I sat in the passenger seat of her Volvo S80, I felt extremely embarrassed. Mrs. Beal had become somewhat of a mother to me, and I did not want to make her upset. My skipping Bible study just to see girls shake their asses was not acceptable to Mrs. Beal. She lectured me all the way back to the college.

Mama Kay was disappointed as well. "You should be ashamed of yourself as a man of God! I'm teaching you to lead by example, but you're out here skipping Bible study to go to the club!" she said sternly.

Moreover, the little popularity that I had garnered among my fellow students dwindled away when I no longer had a car. The girls stopped reaching out to me for rides, and once again, I found myself being picked on by my peers in Chosen. Although I lost my car, I was thankful that I had not lost my life on the highway.

After all this, I should have learned my lesson regarding the negative effects of impulsive curiosity. Wrong! By Thanksgiving, I was failing all my classes. I was more preoccupied with getting a girlfriend and seeing a vagina in real life than with studying my books. I spent weeks trying to be cool with the ladies, hoping to get some ass. Unfortunately, I was always rejected as if I were a scrub. One girl laughed in my face and said, "Look at this church boy trying to be bad." No matter how hard I tried, I was always unsuccessful at getting a girlfriend—the goal was impossible to attain.

Focusing on finding a girlfriend instead of studying my books was a bad decision. My irresponsibility with my books cost me my Thanksgiving break. Rather than being able to relax, I had to spend time catching up on homework. I went to the Beals' house since I did not have anywhere else to go for the holidays. During the Thanksgiving break, I noticed that Mrs. Beal invited several other foster youths from Navarro College to her home. Once I got done with all of my assignments, I remember spending time wrestling with some of the other guys and pranking the girls Mrs. Beal had brought over. In a way, it seemed as if all of the foster youths at the Beals' became a makeshift family. I listened to the other foster youths' experiences with their foster parents, and their stories taught me that I was not alone. All of us were shocked when we recognized that we all had been sexually abused in the group homes. Although we shared the same trauma, we also shared some of the same feelings. Although our foster homes were hurtful, the foster families were the only ones we ever had. We missed our foster parents just as much as we resented our trauma.

As the Thanksgiving holiday came to an end, I approached the latter part of the fall semester with a lot of energy. I submitted all of my makeup assignments, and I was able to pull my grades out of the gutter. As all of the students poured back into the college dorms, I again wrestled with a sense of belonging because the Christmas holidays were coming up, and the other foster youths were going home to their blood relatives. Once again, I started to feel out of place. I knew that I could not go back to the Thibodauxs' home or stay with my relatives—the wounds they had inflicted upon me were still fresh in my mind.

Although the Beals had created a makeshift family environment, my mind continuously wondered if there was someone related to me who would be my family and be willing to make up for lost time. I searched for hours on the Internet, looking for the Obasekis. I remember speaking with several relatives on my father's side of the family. Many of them had strong accents and stated that they were looking for me. Most of them I never called back because I figured they were lying. I was blown away when a genuine guy who introduced himself as Uncle Chukwu extended an offer to fly me out to his home in Alicante, Spain. "Finally, all of my questions will be answered," I thought excitedly. After announcing the news to Mrs. Beal, I quickly submitted an application for a passport, and on December 1, 2007, I was off to Spain.

My mind raced constantly during the eleven-hour flight! All I could think about was what would happen when I finally met the Obasekis. As a child, I was told that I was a prince in Africa and that the Obaseki family was royalty. For a second, I actually entertained the thought of being met with hundreds of my African relatives at the airport. "What if I'm chauffeured in a Mercedes stretch limousine to a massive family estate where I get access to unlimited money?" I thought. As I stared out the window of the plane, I smiled from ear to ear. I actually believed that my life could possibly turn out as Eddie Murphy's did after his character returned to Zamunda in the movie *Coming to America*.

Meeting Uncle Chukwu was not exactly what I had imagined. Reality set in really hard. I was not greeted by hundreds of townspeople and relatives; instead, I was met by Uncle Chukwu's wife and two happy children.

Rather than ride in a limousine to a gigantic family estate, I rode in a taxi from Madrid, Spain, to a decently sized condominium with modest furniture. Uncle Chukwu and I shared a good laugh when I told him all the stories of how I thought everyone in the family would be of royal descent.

"The only thing you will find at Uzubu Quarters is a couple of goats and chickens."

Throughout the Christmas holidays, I had a blast with my newfound relatives. I spent weeks traveling through Spain, sightseeing, and enjoying good food. Uncle Chukwu's wife insisted that I try some of the good food in Spain. I was in food heaven! I enjoyed eating the paella and manchego cheese and drinking sangrias. Because of my skinny size, I was always prompted to eat more. "You need to eat food!" Uncle Chukwu would say in his strong African voice. Uncle Chukwu was also a pastor of a local church, and I spent a whole Sunday at his church, which was filled with people from various parts of Africa, people who spent the majority of the service dancing and singing.

Although I was having a boatload of fun with my relatives, there was something in me that wanted to know more about my history and the meaning of my last name. While we were hiking up Mount Benacantil to visit Santa Barbara Castle, Uncle Chukwu explained that the Obasekis were, at one point, a very wealthy family in Benin. Uncle Chukwu explained that because of family discord, the rich heritage fizzled out in the 1800s, causing most of the Obaseki people to immigrate and start life in other areas around the globe. After Uncle Chukwu talked about our family history for about an hour, I blurted out the one question that I had waited years for someone to answer. I asked him, "What happened to my father?"

For a second, Uncle Chukwu was very hesitant, and the look on his face showed that he was uncomfortable. After I asked several times, Uncle Chukwu explained that my father was murdered. "They call it voodoo in Africa," said Uncle Chukwu in a solemn voice. "After your father returned from the States, he didn't talk or eat. Someone took him to another village, and he died shortly thereafter. Not too long after that, he passed away, and someone confessed that they had poisoned him." Uncle Chukwu was staring at the ground by the time he finished speaking.

By then, we had reached the top of the castle. For some reason, the awesome view overlooking the Mediterranean Sea did not seem as appealing anymore. Reality hit hard, and I became angry after finding out that my father was killed by someone who had most likely been in his immediate family circle.

The remainder of my stay in Spain seemed to pass like a blur. At night when I lay down, all I could think about was one particular fact: my father was murdered. I wondered what life would have been like if my father had been around. On January 10, 2007, I returned to Navarro College, feeling depressed.

As the spring semester kicked off, I had a hard time focusing on my schoolwork because I was preoccupied with trying to accept that my dad was long gone. During that time, I felt as if the weight of the world was on my shoulders. I tried reaching out to my aunts in Houston, and once again, they focused only on comparing me to my cousins. One of my aunts said, "Don't think because you got relatives in Spain that you are all that."

When I reached out to Mrs. Thibodaux, I was met with an earful of how ungrateful and arrogant I was to leave her home and act so disrespectfully. The final comment she made before hanging up was "Nigga, don't call me with this foolishness!"

The news of my father's death, the rejection of my relatives and foster parents, and my low self-esteem caused me to swiftly sink into an abyss. I felt as if I were in emotional quicksand with no way to pull myself to safety. After losing the motivation to attend class, I began to spend every day sleeping. I lost all motivation to even look at other people and had no desire to eat. "I should just die like my father," I thought. "Why should I eat if no one cares about me? If I died right now, all of my troubles would be over." My thoughts raced constantly, and I even had dreams about the sexual and physical abuse I encountered as a child. Images and memories from my past flooded my thoughts like a faucet filling a bathtub. "Why should I continue to live when everything is just pain?" My negative thinking caused me to slip deeper and deeper into a zone of terminal depression.

One day, I woke up at Corsicana Regional Hospital. Mrs. Beal was at the side of my bed. I had no knowledge of how I had gotten to the hospital or why I was clothed in a hospital gown.

"Don't sit up!" said Mrs. Beal. "The doctors performed a spinal tap on you, and it's best you get some rest."

Sitting up anyway, I immediately felt immense pain shoot from the top of my head to my lower back. I felt as if my head were about to explode from all the pain.

"Tyrone, why didn't you talk to anyone?" asked Mrs. Beal. "We are concerned about you! So is Mama Kay!"

In my mind, all I knew was how I felt, and everything in me felt like an unwanted dog. I avoided eye contact with Mrs. Beal, wondering why she cared whether I lived or died. My thoughts were soon interrupted by Mr. Beal, who came walking into the room.

"Tyrone, your foster mother, Dana Thibodaux, is on the phone," he said.

My eyes became heavy; I felt as if I wanted to go back to sleep. I mustered up the strength and grabbed the phone.

"Tyrone, why are you not eating?" asked Mrs. Thibodaux, sounding as if she were merely annoyed. "You got them white folks up there calling my phone and telling me that you have had some type of emotional meltdown! What is going on with you?"

"I just found out that my father was murdered, I don't have any friends or a girlfriend, and life just seems—"

"I've done all I can to raise you into a man of God, and if you don't have the faith to pull yourself together by now, then suffer the consequences, nigga! Since you want to act like Boo Boo the Fool, I told the doctors to take you to Green Oaks Hospital in Dallas! You're going to ride in the back of a police car, and you need to stay there until you gain some sense." Once again, she hung up the phone without waiting for a response.

I remember feeling as if Mrs. Thibodaux could care less whether I lived or died; her tone and careless attitude conveyed her sentiments clearly. Her heart had shifted; she no longer saw me as her son but as a foster child who had only stayed at her home for a season. Perhaps she believed that my emotional meltdown was the Lord's way of making her enemy (me) her footstool, as the Bible says in Luke 20:43. Either way, I knew at this point that Mrs. Thibodaux was still struggling to accept the foolish mistakes of my youth.

Not too long after my phone call with Mrs. Thibodaux, I was handcuffed, placed in the back of a cop car, and driven to Green Acres Hospital. I remember checking in and being placed in the observation room, where all the sick people were recovering from surgery. For the most part, I remember lying in bed and sleeping all day, except for the day I was instructed to sleep in a dark room with a video camera. Once again, I found myself lonely and isolated, just as I had been as a foster child growing up in the system.

After a couple of days, I was transferred to the psychiatric floor. After entering the unit, I was given several shots that kept me heavily sedated. After the medication wore off, I remember the nurse pulling me into a room. "You have two options," she said. "You can take this shot voluntarily or involuntarily. If you refuse to take this shot, these two nurses are going to hold you down while I give it to you anyway."

Out of fear of being wrestled to the floor by two muscular men, I gripped the table, pulled my pants down, and nearly fell over because of the pain. They call it "booty juice" on the streets, and when an individual receives an injection of it, he or she will be out cold in a matter of minutes. I received my injection, and for three days, I lay in the hospital, heavily sedated with no appetite. I remember waking up to Mrs. Thibodaux and her sister praying for me and anointing me with olive oil. This took me by surprise because I thought Mrs. Thibodaux was mad at me still. Instead, while I was in the hospital, she said she was proud of me and wanted me to graduate college. Our conversation was cut short because I vomited all over the couch.

After Mrs. Thibodaux left, I started feeling an eerie presence around me as I slept. I imagined myself in a casket and felt that if I stayed in the hospital one more day, I would die. After signing myself out of the hospital, I requested to be dropped off at Mrs. Beal's house, which was the last place I had felt comfortable.

"Tyrone, you can't stay here," said Mr. Beal as he grabbed the keys to his car and locked his front door.

Although I was sick, I started to see that the people who had said they cared about me were now backing away because they believed I was mentally ill and a liability.

After Mr. Beal dropped me off at the college, I remember walking into the cafeteria and becoming the laughingstock of the students there.

"Damn, that nigga look like shit," said one of the football players.

"That nigga look like he got the bird flu!" yelled a student.

As people walked in and received their meal tickets, several people took pictures of me with their phones. "This nigga look like he's on crack!" another student yelled, laughing and pointing in my direction.

Mama Kay came to my defense. "Boy, get out of here, and mind your business!" she said, pushing the boy out of the way.

The students were relentless, however. Another one yelled, "This nigga look like an emaciated Tyrone Biggums!"

Mama Kay and Mrs. G. did their best to push the students away from me, and I could only sit there like a circus animal. Mama Kay and Mrs. G. took me into the back office, where they prayed for me and tried to encourage me. "Tyrone, you gotta pull yourself together!" said Mama Kay, slamming her hands on the desk.

"Tyrone, you are a grown man and fully capable of making healthy decisions! You are not a mistake," said Mrs. G. with tears in her eyes.

"I promised myself that I would not become a statistic and that I wouldn't let anything stand in my way of graduating. But I just don't have it in me anymore," I said angrily.

"You've come too far to stop now," said Mama Kay.

Their words did help, though. After talking to them, I felt as if I could take on the world. Their attempt to motivate me broke through my sadness and frustration. Their support felt like ice-cold water in a hot desert.

Unfortunately, Navarro College saw me as a liability; on May 5, 2008, one of the deans strongly encouraged me to sign documentation that would dismiss me from Navarro for medical reasons. It seemed as if my dream of graduating college had come to an end.

Looking back on my time at Navarro, I see now that I was foolish to devote the majority of my attention to gaining people's acceptance. Like so many other foster youths, I made the mistake of seeking love and acceptance from biological relatives and foster parents, which they did not want to provide. Everything on the inside of me wanted to make them proud of me, hoping that their approval would make up for the love and affection that I had been denied as a child. Reflecting back on this futile pursuit, I see that I was making one emotional, unintelligent decision after another. Life was teaching me that running behind what I lacked as a child would only distract and deter me from accomplishing my goals and being the man of God that I was destined to become.

CHAPTER 12

Quicksand

AFTER RETURNING TO HOUSTON, I was lucky to have a place to stay. Mrs. Liggins, one of my social workers from CPS, spent forty-eight hours hunting down my two sisters, whom I began to live with. Living with Trish and Tasha started out to be great. Years had passed since I had seen them, and it felt good to reunite with them after so many years of separation.

For the first couple of days, my sisters and I spent time reminiscing about our experiences while in the system. Tasha shared stories of how she was raped in group homes and gave birth to a baby she only saw once. Trish and I shared stories of how we were constantly restrained on the floors for refusing to take psychiatric medications. During that talk, we huddled together on the couch.

"What about all the times we sat at the CPS office for hours and Mama never came!" said Trish angrily.

"Why did we have to go through all this crap!" I said angrily.

"We will make it because all we have is each other," said Trish.

The last sentiment quickly dissolved in a matter of days and was replaced with constant arguing. We took sibling rivalry to the next level. I do not know if it was because we were all super emotional or because we were confined to a tiny apartment. Trish became increasingly moody and enraged. I often felt as if she purposefully picked on Tasha just to intimidate her. I broke up several of their fights, and I was always amazed at how my sisters would fight each other. One day, the fighting got so bad that I had to stop Trish from hitting Tasha in the head with a TV!

As the weeks progressed, I started to work at a local shelter for wayward youths, just to get out of the house. Once I took myself out of the picture, it seemed as if my sister started to direct all of her anger toward me.

"Nobody else wanted your big lips around, but you won't give me any money? yelled Trish. "Everybody wrote you off as crazy after your little emotional meltdown at Navarro College. Aunt Shy, Meme, and everyone in the family don't want your black ass around! Mrs. Thibodaux, the woman that raised you, told me point-blank to leave your ass in the psych hospital because you're crazy! All these people turned their backs on you in your lowest moments, but you won't give me—"

"Look, I already gave your ass two hundred dollars. I don't have any more money!" I shouted. "If people in this family had supported me in college, I wouldn't be here right now." I went to grab my things. "All this family does is sit up and talk about each other like crabs in a bucket—and I'm tired of it!" I stormed out of the door to catch the bus.

Arguing with my sisters about petty stuff became part of our morning routine. I looked forward to getting out of the house and going to work just so I could be away from them. In comparison with living with my sisters, work felt like a vacation. After I described to Mrs. Liggins the violent arguments that happened in the house, she constantly encouraged me to trust Jesus and to not lose sight of my educational goals. I liked to work with Mrs. Liggins because she was a genuine person and treated me in a motherly manner. She summed up my predicament in this way: "Tyrone, you need to focus on school and keep Jesus first. Sometimes, you have to leave the negative people in your life alone."

While working with her, I received the mental stimulation and encouragement that I needed to stay true to my promise of not letting anything prevent me from graduating college. All of our long talks at restaurants and late-night discussions carried me out of my depression. When I felt better, I decided to apply to the University of Houston, and in August 2007, I was accepted into the university, which gave me a sense of fulfillment.

I remember walking throughout the university and feeling excited and in awe of the campus's enormous size. Everywhere I looked, there were so many students moving around and going places. I admired the fine architecture of the buildings and how the sunlight broke forth through the trees. When I walked through the campus, I felt as if I were taking a stroll through Central Park.

After a couple of weeks into the semester, I recognized that I needed help with my classes, so I joined an academic program for minority students with low incomes. When I went to sign up for the program, a lady named Mrs. Nelly greeted me: "Welcome to CEP. You're just in time for lunch!" She took a bite out of a slice of pizza she was holding.

"My name is Tyrone, and I was wondering if I could sign up for tutoring. I'm kind of a slow learner and—"

"No problem!" chirped Mrs. Nelly. "This program was designed to help low-income students acclimate to the university."

She and I continued to talk as I filled out the appropriate paperwork to get into the program. Mrs. Nelly seemed to be a motherly person, and she had a way of getting you to tell all of your business; by the end of lunch, I had divulged all of my experiences in foster care and had moved her to tears. "I want you to check in regularly with a good friend of mine," she said calmly, wiping tears from her eyes. "Dr. Lee is the vice president of student affairs, and he has mentored several students over the years." She then handed me his business card.

I took the offered card and thanked her for lunch and for lending a listening ear. I felt at ease knowing that I was now part of a program that would help me acclimate to the university and provide mentorship.

Dr. Lee and I became acquainted after I bought a car and was arrested in Liggins County for speeding. He helped me get out. I returned to campus with a new appreciation for being free after my brief incarceration. I was so happy to be out of jail that I searched for his office to personally thank him for helping me. To my surprise, my act of expressing thanks took a sharp turn. He proceeded to give me a two-hour lecture on not making foolish and impulsive decisions.

"Tyrone, you are a black man in a nation where cops won't hesitate to shoot you or lock you up," said Dr. Lee sincerely. "Mrs. Nelly told me that you were in foster care. Is that correct?"

"Yes, sir," I said softly.

"This may sound harsh, but society could care less about what happened to you as a child. You are a grown man now, and it's up to you to take charge of your life and reach for success. People who make foolish decisions play Russian roulette with their future."

The conversation between Dr. Lee and me covered all subjects that men deal with in life. I left his office with the imperative phrase "Take charge of your life!" ringing loudly in my ears.

Checking in with Dr. Lee on a regular basis started to play an integral part in my growth and development. There were days when Dr. Lee would pick me up in front of my dorm in his purple Lexus. One day when he pulled up, he yelled, "Get in! Let's go eat!" After grabbing some chicken wings, Dr. Lee would drive me around the city, pointing out places that were going through a process called *gentrification*.

"Do you see that bus stop right there?" asked Dr. Lee, squinting his eyes and pointing to the opposite side of the street. "Before the wealthy people start moving back into the urban areas, the city wants to fix things like stoplights and bus stops," he explained, the golden evening sun beaming across his forehead. "They're going to bring the metro rail all through this area."

Dr. Lee and I continued to talk as he ran errands, and he had my undivided attention when we talked about women. I listened to him for what seemed like hours as he talked about "the ladies," as he would say it. "Women are like the stars in the sky, Tyrone. They're not going anywhere, so focus on school."

Despite Dr. Lee's wisdom regarding women, there was something in me that still longed for a girlfriend. After class one day, I used my financial-aid money to buy clothes so that I could look cool enough for a girlfriend. I figured that since I was no longer at a smaller college like Navarro, finding a girlfriend would be easier. To my surprise, my Nike Air Force 1 shoes, expensive jeans, and expensive shirts did not work.

I even tried to join several fraternities, hoping to increase my social network of friends. I thought, "If I go Greek, I would have all the girls." Unfortunately, my plans blew up in my face, once again. After approaching several guys in the cafeteria who were alphas and asking to join their fraternity, I was laughed at. I remember standing there for a good forty-five seconds as the guys laughed so hard that they almost choked on their food. "What's funny?" I replied, looking around with a halfhearted smile. The alphas just walked away laughing and did not even bother to respond. I remember walking away and feeling so angry that I wanted to fight.

As my first semester at the University of Houston progressed, I felt consumed with loneliness. Something in me yearned for acceptance and validation. I wanted to feel loved and accepted by a woman. I wanted to be cool and a part of something. It seemed as if I had a mark on my head that caused girls to run the opposite way. I remember days of sitting in my dorm room after studying, just staring out the window. I would see guys walking with their girlfriends, and I would become instantly frustrated. "When will girls like me?" I yelled internally. "Why is it that all the other guys have girlfriends, and I don't?"

One day, something in me just snapped, and I decided that I was going to be with a woman—no matter what. During this time, I used my financial-aid refund money to pay a prostitute to sleep with me. In a way, I was scared because I had never been that close to a vagina. I did whatever she told me to do during our sexual encounter. "Suck this," she would say, guiding my head around her erogenous zones. As she bounced up and down while gripping my chest, I found myself enjoying every minute of this strange woman's affection. When it was over, I was disappointed because I was out of $200 and still did not have a girlfriend.

My desire for intimacy and affection became insatiable, to the point where I could not sleep at night. Once again, the thoughts of my sexual abuse filled my mind, and I began to question my masculinity. "Why do I have to live with the memory of a man slapping his genitals in my face when I was a child? Maybe life wants me to be gay," I thought. During that time, I believed that women refused to talk to me or date me because they believed I was odd and gay. I would spend hours looking for sex on gay chat sites. At that point, I did not care how I received affection; I just wanted something to carry me far away from the memories of my pain. I remember sleeping with well over four hundred men. During my sleeping with men, I would think, "Well, at least no one will get pregnant." I felt at ease knowing that by engaging in these acts, I would not bring an innocent child to suffer alone in a heartless world, as I did.

Sleeping with men also opened several other portals of sexual perversion. While riding the roller coaster of sexual deviance, I would hook up with numerous guys throughout the city of Houston. I would lie with men as I had with the female prostitute. While engaging in this sexual deviance, it seemed as if all the memories of being forced to rub people's feet in foster care flooded my mind. I began to act out everything that was done to me as a child with other men. I began to engage in fetishism and became obsessed with various areas of the human body. I delved into a realm of sexuality that was mysterious, abominable, and forbidden as a Christian. I did not care. After all, I was lonely and felt that no one cared about me anymore.

The memories I had of being slapped in the face by another boy's genitals as a child and seeing older boys have sex with each other at night urged me on and made me feel that it was OK to engage in that type of behavior. I became buck-wild sexually but in a quiet and reserved way. Around the college, I was a skinny nerd with no friends; however, behind closed doors, I was becoming a raging freak. I plunged so deeply into homosexuality that I would spend hours sucking and smelling my sexual partners' feet and nipples. Afterward, I would spend an additional two hours sucking on my sexual partners' booty holes and penises before engaging in sodomy. On Saturday nights, I would take my financial-aid refund money and would pay men to allow me to swallow their seminal fluid. I grew to like the milky taste of seminal fluid and would eat cranberry sauce out of my sexual partner's booty hole. Sometimes I would even eat chocolate syrup off of mens feet. After having orgies that lasted into the early hours of morning, I would wake up with the scent of other men's pheromones on my top lip. Without wasting time, I would proceed to spend forty-five minutes to an hour on gay chat sites to arrange my next sexual encounter. Then I would brush my teeth and rush to church.

The depth of my sexual deviance was sending me on a collision course with hell; I was worshipping pleasure at the cost of my dignity and undiscovered purpose in life.

After class, I would often check in with Dr. Lee and Mrs. Nelly, do my homework, and then run to my room just to flood my mind with pornography. I did not like how I felt on the inside, so I allowed the haze of sex to carry me far away from my reality. I was a raging sexaholic. The euphoric feeling of pleasure allowed me to momentarily journey past the years of internal pain and unanswered questions. Deep in my gut, I knew that my sexual deviance was wrong; however, I equated someone loving me with having sex, so I placed more emphasis on experiencing multiple orgasms than on being a Christian. After class, I would often feel extremely remorseful for sleeping with men, so I tried drowning my guilt in alcohol and marijuana. Drugs became another avenue I used to escape the pain. The pain of being rejected by my foster family, biological relatives, college peers, and women hurt me to my core. To my chagrin, whatever I tried to fill the void with was never strong enough.

After contracting an STD in my mouth, I remember driving to Ben Taub Hospital to take a shot. Afterward, I bumped into my biological mother in the parking lot. "Mom? What are you doing here?" I asked, feeling bewildered.

"Hey, baby," said my mom, covering her teeth. She looked extraordinarily frail and smelled like raw fish because she had urinated on herself and was on her cycle. "Look at you—looking like your father," she said, smiling.

We continued to talk in the parking lot. I learned that my mom had just gotten a checkup because she had been raped two days ago at the bus stop. Rather than leave my mom on the streets, I drove her to my dorm room and allowed her to stay with me.

"I stay in a small dorm room. It's not much," I said, opening the door. My room consisted of a twin-sized bed, desk, small closet, kitchenette, and bathroom that I shared with another roommate. "You can sleep on the bed, and I'll sleep on the floor, Mom," I said.

My mom was so happy to see me that she wrote poems and read them to me. We spent time catching up on old times, and my mom answered a lot of my questions. I took her to a Luby's to ask her some serious questions. Although there were some questions that I knew the answers to, there was a part of me that wanted to hear the words come out of her mouth. When

I asked my mom why she left my two sisters and me in that old apartment, she hung her head down. "I couldn't raise you, baby. I was still trying to recover from my childhood pain inflicted by your grandfather. I knew that CPS would come in and get you and raise you better than I could," said my mom, her head still cast downward. "I didn't want you and your sisters with the family because of how they treated me."

My mom and I then experienced a long, awkward silence. Eventually, I said, "Meme and Aunt Chy told me what Grandpa did to you, Mom. Is it true?" I said, my eyes wide open. The words that then came out of my mother's mouth caused me to put my hands on my head in shock.

"Not only did he rape me, but he also raped my friends and your uncle repeatedly. Your uncle died of AIDS after living life as a homosexual." My mom was back to looking at the floor. "He never got over what your grandfather did to him." Tears were running down her face.

By the time we were done talking, I did not know whether to burst into tears or seek revenge for the damage that my grandfather inflicted. My mom and I rode back to my dorm room in silence. That night, I slept on the floor again, and all I could think about was what a monster my grandfather was. Although I previously knew some of what had happened to my mom, I still could not understand *how* anyone could do such things. I kept thinking about how my grandfather had sex with my mother repeatedly and then raped her friends. I wondered how my grandfather could let himself have anal sex with my uncle. And I thought of my unfortunate uncle, who had died from AIDS. As I drifted off to sleep, I envisioned myself ripping out my grandfather's esophagus.

Hiding my mom in my dorm room became a problem after I returned from class one day and found her on my laptop. After finding out that I had downloaded gay porn and created a profile on a gay website, my mother was terribly upset.

"Boy, I'll kill your ass!" said my mother angrily. "Your uncle died of AIDS after living that lifestyle, and you don't have enough common sense to stay out of that mess?" She was flailing her arms.

I stood in front of her, my eyes filling with tears, and she continued to yell and scream in frustration. Then I snapped, and my words poured out of me: "No one cares about me! Maybe I wouldn't be a faggot if you had been a real mother and hadn't left me in an environment where people were trying to fuck me in my ass! So guess what! I got a foot fetish now—did you see that too? I like smelling people's stanky feet! I guess the psychiatrist was right! I'm crazy! I'm addicted to foot stank, booty licking and nipples! Where were you when I was forced to rub people's feet as a child?" My anger was escalating, and I ended up blurting out the worst sentence a child could yell to a drug-addicted parent: "You were too busy sucking that glass dick of a crack pipe instead of taking care of your own damn kids!" I paused to breathe. "Why the fuck did you bring us into this world?" I asked, raising my voice.

An awkward silence lasted for a few moments. We were standing face to face.

"My point precisely!" I said. "Your ass was more focused on trying to bust a nut, rather than—"

Bam!

I gripped my jaw in pain as I struggled to pick myself off the floor. "Don't you talk to me like that!" said my mother as she punched me in the face. My jaw caused me agony, and I could only stare at the floor. "I haven't been the best mother, and I couldn't protect you from what happened, but I did what I could, boy," said my mom, who was now crying. "I put you in a little boat and set you afloat in this world, hoping that God would take care of you because I couldn't!"

After I explained to her all of the abuse that I endured while growing up in the system, we both sat on the bed in silence. Regardless of my yelling and screaming, my mom was adamant about me steering away from a homosexual lifestyle. I remember leaving my dorm room, jumping into my car, and driving away. I had no clear destination in mind. All I knew was that I wanted to get far away from Houston.

I eventually parked my car behind a hotel on Tidwell and Lockwood. I frantically searched through my glove compartment for the small bag of weed

I had stashed. As I leaned back in my seat, I noticed there were three kids playing across the street in front of a grocery store. "I wonder what life has in store for them," I thought. As I leaned back further, I allowed the haze of marijuana to carry me away; my mind began to drift. I thought a lot about that song Mrs. Thibodaux used to sing: "Changed," by Tramaine Hawkins. I thought about how my foster mother used to lecture me for hours about how I was going to be a man of God one day. All the prophecies that were spoken by ministers in the church flooded my mind. "My mind is playing tricks on me," I thought as I drifted to sleep.

A couple of hours later, I awoke to police sirens and started to cough because of the horrible taste in my mouth. I jumped on US Route 59 and drove south, heading to my dorm, where I eventually found my mom sleeping with a Bible in her hand. After tucking her into bed, I lay on the floor, feeling angry and frustrated as the tears began to flow.

I remember waking up the next morning to a large banging noise. "I'm sick of these motherfuckers always trying to kill me!" yelled my mom. "The government owes me money, and all I know is that I have a case coming to me and that someone owes me some damn answers!"

"Mamma, what the hell are you doing? It's six in the morning!" I said, rubbing the sleep matter out of my eyes. The words were coming out of my mother's mouth so fast that I could barely understand her. I did not know it at the time, but my mother was experiencing an extreme case of mania and was having a psychotic episode. Scared and having no clue about what to do next, I called Trish, who instructed me to take our mom to Memorial Hermann Hospital, which was southeast on Astoria Boulevard.

After verbally fighting with my mother and forcing her into my car, I spent the next fifteen minutes hearing her ramble and verbalize her paranoia. Her speech was pressured, and her thoughts were extremely disorganized. My mom thought that the government was trying to steal her poems. "Everybody is trying to steal my poems, and all I know is that this is my life. All the money the government owes me is coming to me!" said my mom. She talked about how my car radio was recording her conversations, until we pulled up in the driveway of the hospital.

"Mom, are you sick?" asked Trish with wide-open eyes. I could see my other sister, Tasha, in a corner eating chips; however, the astonished look on Trish's face caused me to abruptly stop walking.

After three long hours at the hospital, my sisters and I found out that our mother had tested positive for HIV. The doctor said, "At this point, your mother's viral load is so high that it could be a significant threat to her health if she is not stabilized with the appropriate antiviral-medication regimen." I remember that the doctor was a bald-headed, heavyset Caucasian male with a big belly and extremely thick gray beard.

After the doctor walked away, my sisters and I were left standing in shock. "Mom is going to die of AIDS?" said my older sister, looking at the floor with a blank stare.

"He's lying. Mom will be fine," I said, reeling in disbelief.

Our mother sat in a catatonic state, and after an hour of trying to engage her with small talk, my sisters and I dropped her off at a shelter.

―⁂―

My first semester at the University of Houston came to a dull and boring close. I remember spending the holiday season with Mrs. Nelly, the director of the social-service program. All I could think about was my mother, who was now sick with HIV.

"Are you OK, kiddo?" said Mrs. Nelly. She saw that I was not eating my food. "You never pick over food, so something has to be wrong," she said, trying to figure out what was bothering me.

"I'm OK," I said, smiling and trying my best to mask my true feelings.

The holiday season flew by swiftly, and as the spring semester started, I found myself struggling to focus on school. A battle seemed to be taking place on the inside of me that I did not understand. After learning about my mother's illness and after engaging in some deep self-reflection during the holidays, I decided to get baptized and to stop sleeping with men for affection. In my spirit, I felt that one day, God would honor my obedience and bless me with a wife if I abstained from sleeping with men for affection.

During that time, my body was screaming yes to whatever pleasurable activity I could find, but my spirit and love for Jesus were screaming no. After a month, I slipped up and had a sexual encounter with a student at the University of Houston and felt horrible. What I had done was unbearable, causing me to spend several days crying myself to sleep. The intense feelings of loneliness arose again, and I found myself battling the urge to drink alcohol and smoke weed.

I reached out to Mrs. Thibodaux; however, she refused to return my phone calls. I called the HAY Center, a support center for foster youths, and told one of the social workers about how my mom was sick and how sad and lonely I was in the world. I spent at least twenty minutes pouring my heart out to the social worker, who simply listened and prayed. I remember hanging up the phone and feeling an increased sense of loneliness. Although I could not prove it, I felt as if life wanted me to fold mentally and emotionally under loneliness and rejection. It seemed as if sexual perversion was stalking me; life was patiently waiting for loneliness and rejection to cause me to run back to the homosexual lifestyle.

About two months into the spring semester, I gave my car to my biological mother, dropped out of all my classes, and was kicked out of housing for not being enrolled.

"The only thing the state can do for you right now is pay rent for a couple of months at the YMCA," said Mrs. Liggins, whom I called for support.

After moving the few things I had into the Cossaboom Family YMCA on Highway 610, I sat on my bed, feeling confused. The room was as big as a shoebox and stank like an old nursing home. After a couple of weeks of staying at the YMCA, I became extremely uncomfortable because I was the youngest person living there. The place was filled with old, weird men who gave me dirty old looks.

During that time, I prayed and reached out to Jesus as much as I could. Everything in me wanted to know Jesus for myself, especially since all those I knew seemed to turn their backs on me. During the day, I tried to take a couple of classes at Houston Community College to finish my associate's degree. I continued the same routine of going to school and reading my Bible for a couple of months. I walked one half of a mile to the nearest bus stop so that I could attend classes at HCC downtown and rode back to the YMCA in the evenings. Every night, I replayed the gospel song, "Shake Us Again," by Juanita Bynum. As the song played at night, I would envision myself in the arms of Jesus, safe from the confusion of this chaotic world. I felt as if my love for Jesus was keeping me from drugs, alcohol, and gay sex. Although I was lonely, everything seemed to be going fine until a dreadful night, in which my peace was disrupted with foolishness. I awoke one night to a large Hispanic male rubbing my nipples and ferociously jacking off in my face. To this day, I remember the words that came out of his mouth. "It's OK," he said as he massaged his erect penis continuously.

After I cussed and screamed, the guy ran downstairs. I thought, "I can't even rest in peace!" I called the cops and explained what had happened, hoping that the guy would be arrested. When the four officers arrived at my room to take a report, I felt even more humiliated! The smiles on the officers' faces suggested that my safety was not a priority.

"So let me get this straight," one officer said, rubbing his nose. "The guy was jacking off in your face?"

The other officers chuckled when he said this. Explaining that a guy had tried to masturbate in front of me to cops and seeing their laughter was like a sucker punch to the head.

The next morning, I explained the situation to the site manager and was informed that I was being put out of the YMCA. "We've never had this problem until you came," said the manager. As I packed my things, I became enraged by the irony and futility of my situation. It seemed as if no matter what I did, a spirit of sexual perversion would always haunt me. Fighting to be free from bondage seemed to attract incredible resistance. It was almost as if Satan himself were yelling, "You will bow to perversion voluntarily or involuntarily. Either way, you will bow."

Having nowhere to go, I left a lot of my clothes at the YMCA and caught a bus to the Dryden/TMC Station downtown, which was part of a metro-rail network. As I sat with my head in my hands, I began to feel an increased sense of despair. I felt as if my life were coming to an end. "This is rock bottom," I thought repeatedly. "God, just take me far away from here!" I yelled internally. The heat of the sun caused me to sweat bullets as I sat watching people get on and off the bus at the transit center. "Everybody is in a constant state of motion, yet here I am once again flat on my face."

After sitting at the transit center for almost an hour, I came to the conclusion that I would never reach my dream of becoming a college graduate. For the next couple of days, I slept on the streets and ate at homeless shelters throughout the city. After spending one night sleeping on the floor of a Salvation Army on South Main Street, I decided that it was time to be a man and grow up. On June 18, 2008, I enlisted in the US Army as a chaplain's assistant. When I enrolled, I did not know what would come next; all I knew was that I was hungry, was losing a lot of weight, and was growing tired of living life as a homeless vagrant. I was ready to escape the emotional trauma and sexual quicksand that was trying to destroy me. Life in Houston was growing increasingly confusing, and I was happy to take the first flight out of this city by any means necessary.

CHAPTER 13

Army Life

AFTER A FULL DAY OF being processed into the army's training base at Fort Jackson, South Carolina, I was bored to the point of mental exhaustion. Most of my first day was spent signing papers and getting medical exams and shots. When everyone finally boarded the bus to go to our barracks, I was excited. "My life will change for the better, now that I'm in the military," I thought as I dozed off to sleep. After what only seemed like ten minutes, the bus driver slammed on the brakes when he pulled up beside the barracks. I awoke dazed and confused as my head hit the seat in front of me.

"Get off the fucking bus right now!" the drill sergeants yelled fervently.

My heart began to beat so hard that I thought my chest was about to explode. I nearly toppled over another soldier as I struggled to grab all of my bags and to exit the bus.

"Welcome to hell, assholes! Lift your bags above your damn heads right now!" the drill sergeants hollered.

I did not know whether to cover my ears from the screams of the drill sergeants or cover my nose from the strong scent of diesel exhaust fumes coming from the buses. The booming voices of multiple drill sergeants caused my ears to ring. Suddenly, I could not help but laugh as the guy next to me fell over under the weight of his bags. Seeing him on the floor with his bags on his head was downright comical.

"Looks like we have a big-lipped chuckle bunny over here," a drill sergeant said, stepping directly in front of me, bringing himself face to face with me. The drill sergeant repositioned his hat and wiped his forehead. "That funny to you, boy!" the drill sergeant yelled. I could see the back of his throat as he spoke, and he spewed spit onto my face.

"No!" I yelled awkwardly.

"That's 'Sir' or 'No, sir' to you, asshole!"

I quickly learned not to laugh or smile in the military. My arms felt like bricks after being forced to do what seemed to be one hundred push-ups.

Acclimating to military life was not that bad after I got past the cussing and constant exercise. Although it took a few days for me to get past the shock of the forceful drill sergeants, overall I was happy to be in the US Army. One of the reasons why I joined the military was because I had been a hungry vagrant in Houston. Knowing that I would be able to sit down to a table full of food three times a day put a smile on my face. Very quickly, I learned to appreciate the simple things that basic training had to offer. After living on the streets of Houston, Texas, three hots and a cot—coupled with free fitness training to sculpt my body—was a good deal. Basic training seemed to lift my spirits and took my mind far away from my horrible life in Houston.

Although there were no average days in the military, exercising was a daily requirement. Each morning before roll call, I awoke to the sound of Sergeant Brown screaming and critiquing everyone's bed-making skills and the cleanliness of our lockers. Sergeant Brown was a tall, muscular black man with a gold tooth and an extremely short temper. His resemblance to Damon Wayans in the movie *Major Payne* was uncanny! After roll call, everyone in my platoon would journey outside for fitness training. I enjoyed the push-ups, sit-ups, and early-morning runs. There was something about nature that always put a smile on my face. Running with my platoon became easy because I began to focus more on how the sun's rays pierced through the trees rather than the lengths of the runs.

After our morning fitness regimen, we engaged in my favorite activity of the day—eating! Sitting down to pancakes, waffles, eggs, and tall glasses of orange juice every morning was heaven! On some days, I would sneak to the other side of the cafeteria and eat twice before joining my platoon. After breakfast, there was a period where we were all tossed into a room and lectured by various drill sergeants. Most days, breakfast made me so sleepy that I could barely keep my head up and focus on what the drill sergeants were saying.

"Obaseki, get in the push-up position right now!" the drill sergeants would yell when they would see me dozing off. Yep, I was quickly known in my platoon as the soldier who was always getting grilled by the drill sergeants for sleeping.

Midday was when we engaged in team-oriented activities. What made basic training exciting was that we never knew what activity the drill sergeants had planned. There were days when we spent time practicing our shooting. "Ready, set, fire!" the drill sergeant would yell after coaching us on how to shoot between breaths.

One drill sergeant said, "Obaseki, if our lives ever depend on your ass shooting a damn target, we would all die! Get your sorry ass to the back of the line!"

I was not the best shooter, but at least I gave it all I had.

Some activities were actually cathartic, allowing me to ventilate my frustration. After being trained on how to attach our bayonet knives to our M16 rifles, we were led into a forest and instructed to run and slice the wooden targets with the knives. The targets resembled Chinese soldiers, and I could not wait to have my turn to run through the forest and slice and stab the targets with my bayonet knife. These targets became more than just targets; they started to represent the sources of my pain and frustration up to that point.

When it was my turn to charge, I would run through the forest, whacking the targets, screaming loudly as if I were on a battlefield. When I would reach the last target, all of my frustration and anger would compel me to ravage the target maniacally. One time, I must have spent five solid minutes beating and stabbing the final target, causing large pieces to fly everywhere in a storm of splinters. Every blow caused a large gash on the chest of the target. I thought, "This is for all the hell I've gone through!"

My thoughts were, of course, interrupted by Sergeant Brown. "That's right, Obaseki! Get that anger out!" he yelled before telling me to rejoin my platoon.

Not all of the activities in the military were easy. For instance, I remember Sergeant Brown marching us onto a field and to a huge wooden tower, which we would end up having to climb. The top of the tower had to be at least twenty-five feet in the air. The objective of the assignment was for soldiers to overcome any fear of heights and to use their legs to repel off the tower while holding on to a rope. Initially, I was excited, and while on the ground with the other soldiers, I spent time flirting with the ladies, joking and laughing.

"You ready, Obaseki?" yelled Sergeant Brown.

"Sir, yes, sir!" I replied while jumping up and down to show I was ready and unafraid. There was no way I was going to show any signs of weakness to Sergeant Brown. "I'm not scared!" I yelled, bracing myself.

All of my confidence evaporated when I was twenty-five feet up in the air. I was consumed with fear. Sergeant Brown handed me the rope, and as I jumped off, I lost my footing and hit the side of the wooden tower with a loud thud! I winced, and my eyes clenched shut. I held the rope for dear life before Sergeant Brown let me down. "Use your feet next time, egghead!" yelled Sergeant Brown.

Of course, I had to deal with other soldiers' laughter, but I was just happy to be alive.

Boot camp initially started out to be a place where I finally began to feel connected and accepted. What was making basic training so enjoyable was the sense of camaraderie. We exercised, solved problems, and marched together, regardless of rain, sleet, or snow. Despite the mean drill sergeants and the difficult team-building activities, at the end of each day, I appreciated sitting down and eating with people from all different walks of life, who all shared the same goal of defending the country.

The military was my new family and home, and at first, I believed that things would turn out for the better. As time progressed, however, the appreciation and happiness that I felt while in the military began to dissipate. To be disrespected by the drill sergeants was one thing, but to be disrespected by my peers was a whole different story.

His last name was Collins. To be honest, I never noticed him up until he started opening his mouth and bullying people in the evenings after training. Although most of the other soldiers just ignored him, I was irritated at the fact that someone would join the military and proceed to bully his peers. I thought, "We're here to defend the country, but this idiotic quack takes pleasure in harassing everyone." Rather than address the situation immediately, I decided to wait to see if his behavior would change. After a couple of days, his bullying became worse! As a matter of fact, his horrible comments were far worse when the bullying was directed toward me! "Look at this big-lip nigger right here!" Collins would yell.

After a while, Collins ignored all the other soldiers and devoted a lot of his time to bullying me directly. One day, as I marched to a rhythmical cadence with the other soldiers, Collins remade the lyrics: "Tyrone is a fucking faggot, and he looks like a crab! Sound off—one, two, three, four!" After a couple of days, his taunts reached a point where it became too much to bear. I could not take his harassment anymore.

One evening after dinner, I was cleaning my gun, and Collins decided to leave his area to comment on how poor of a job I was doing with my gun. "This dumb-ass nigga don't even know how to clean a gun!" he yelled to the other soldiers. "Nigga, you need to—"

Wham!

Before he could finish, my fist landed hard on his nose. "I'm tired of your bitch ass always talking shit," I yelled, hitting him again in the jaw. Before I knew it, Collins had landed a right punch to my jaw.

"Y'all break it up!" Sergeant Brown yelled, walking into the room. "Looks like I got two lovebirds! Since you idiots want to fight, both of you can grab your tents and sleep outside!"

My fist was still clinched, and my face filled with rage when Collins flashed a huge grin. The situation angered me even more because he found the whole ordeal comical. I refused to accept this punishment and had to provide a rebuttal. "There wouldn't be a problem if this dude would just—"

I could not finish my sentence. Sergeant Brown forced me to the ground and made me do push-ups. As a consequence, Collins got to remain in the barracks, and I had to sleep outside in my tent.

For several weeks, Collins and I continued to argue and fight continually. My frustration got to the point where I began to submit requests to see the army counselor. Each time, I was given the same response: the counselor only told me to focus on myself and remind myself of why I was in the army. As time progressed, the counselor's advice did not work! What made things worse was when I caught two drill sergeants hiding behind a bush while Collins and another soldier were picking on me. When I looked and saw the drill sergeants smiling while peering over a bush, I immediately put two and two together. I thought, "The drill sergeants were putting him up to this on purpose. Why else would two drill sergeants hide behind a bush and smile as another soldier bullied a member of his team?"

After I became aware that the drill sergeants were encouraging soldiers to bully me, I began to fight Collins and every soldier in my unit who had something negative to say. My motto was "If you're man enough to talk shit, then you're man enough to get your ass whooped." Unfortunately, my bad attitude did not end well for me. After submitting another request to see the counselor, I was called into an office. I could not wait to tell the counselor my frustrations.

I thought I would be able to connect with a psychologist like Denzel Washington's character in the *Antwone Fisher* film. His character is the psychologist who comes in and saves the day by helping the angry soldier with all his anger issues and childhood trauma. I just knew that if I talked to a counselor one more time, that I would find someone to mentor me through basic training and guide me into a successful career as a US soldier. Boy was I wrong! Instead of seeing my usual counselor, I was met by an Asian psychiatrist with a long white coat. He looked at my case file for a few seconds and then immediately walked me over to the army's psychiatric hospital.

"Why am I not going back to my barracks?" I asked, feeling confused.

"You're not adapting to military life," the psychiatrist replied.

"What do you mean that I'm not adapting to military life? I mind my own business, but the same guy keeps bullying me while the drill sergeants watch in the corner!"

However, my explanations fell on deaf ears; the psychiatrist did not seem to care. Nothing I said could convince him to allow me back into my unit. I did not understand it at the time, but the military had already made up its mind to discharge me because of my history as a ward of the court. My US Army records listed the following statement on July 27, 2008:

> Past treatment records were obtained, confirming a history of bipolar disorder and treatment with various medications over the years including Abilify, Lexapro, Depakote, Effexor, Adderal, Remeron, Dexedrine, and Mellaril. Soldier's mother is schizophrenic, and he was taken from the home by child protective services at a young age and had multiple foster-home placements from two months to eighteen years old. It is recommended that the soldier be separated from the US Army for failure to meet medical procurement standards IAW AR 40-501, Chapter 2-27 d.

A week or so after the statement was made, I was called into a room by a psychiatrist and informed that I was bipolar. As the psychiatrist continued to talk about the National Alliance on Mental Illness, I could not help but tune him out. All I could think about was the numerous times I had had this conversation as a ward of the court. I thought, "All my life, people have been telling me that I was crazy, retarded, chemically imbalanced, and bipolar. The problem has to be the system, not me." Eventually, I just got up and walked out of the doctor's office. I refused to listen to the psychiatrist stressing the importance of me adhering to a regimen of psychiatric drugs. As far as I was concerned, the psychiatrist was the one who was crazy, and his attempts to convince me to believe that I was mentally ill and needed pills to live a normal life was falling on *my* deaf ears.

The few weeks I spent at the psychiatric hospital were filled with watching TV, doing puzzles, and suffering through informational sessions about psychiatric medications. For days, I sat in the hospital, feeling nothing but angry. I was angry because I felt as if I was a failure and now had no future. To make myself feel better, I would sing gospel songs loudly at the top of my lungs. Although this behavior was viewed as odd, I found it to be cathartic. It made me feel better. At night when I could not sing loudly, my thoughts filled with fear and uncertainty. "What if, somehow, there is some hidden force that is intentionally pushing me over the edge?" I thought while lying in bed one night.

For the life of me, I could not understand why I was bullied and singled out everywhere I went. Being discharged from the military brought forth feelings of worthlessness. I thought, "You're too sorry to even fight for your own damn country, you retarded-ass nigga." Intense feelings of nervousness began to consume me because my backup plan had failed. My attempts to become a college graduate had failed; now, what seemed to be my only shot at becoming someone had also gone down the drain. As I sat in the psych hospital, feeling bored and lonely, I began to believe that I lacked the ability to bring my dreams into fruition.

On September 5, 2008, I boarded a plane back to Houston, Texas, without a clue as to what I would pursue next. Although I had no ideas about the next road I would take in life, I knew I could not give up. Giving up meant failure, and failure would mean that life would have somehow succeeded at breaking me down.

CHAPTER 14

Full Circle

"My life is over," I thought as I sat in the airport. Calling the Thibodauxs or my biological relatives would be pointless because of how they usually treated me. I decided to call Mrs. Nelly at the University of Houston and ask her to come pick me up from the airport. By the time we got into her small office, she immediately started to place phone calls to social-service organizations around the Houston area. I tried to help too by searching the Internet for safe homeless shelters, but after about an hour, I started to feel as if there was no hope for my getting into a shelter.

"There's nothing else we can do for him," said a representative from the HAY Center.

"What do you mean that there's nothing else you can do? All I'm asking for is a list of homeless shelters," said Mrs. Nelly in frustration. "Who said anything about being reimbursed? I'm trying to help this young man stay off the streets and get into a shelter!"

As I sat in Mrs. Nelly's office, I could see the frustration bubbling up, and she hung up the phone and placed her head in her hands.

"Well, look who decided to surface all of a sudden," said Dr. Lee as he entered the office. "Did you find any information, Nelly?"

"I've searched all afternoon but haven't gained any ground," she replied softly.

"Well, let's go to the Luby's on Old Spanish Trail," said Dr. Lee, yawning and looking at his watch. "Looks like we got some catching up to do." He patted me on the shoulder.

As we sat and ate, I would spend the next forty-five minutes talking about my experiences in the army. The disappointment was clearly visible in my tone when I explained how the drill sergeants made the other soldiers pick on me. Of course, Dr. Lee and Mrs. Nelly were looking for an explanation for why I had not called them to let them know I was joining the military.

"All I wanted to do was fight for someone else, to have a chance at achieving the American dream," I said. "I wanted to be my own man. What would you do if you were homeless and hungry?"

We continued to talk throughout lunch, and Dr. Lee decided to turn the conversation into an opportunity to teach me a life lesson. "Tyrone, from what you told me while at the University of Houston, you spent eighteen years in a system where you were beat down. I would have told you that joining the military was a bad choice because you needed to surround yourself with people who could build you up," said Dr. Lee before shoving a large forkful of liver and onions into his mouth.

"I always thought the military tears people down before building them back up," said Mrs. Nelly as she scrolled through her cell phone. By the end of lunch, I got the point that I should make better decisions regarding my backup plans. Perhaps Dr. Lee was right: just because something was optional did not mean that it was the best thing for my growth and development.

After lunch, Dr. Lee and Mrs. Nelly paid for me to stay in a motel, while they helped me get into a safe shelter. The next three days at the Sunshine Inn and Suites was filled with extreme boredom. The television in the hotel did not work right, and I had no friends I could visit, so the only thing I could do was daydream. All I could think about was what move to take next in life. Although I promised myself that I would get a higher education and not be a statistic, I felt very apprehensive about returning to college. I thought, "I'm too dumb to go back to school. The least I could do is find a trade and try to live a normal life."

As each day passed in the hotel, I wondered if I would ever experience the happiness that comes with earning an honest living. I began to think about what my life would be like if I were to come home to a beautiful wife and kids every day. The following scene unfolded within my imagination:

A vivid little girl with curly pigtails ran into my arms, yelling, "Daddy!" as she showed me her artwork from her kindergarten class. The fact that she had found my chocolate stash was clearly evident; there was a brown residue on the side of her mouth and on her fingers, making them sticky.

"Let's go see what Mama's making in the kitchen," I said, and I picked up and carried my daughter toward the kitchen.

The aromatic scent of a clean house, smothered chicken, turnip greens, candy yams, corn on the cob, and corn bread put a smile on my face as my nose rejoiced.

"Looks like someone came home early and outdid themselves again!" I said to my gorgeous wife, grabbing her waist and giving her a long kiss.

"Don't get too happy now. That's how we got the kids we have today," said my wife as she pulled the corn bread out of the oven. "Oh yeah, your son is waiting for you to change him. It's your day." My wife patted me on the butt before shooing me out of the kitchen.

"All right, calm down," I said as I walked over to the crib next to the wooden dresser. As I stared into my son's eyes, a warm, fuzzy feeling filled the center of my chest. I was feeling a sense of accomplishment and comfort in knowing that I had reached a point where I could care for my family, who loved me as much as I loved them. My son gave me a slight smile before blinking his eyes and slowly drifting off to sleep. That brief smile conveyed that he felt safe. It was as if he and I had a nonverbal understanding; he understood that he could rest peacefully because his pops was going to always be there for him. I then wondered about what career my boy might choose, while I changed his diaper with a smile. My smile was cut short when my son unleashed a powerful stream of urine, which struck my face. "Ahh!" I yelled, trying to shield my face.

"Sir, are you OK?" asked a male attendant in the hotel's computer lab, interrupting my dream. "The lab is closing in five minutes." He tapped me vigorously on my shoulder.

"Sorry, I must've fallen asleep," I said, gathering my things and leaving the lab.

My continued efforts to map out a plan for my future became futile. I had no idea about what path to take next in life and wondered if being a happily married man would ever be a possibility.

Eventually, Dr. Lee and Mrs. Nelly were able to help me find the homeless shelter called New Faith Home for Men, which was in southwest Houston. Initially, I thought the shelter would be a massive complex like most shelters in Houston. To my surprise, it was a small storefront church with beds in one of the rooms. After being dropped off, I was amazed at how welcoming the pastor was.

"Welcome to New Faith, Tyrone. I'm Pastor Kirk Higgins, and this is my wife, Iris." Pastor Higgins was a tall, barrel-chested guy with serious eyes and thick glasses.

His wife was dressed in a white pantsuit and a large church hat. "You made it just in time for Bible study," she said, smiling largely.

Bible study was filled with singing and excitement about Jesus. My face depicted my thoughts during the church service. All I could think about was how my life seemed to be going down the drain. Jesus was the last thing on my mind. "I don't have anything to be happy about right now," I thought, folding my arms and leaning back in my chair. I slept through the service and woke up when everyone started clapping. The clapping meant that the pastor was about to give the benediction.

Before walking out of the sanctuary to take my bags to the bedroom area, I was stopped by Pastor Higgins's booming voice. "Tyrone, let me talk to you for a second in my office," he said with a sincere look.

I thought, "The last thing I need is another pastor who doesn't even know me trying to be my daddy."

For the next thirty minutes, I was told how I had a mighty calling on my life and how God was calling me from the sidelines to the forefront. As I sat and halfway listened to the pastor encourage me, all I could think about was whether I was going to sleep on the floor or in a bed. I sat nodding my head, but my mind was elsewhere. I was released to go back to the living area and was instructed to meet with him every week as a requirement of being in the shelter.

Acclimating to the shelter was smooth and easy. The shelter comprised men of all different ages and backgrounds. Ex-convicts, mentally challenged youths, and drug addicts became my confidants during this homeless stage. A lot of the people in the homeless shelter seemed to be drifting aimlessly with no plans for the future. Our days were filled with looking for jobs and playing card games or dominoes. I started to work for the shelter after my first week and was moved into one of the apartments around the corner. The loneliness, extra freedom, loss of hope, and lack of drive became a dangerous combination for me. I quickly reverted back to my street mentality.

I can recall numerous days of smoking weed and getting drunk with my roommate, Jason. My reopening the door to alcohol and marijuana also prompted me to open the door to forbidden pleasures as well. Once again, I yielded my body over to vile engagements with men and did not care about the consequences. The affection helped me cope with the pain of being rejected from the military and being on the streets again. Day in and day out, I found myself drifting to the desires of my body. I felt that since I was on my way downhill, I might as well enjoy the ride to hell.

My self-destructive behavior came to a halt when Pastor Higgins caught me trying to arrange a hookup on his office computer. I remember becoming angry when the pastor turned the computer off. All I wanted to do was smell folk's feet, eat booty, swallow seminal fluid, and I was mad that Pastor Higgins had interrupted my plans. The first thought that came to mind was that I was going to be put out of his shelter. To my surprise, Pastor Higgins did something that I had not experienced in a long time. "Tyrone, you don't have to be gay—you're a man of God, and he has purposed you to be set aside for his glory! Allow his grace to shine upon you," he said with a serious face. Pastor Higgins was validating my identity in Jesus during a time when I was clearly lost.

During the couple of weeks before he caught me in his office, I had not been saying much in our weekly meetings, but then right after his show of support, I felt the need to let it all out. "Everything that I try to do in life seems to wither up and die before I get a chance to enjoy it," I responded angrily. "All I have left in life is to enjoy pleasure by any means necessary." I explained how smoking weed and alcohol were coping mechanisms.

As I continued to pour my heart out about my experiences in foster care, Pastor Higgins listened intently for about fifteen minutes before interrupting me: "Tyrone, you have a choice to make. Do you want to rely on homosexuality, alcoholism, and weed or rely on Jesus and watch him work a miracle in your life?"

"You don't understand. I was molested, and no one—"

"I don't care what happened!" replied Pastor Higgins, interrupting me with his booming voice. "God ordained you before the foundations of the earth as his royal priesthood, and it's time for you to start acting like it. I've spoken to the Thibodauxs about you being in their home, and I know you were raised in church."

All I could do was express my desire for Jesus. As a man, I felt as if life was kicking my ass so bad that Jesus was the only option I had to survive.

"If it is Jesus that you are going to rely on, then from this day forward, let go of what you know and engage in behaviors that are pleasing to him," said Pastor Higgins. He continued to impart wisdom into my mind and ended his conversation by encouraging me to use my tuition waiver to go back to college.

By the end of the summer, my fire and drive to accomplish my goal of finishing my education was fully blazing. After submitting my application to Texas A&M University–Commerce, I was accepted within a matter of weeks. I knew that I had not gotten in because of my intellect but because of the prayers of the church. After talking to a college counselor about my interest in joining the FBI, I decided to major in sociology and get a minor in criminal justice. I was surprised that all I needed was three semesters of classes before I could graduate with a degree in sociology.

The weekly meetings with Pastor Higgins and the lessons I learned in church exchanged my sorrow and anger for joy and renewed passion to stay on the course toward college and beyond. Before I left New Faith, Pastor Higgins invited me to his house for his wife's birthday celebration. I could not remember the last time I had celebrated with people. For the first time in a long while, I was smiling again; it felt good to see people dance and laugh and enjoy the simple things of life, and just being there made me feel more connected. This was one of the last good memories I had at New Faith before boarding a Greyhound bus to go to Texas A&M University–Commerce.

Looking back on my time at New Faith, I now see that sometimes Jesus places people in our lives to bring out the best in us. In a period in which I was a homeless vagrant, Jesus provided shelter and encouragement to help me recognize and remember who I was in him. I believe wholeheartedly that if more men and women would encourage young minds to walk in their Christ-given identity, then more of our youths would bloom into stronger men and women of valor and of love.

Transitioning from New Faith to a college university required a leap of faith, which I would not have taken if I had not received the support of a man of God—that is, Pastor Higgins. He had reminded me of something powerful in me that I had forgotten or never truly embraced.

Making the jump to Texas A&M University–Commerce turned out to be a rewarding move for me. This time around, I was able to make friends quickly rather than be bullied. Two of my best friends at the college were Phillip and his girlfriend, Randi. I met them at a Christian concert in the student center, and they invited me to a Bible study at the home of one of his church members.

What made that Bible study unique was that before delving into the Word of God, we would eat, play games, and chat with each other. It felt good to bond and be a part of a community of people that was positive and uplifting. As the semester progressed, I gave Phillip the nickname "Ned Flanders," which I got from *The Simpsons*, because he was holy and always encouraged me to be a man of God.

Another good friend that I made at the university was a country girl named Jackie. She was dark skinned and had long black hair, and she cooked better than anyone's mother. After joining the school's gospel choir, I was invited to her house through the choir director. After choir rehearsal, some of us would go to her apartment and enjoy the best soul-food dinners in Commerce. Once again, this was another venue in which I was able to worship alongside Christian believers and enjoy the Word of God. My attending Texas A&M opened me up to experiencing the kindness of people my own age, and it felt great to be in an environment where I could enjoy my college experience.

Texas A&M was different than any other college I attended because of the compassion that I felt from the people who worked at the university. After recognizing that I needed help with my college courses, I joined the Student Support Services Program. A lady named Mrs. Mable and her sister, Clarenda, were the directors of the program and became my mentors while I attended the university. After meeting them for the first time, it seemed as if I had known them for years.

Their support was unwavering. For example, Mrs. Mable would often remind me that I needed to "develop a study routine" to pass my classes and to stop chasing the "little, nappy-headed girls." They were not only my mentors but also my pushers and motivators. What made me so receptive to them was that they successfully balanced being serious with being comical. Mrs. Mable would often joke and laugh with me. One time, she said, "Tyrone, you need to stop walking around campus with them crusty lips; go look on my desk, and put some lotion on them thangs." Both of us would share a laugh when she made such comments. In general, Mrs. Mable seemed to be a parent figure for everyone, especially the young men.

There were many days when I spent hours in the computer lab studying to pass classes that I would not have passed without the help of the student-support services. I remember spending countless hours in the computer lab with tutors who helped me find T-scores for my statistics class. In addition to student-support services, several of my sociology and criminal-justice teachers helped me make it through college by taking extra time to answer all of my questions. Passing their classes became less difficult because the professors always had an open-door policy. I appreciated being able to sit in their offices and ask any questions I had regarding my coursework.

After enjoying four long semesters at Texas A&M, I was able to graduate on my birthday, May 15, 2009. All the assistance from my teachers and the Student Support Services Program had paid off for me. As I stood excitedly in the graduation line, all I could think about was how much of a struggle it had been to reach this seemingly impossible goal of graduating college. The excitement was contagious as I watched my peers walk on stage, one by one, to receive their degrees. When I looked to the audience, I recognized that the people who were cheering me on and supporting me were random people I had met during my journey toward graduating college. Although my biological relatives and foster family had pushed me aside, there was still something in me that wanted them there; I wanted them to see me at that point of my self-actualization. After all, it was Mrs. Thibodaux who had looked me in my eyes and told me to get an education. Although I had promised myself that I would not run behind them anymore, I still yearned for their acceptance and approval.

I remember learning a valuable lesson that day: just because a person reaches a point of success in life does not mean that everyone will congratulate him or her or offer support. Sometimes in life, we have to embark on journeys simply by placing one foot in front of the other, while trusting and believing that as we keep walking, everything will work out along the way. The absence of my biological relatives and foster family taught me that in going forward, I must be careful not to allow people's absence and lack of involvement to keep me from becoming the person that Jesus called me to be.

When the president of the university called my name to walk across the stage, I knew that I was not walking for myself. I was walking for all children who would be removed from their homes by CPS and would spend about eighteen years of their lives being restrained in group homes, fed psychiatric drugs, and treated as if they were mentally ill. I was walking across the stage for all children in foster care who had been molested and had aged out of foster care questioning their identities. I was walking across the stage for the little boy who thinks he's not smart enough in school because his counselors or teachers told him he was retarded. Yes, this was for all the children in America who would grow up in the system as I had.

CHAPTER 15

Present Day

"Don't allow the pain from being mistreated, abused, rejected, and molested to destroy your purpose and destiny. It hurt, it wasn't fair, and it was wrong for someone to abuse his or her free will to take your innocence, but you can't give up—you have to keep moving! Blaming God because someone abused his or her free will and hurt you will only cause you to wander around in the wilderness. How about seeking Jesus and trusting that he will light your life up with his love and fill you with everlasting joy? Ladies, I want you to know that just because you didn't have a dad does not mean that you have to open your legs up to all the men who say they love you. Men, listen up! Real men don't validate their masculinity by how much ass they get. Always remember that the true measure of a man is determined by whether or not he allows the Word of God to be the fulcrum between his thoughts and his actions. One day, every one of you in this room will look back on what happened to you and laugh. You're going to laugh because on that day, you will understand that the very thing that tried to destroy you is what the Lord is using to take you to the next level."

As I peered into the audience of emotionless foster youths, I began to question whether or not my passion and words of wisdom were rubbing off on them. The room was so silent that I could hear the kitchen faucet drip water. "Does anybody have anything to share or ask?" I asked, glancing around the room. I twiddled my thumbs as the awkward silence continued. Finally, a hand rose. "Yes, Trent?" I said happily.

"Mr. Tyrone, I don't know how to say this, but—"

"But what?" I asked, leaning in intently and listening. I thought, "Yes! I'm finally getting through to them."

"I just wanted to say that I sharted!" said Trent, flashing a huge, mischievous grin.

I dropped my head down to my hands. The whole room began to smell unbearably like rotten eggs and old garbage. The room thundered with laughter, and people grabbed their stuff and ran out of the house.

"Eww, Trent, you're so freaking nasty!" one of the girls yelled, and she slapped him across the head before following the crowd out of the room.

"Open your mind and close your asses," I said, shooing everyone out of the room. "Everyone, make sure to bring your journals next week."

The days at the Heaven's Arms Transitional Home were filled with such unpredictable scenes as the one just described—but I liked every bit of my time there. I liked that my work there afforded me the right to empower my younger brothers and sisters in foster care. It made me feel good on the inside, made me feel as if I were a protector for all of the people coming out of the system.

After graduating from Texas A&M, I went on to pursue a master's degree in counseling at Prairie View A&M University and later passed the state exam to be an intern for a licensed professional counselor. I never thought I would be in the seat to provide counseling to aged-out foster youths, nor did I think I would ever be the one to aid them as they strived to find their way through adulthood. Although the wild and crazy days were many at Heaven's Arms, I loved them. Of course, there were days when my job was very offensive, but I understood the children. I did not mind being cussed out and called a skinny-ass bitch, faggot, stupid counselor, or lame-ass nigger. I figured if my young brothers and sisters in the system needed someone to cuss at, it might as well be me since I had grown up as they were. However, dealing with a twenty-year-old man who thought that farting in my group counseling session was funny was a whole different story.

Moreover, it did not compare to what I was about to deal with ten minutes after that session had ended.

New foster youths who arrived at Heaven's Arms always had something jaw-droppingly devastating to tell me about their growing up in the system and aging out of care. After I ran upstairs and grabbed the chart out of the box for new clients, I quickly perused through the chart and read the name "Jason Lennox." He had been out of the system for one year and had just left a homeless shelter near downtown Houston. I was not surprised about where he was coming from because many youths came from the same place—that is, passing through homeless shelters seemed to be a rite of passage for aged-out foster youths.

With every word that Jason spoke, my throat seemed to throb. The painful lump in my throat began to intensify and grow as Jason described years of horrendous abuse at the hands of caretakers and his peers in the shelters. In a way, my feelings vacillated between anger and sadness.

"No one gives a damn about me, man! What am I supposed to do out there?" yelled Jason. He was staring at the floor. His thick Afro was matted on one side because his head had been resting on the sofa pillow in my office. After disclosing years of molestation, physical abuse, and rejection, Jason described how he had hit the streets hard—so hard that he contracted an irreversible STD from having unprotected sex. He also did a lot of drugs.

I broke the awkward silence by offering a powerful statement of encouragement. "Jason, you've been through more than most, and you feel as if you're an island out there in the big world. There are people out there who would enjoy nothing more than to love and appreciate you for you. More than your pain, insecurities, and foolish mistakes."

I saw tears welling up in his eyes when he briefly glanced at me, but then he went back to avoiding eye contact. "That's easy for you to say, man. You're probably married and get to crawl up in bed every night to someone that's happy to see you," he retorted. "You fucking counselors get on my nerves! I don't need this damn psychobabble." He stood up and reached for the door.

"Looks like we've covered a lot for a first session. Let's talk next week," I said, ending the session.

Later that evening, I arrived at my small, one-bedroom apartment, tired and at a loss for words.

Although one rule for counselors was to never take our clients' problems home, I could not help but think about Jason and his trauma, primarily because his story reminded me of mine—in more ways than one. I also thought about the hard reality of my life up to that point. The truth was that at the age of twenty-eight, I did not have a girlfriend or anyone to come home to, nor did I have anyone in my life who sincerely missed me or wanted to spend time with me.

I had fallen in love and dated a girl from Mississippi for two years, and we became engaged, but I had to cancel it because of the constant arguing and manipulation. Nothing seemed to make her happy. I bought her plane tickets, clothes, and jewelry; I wrote her poetry and spent late nights talking on the phone with her. Such things were not enough, and it seemed as if she was intentionally becoming what I disliked to end the relationship. For some reason, there was always something she wanted to argue about. I also could not deal with the fact that her mother relentlessly attempted to control my relationship with her daughter. After finding out that her mother was using her daughter's phone and social media to message me, I became leery of trusting my fiancée. My fiancée and I sent nude photos to each other, so I became nauseated when I realized that her mother had probably seen my naked body.

As I sat in my one-bedroom apartment, lost in self-reflection, I thought about other relationships that came to a screeching halt after college. After my relationship with my fiancée failed, my relationship with the Thibodauxs went further down the drain as well. While working for CPS as an investigator, I received a call from Mrs. Thibodaux's sister, who informed me that Mrs. Thibodaux had sexually abused one of the foster girls. She had conducted an invasive vaginal test to see if the foster girl was pregnant and spanked her to the point of bruising. Recognizing that I had a duty as an investigator to report the claim, I reported the story, with no little prompting from her sister and my supervisor. All I could think about was the safety of my little foster sisters and where I would live if the agency fired me for not reporting suspected abuse. So much was going on in my life with grad school, work, and my fiancée that I felt I was being tested by God. How could I explain my reasoning for failing to report suspected abuse if my little foster sister told someone at school about what had happened? I could see the agency conducting a roundtable discussion and saying, "Well, Mr. Obaseki, your foster aunt stated that she failed to report what happened because she had told you about the incident. We're sorry, Tyrone, but you're fired."

After speaking with my foster mother's older sister, Letta, I was shocked to find out that the very one who suggested I report her, in order to protect the kids, turned on me. Her words still rang loud and clear in my ears. "Don't you ever, ever, ever in life come back around this family!" she yelled.

After speaking with Mrs. Thibodaux I remember her telling me the following with emphasis: "I don't have to deal with you anymore, and I won't! Stay away from my children, my church, and my husband." My foster mother went on to paint me on social-media websites as some mentally ill lunatic who was out to kill her. I knew that my foster mother was angry with me and was saying things out of spite because she had begun to post on social-media websites that I was stalking her and hiding around her house. Although she had previously raised a boy that everyone called LA, who actually did stalk her, I was disgusted that she would blatantly lie about me. This event led to me distancing myself from people in the Church of God denomination that I was raised around. Many of them believed her lies and began to ostracize me, although I was a minister in training.

I had become an island unto myself at this point in life, driven by nothing more than my faith in Jesus and my passion to be a voice for foster youths. As I continued to reflect and sit in my one-bedroom apartment, I could not help but think about all the foster youths who probably felt isolated and rejected as I did. I thought about young Derrick, who had been sleeping in an abandoned house when Heaven's Arms found him. I thought of Crystal, who had been raped in her anus and vagina by caregivers. I thought of young Kristopher, now a homosexual, who had been raped repeatedly by his foster parents and his peers. I thought about young Jesus, who recently turned eighteen and came to Heaven's Arms with a large Ziploc bag full of psychiatric pills. I thought about all the young, aged-out foster girls who started having premarital sex because they wanted a baby that would love them, hoping to fill that void from not having a male role model. Most important, I thought about Bianca, whom I had dropped off the previous week at the IntraCare Psychiatric Hospital for swallowing pills to commit suicide. My stomach began to sour as I thought about the constant stories of abuse, rape, and degradation. Something had to be done.

My own trauma was the icing on the cake. I thought about waking up to sexually abused teenagers sucking on my toes and feeling my groin while in foster care. I thought about the pressure in group homes to engage in gay sex. I thought about the psychiatric pills that were forced down my throat. I thought about having to rub my foster mother's feet and lower back for hours. I thought about being body slammed by staff members in group homes. I thought about being placed in straitjackets. All of my memories flooded my mind. My reflecting led me to conclude that the only remedy was to take these all of these issues to Capitol Hill in Austin, Texas.

With each passing day, my desire to do something about the abuse in foster care intensified. The fun activities that I did with my foster youths, such as swimming, eating, and playing basketball, became dull to my thoughts about changing the system for others coming after us. I decided to speak with my boss about the issue. After excitedly explaining the issues of abuse to Susan, the director of the program, I patiently waited for an answer. She said, "If you believe this will help the youths and aid policy makers in making the needed changes, then Heaven's Arms will support you in this activity. But I want you to remember to calm the hell down, to keep your anger in check. However, don't forget to let your light shine."

After working with the youths for months, I loaded them in the fifteen-passenger Ford van, which we had named "Big Bertha," and we did our best to present solutions to legislators. We called ourselves the "BRAVE Champions" (bringing resiliency, advocacy, valor, and excellence), and we were proud of that name. The Heaven's Arms group became somewhat of a spectacle in Austin, Texas, when we fought to have our voices heard. Some of the other foster-care groups thought we were unorganized, radical, and unprofessional. We did not care. As far as I was concerned, we were the child-welfare experts, and we knew what was needed to overhaul the system. We refused to be preoccupied with idle chatter because we wanted to stay focused on the goal.

After months of testifying in the eighty-fourth legislative session, we continued to feel as if the policy makers were not hearing our voices and not moving quickly enough. On September 4, 2014, we decided to do something that would ensure our voices were heard on a different level.

"All right, everybody, shut up and listen," I said, slamming Big Bertha into park. "Today, I want you to just be yourselves when you go into this building. I know you have scripts that you've rehearsed, but remember that the important thing is to just be yourselves. You're not speaking for yourselves today but for every foster child in America! Let's win one for every foster youth in America." As we walked briskly into the Texas capitol for the joint hearing on higher education and human services, I could not help but feel proud of all the aged-out foster youths who wanted to make a difference. All of them were dressed in nice outfits and had diligently worked on crafting six-minute speeches about their experiences in the Texas foster-care system. Today would be the day that we would attempt to make a difference for our younger brothers and sisters who were still in the system. After two hours of listening to invited testimonies, it was finally our turn.

"At this time, we would like to invite the foster youths in attendance to come to the stand," said one of the state representatives with a booming voice. As we walked to the podium to sit down, some of the youths flashed posters that read, "Stop raping us!" Another poster shouted the following words in bright-red letters: "Stop psychiatric drugging of foster kids!" After we sat down, we all shared our individual stories of what had happened to us in foster care.

"All I know is to steal, kill, and get locked up," one youth said loudly.

"I was raped to the point where my rectum fell out!"

"I was restrained over and over again in foster care!"

"It seems like CPS does not care about us!"

After I took the microphone, adrenaline was pumping so hard that I thought my head would explode. I began to blurt everything I had wanted to say in the Texas legislature, speaking as if my own children had been raped, molested, and beaten in a system that had been entrusted with their protection. After ten minutes of addressing my concerns, I was still saying whatever came to my mind: "If these young people were your own children, what would you do? As a child in foster care, I couldn't even watch *Looney Toons* without some staff member in a group home trying to restrain me and stick his or her knee up my ass! When will legislators focus on the real issues at hand instead of trying to be reelected? How many more of us have to die? If we want to change this system, then we need legislators who don't mind walking through the group homes to ensure our young people's well-being. We need legislators to focus on more than data and numbers."

After testifying at the capitol, all of us were excited about the effect that we had that day. Although we did not get invited back to meet with a state representative, we could tell by their facial expressions that they understood that change needed to happen soon, not the next year or next decade—now. The excitement was evident on our faces as we ran out of the capitol, jumping and screaming.

"We made a difference!" yelled Kristopher.

"Did you see their faces?" asked another youth.

I was happy to see that they had experienced the magnitude and the power of their voices unified in a team effort. They had not been perfect; they had not used a script, but they had raised their voices and expressed how they felt.

By the time I was able to fight the traffic out of Austin, everyone in the van was sound asleep. The evening sun created a golden glow on their sleeping faces as I drove up and down the rolling and hilly landscape. As I stared at them in my rearview mirror, I wondered where some of them would be in six years. I wondered whether speaking their truth had empowered them enough to go forward and defy the odds. Only time would tell. At that moment in time, I was proud to know that collectively, we had turned a negative into a positive. The warm, fuzzy feeling we had all felt was *purpose*. Life had taught me, through all of its ups and downs, that reaching purpose is like reaching a finish line. It takes diligence, sweat, and tears to get there, but once a person or people arrive, nothing compares to the feeling on the inside. The journey toward living with purpose can make us feel as if we are knights in armor going to wage fierce battles or as if we are weathering stormy seas. We cannot remain faint of heart if we want to get there. And when we do arrive, we then recognize that the battles toward purpose are not just for ourselves, but for everyone connected to our elevation.

CHAPTER 16

Spiritual Warfare

I OFTEN THINK THAT LIVING life is analogous to a horse race; there are some horses who are laughed at, beaten down, and put through pure hell just to get to the gate. That is not all; then they are beaten, pummeled, and put through additional hell just to get to the starting line to run the race. All the memories and still images through the years remind me of how brutal and cynical life can be. It seemed as if every time I explained my story to people or hit a speed bump in life, there was always someone in the background saying, "That's just life, sweetie. Keep moving." That comment (or similar ones) has become a vapid platitude that I have grown to dislike with a passion. It seemed that life was always being cynical and laughing in my face while it continuously punched me in the stomach. It took a while, but I have finally come to terms with the fact that what I endured thus far in life was no coincidence. It was demonic, deliberate, and orchestrated by Satan and Jezebel to lead me to my physical and spiritual destruction. The plan was to kill me before I could commence to walking in my Christ-ordained purpose and destiny. Listen to me carefully; there are some people who battle obstacles gained through no fault of their own, and this battling has nothing to do with the obstacles "just being life" but everything to do with spiritual warfare. This battle between mortal humans and demonic influence is the reason why many children are intentionally thrust into spiritual warfare like tumbleweeds with no way to fend for themselves.

In order to fully comprehend the reason behind all the pain, confusion, and adversity as a foster child, I had to turn to the most constant force I knew—the Word of God. I desired to seek God to gain a heightened understanding regarding perversion and spiritual warfare. Where did spiritual warfare begin? Why are some people raped and abused and forced to endure affliction more than others? I wanted real answers that revealed why it seemed so hard just to live and inhale my next breath of air. I wanted answers as to why I was enslaved and afflicted with so much sexual, emotional, psychological, and physiological pain while other people seemed to just hop, skip, and leap through life, smiling and untouched. As I turned to the Bible and conducted in-depth research, I was amazed at the answers to my questions.

In this chapter, you will receive a detailed understanding as to who Satan is, his first infraction, and how he tried to sift me and is relentlessly trying to destroy other foster youths and orphans. As I take you on this journey to understand spiritual warfare, I need you to lean in closely and remain present while reading this chapter. You must understand that Satan is real! I think I will reiterate that again so it can sink in: Satan, the evil one, is on assignment in the earth realm to kill, steal, and destroy as many people as possible, before he is placed in his eternal, fiery abode. You also must understand that the Bible is not an old story that people share, but rather it is the only supreme truth that operates as a force field and a catalyst to set people free from bondage. Now that we have laid our foundation, let us jump right to what the Lord revealed to me about perversion and spiritual warfare.

If you look up *perversion*, it is defined as the "alteration of something from its original course, meaning, or state from what was first intended." It is also described as the act of turning aside from the truth and is synonymous with corruption and distortion. To my surprise, perversion started with Lucifer in heaven! Lucifer was created as a beautiful and covering angel on the holy mountain of God but was expelled when he tried to usurp God's throne. The word of God in Ezekiel 28:13–16 gives us a good description of who he is:

> Thou hast been in Eden the garden of God; every precious stone was thy covering, the sardius, topaz, and the diamond, the beryl, the onyx, and the jasper, the sapphire, the emerald, and the carbuncle, and gold:

the workmanship of thy tabrets and of thy pipes was prepared in thee in the day that thou was created.

Thou art the anointed cherub that covereth; and I have set thee so: thou wast upon the holy mountain of God; thou hast walked up and down in the midst of the stones of fire.

Thou wast perfect in thy ways from the day that thou wast created, till iniquity was found in thee.

I continued researching the scriptures to get a deeper understanding and found out that Lucifer committed an intentional infraction and caused war in heaven! It sounds like a science-fiction war movie set in outer space, right? Isaiah 14:12–15 describes the scene of Lucifer's trespass against God's throne and its consequence:

How art thou fallen from heaven, O Lucifer, son of the morning! How art thou cut down to the ground, which didst weaken the nations!

For thou hast said in thine heart, I will ascend into heaven, I will exalt my throne above the stars of God: I will sit also upon the mount of the congregation, in the sides of the north:

I will ascend above the heights of the clouds; I will be like the most High.

Yet thou shalt be brought down to hell, to the sides of the pit.

Lucifer operated in perversion and turned aside from the truth, desiring to ascend above God's throne. We can clearly see that his actions were a deviation from what God had originally intended him to do. God's original plan was for him to function as the anointed covering angel. Scripture shows that Satan's defiance against God's original plan led to his expulsion and then to the expulsion of numerous other angelic beings as well.

Revelations 12:7 gives us a detailed look at what transpired when God put the smackdown on Satan and his army:

And there was war in heaven: Michael and his angels fought against the dragon; and the dragon fought against his angels, And prevailed not; neither was their place found any more in heaven. And the great dragon was cast out, that old serpent, called the Devil, and Satan, which deceived the whole world: he was cast out into the earth, and his angels were cast out with him.

As I continued to study, I found out that although perversion began in heaven when Satan deviated from God's instruction and purpose for him, Satan and his angels did not stop after the expulsion. If you look closely, scripture shows that when the angelic beings were expelled from heaven, they perverted God's plan by mating with the women on earth, who gave birth to giant offspring that infected the human race. Genesis 6:1–4 describes what happened:

And it came to pass, when men began to multiply on the face of the earth, and daughters were born unto them,

The *sons of God* saw the daughters of men that they were fair; and they took them wives of all which they chose.

And the Lord said, My spirit shall not always strive with man, for that he also is flesh: yet his days shall be an hundred and twenty years.

There were giants in the earth in those days; and also after that, when the sons of God came in unto the daughters of men, and they bare children to them, the same became mighty men which were of old, men of renown.

And God saw that the wickedness of man was great in the earth, and that every imagination of the thoughts of his heart was only evil continually.

And it repented the Lord that he had made man on the earth, and it grieved him at his heart.

And the Lord said, I will destroy man whom I have created from the face of the earth; both man, and beast, and the creeping thing, and the fowls of the air; for it repenteth me that I have made them.

After bringing all these scriptures together, I was able to clearly see that Satan and his demons represent the kingdom of perversion. Mankind would not have a clue about perversion if Satan had not committed his actions! Satan's prime objective is to destroy the sanctity of everything that Jesus deems as holy—by any means necessary. Understanding the genesis and source of perversion helped me figure out how Satan operates and why his right arm, Jezebel, attacked me so ferociously!

Satan had open access to wreak havoc and afflict me because my grandfather opened the portal of sexual perversion, which he did when he penetrated and sucked on my eight-year-old mother's vagina repeatedly. Even as I write this, I am baffled as to how a father could take pride in smelling, sucking, nibbling, and penetrating his daughter's genitals—before and after church. I stated this in a previous chapter in my book: my aunt Chyanne told me that early one morning before church, she heard a noise and saw my mother sitting on a dresser with her legs gaping open while my grandfather ferociously performed oral sex. How could my grandfather sleep at night while his top lip smelled like my mother's vagina? That is not all: my grandfather drugged and raped my mother's friends and anally raped his only son repeatedly. According to my grandmother, he was a raging alcoholic who beat everyone in the house and used a gun to intimidate my grandmother to let him do whatever he wanted. My grandfather's refusal to adhere to the word of God regarding sexual purity shows that he made up his mind to yield his flesh over to Satan and Jezebel. I firmly believe that the collateral damage of my grandfather's actions was so strong because he was called to the ministry and was a devout churchgoer at one time. He refused to accept his call and knew that what he was doing was wrong and displeasing to the Lord. His fleshly decision thrust my uncle into homosexuality, eventually leading to his death from having AIDS.

Because my grandfather opened up the portal of perversion, my mother became a crack-addicted prostitute, who still wanders the streets of Houston to this very day. My mother cycles in and out of the Harris County Psychiatric Hospital and the prison, and she is battling AIDS. I reckon that she is still struggling emotionally with the abuse she endured at such a young age. In many ways, my mother is "Felicia"—that is, the well-known prostitute character that the black community likes to mock and laugh at. This is what happens when men yield their flesh over to perversion.

All of this happened because my grandfather had formed an alliance with Jezebel by setting aside his headship as the protector and father to satisfy a demonic sexual desire.

As men and women of Jesus operating as the body of Christ, we must understand that Satan's plan is to use people like my grandfather to execute his original sinister plan of destroying the male seed by any means necessary. If you take a look at the demeanor of Satan after his trespass against God, it will show you that Satan is a brute beast with death constantly on his mind. After Satan failed to usurp God's throne and was expelled from heaven, he did not show any remorse or seek to rectify his behavior! His primary objective after he was expelled to earth was to pervert and kill mankind because he was jealous. Man represented the existing embodiment and authority figure of God; that is why he was jealous. Revelations 12:12–13 proves his jealousy to be true: "Therefore rejoice, you heavens and you who dwell in the earth and the sea, because the devil has gone down to you! He is filled with fury because his time is short. When the dragon saw that he had been hurled to the earth, he pursued the woman who had given birth to the male child."

Based on the scripture above, this lets us know that Satan is on the prowl and has made it his business to hunt men down—hunting like a lion searching for prey. Revelation 12:17 describes the unrelenting and ferocious tenacity that Satan utilizes to sift people: "Then the dragon was enraged at the woman and went off to wage war against the rest of her offspring—those who keep God's commands and hold fast their testimony about Jesus." This, dear reader, is why life has been so hard for some foster youths—especially young boys in the system—just to breathe. Satan deliberately waged war against me by physically, emotionally, mentally, and sexually abusing me.

Some people refuse to see sex as sacred (yes, that is their prerogative), but what I have come to understand is that the Word of God should be the fulcrum between our thoughts and actions. When we refuse to allow the Bible to be this fulcrum, we leave ourselves wide open to being blindfolded and puppeteered by Satan. In fact, 1 Corinthians 6:18 states, "Flee from sexual immorality. All other sins a person commits are outside the body, but whoever sins sexually, sins against their own body." Instead of fleeing and maintaining sexual purity, my grandfather sinned sexually against his own family unit, thus exposing the entire lineage to a higher level of demonic influence.

At some point, people need to understand that the Word of God is not an old fable but rather the tool that God blessed us with so that we can understand how to overcome the attacks and troubles of this world! As a person who sought to understand spiritual warfare and sexual perversion, I always remind myself of two questions. If the word of God shows us that the demonic beings that committed sexual perversion are now bound in utter darkness, what is going to happen to people who reject God's word and continuously yield their bodies to sexual perversion? What is going to happen to people who deliberately refuse to live their lives in praise of Jesus Christ?

Jude 1:6–7 may answer those questions: "And the angels which kept not their first estate, but left their own habitation, he hath reserved in everlasting chains under darkness unto the judgment of the great day. Even as Sodom and Gomorrah, and the cities about them in like manner, giving themselves over to fornication, and going after strange flesh, are set forth for an example, suffering the vengeance of eternal fire."

Based off God's word, we can see that there are serious consequences for sexual misconduct, especially when it relates to our children. If men, the protectors of women and children, do not guard the sanctity of sex, how will their children honor God sexually? My grandfather's inability to be a protector, priest, and provider for his family unit not only affected my mother but also affected me because my mother abandoned me and left CPS to do what she could not do. If you have read my book consistently up to this chapter, you know most of the issues I have dealt with. In this next segment, I am going to take the time to explain in detail the spiritual warfare I had to face as a consequence of my grandfather's decisions.

One of the most important lessons I learned while praying for the strength to recall and deal with my sexual trauma was that in order to break the generational curse or cycle of abuse, I had to understand how the cycle began and what the word of God says about being set free. Although John 8:36 says, "Whom the Lord sets free is free indeed," I struggled to embrace God's word regarding my freedom. For years, I became fearful of standing up and embracing my independence and identity in Christ because all my life I had been relegated to the status of a dog and was constantly knocked to the ground for taking the first step toward freedom. One of the most powerful things that I have ever heard was from Dr. Juanita Bynum, a powerful woman of God, and I consider her a spiritual mother to this very day. After conducting a radio interview and disclosing her own journey to recovery, she said, "If my life's testimony offends you, then good. Now you can go serve Christ for real because he will never disappoint you ever! Testimonies are what you get after something has been put to death; maybe that's why we don't see a lot of them. You have to kill it to tell it. A real Christian is not ashamed of the gospel or what the gospel has done and will do! Remember that!"

After I read Dr. Juanita Bynum's words, the power of the Lord came upon me and broke every form of shame regarding not only my experiences of sexual molestation but also everything I had to fight my way out of. The shame and desire forcing me to hide my sexual abuse and testimony were shattered! I will never forget what happened after reading Dr. Juanita Bynum's words! While lying on the floor of my one-bedroom apartment in Pasadena, Texas, I heard a voice that pierced through my body. The voice stated, "Tyrone this is the Holy Spirit! Don't be ashamed of nothing I have done for you! Tell your story like you know I delivered you from something that was deliberately orchestrated by the devil to destroy you! Remember how I delivered the Israelites out of Egypt? Don't forget that I destroyed those who operated in disbelief. If you had enough faith to believe I could deliver you out of bondage, you had better have enough faith to tell it!"

Although I felt as if I had every right to hide my history and throw it in the bottom of Lake Erie, I had no choice but to yield to God's instruction, after the above experience, to specifically write in this book all of the embarrassing things I had to fight to escape and war against. After all, the Holy Spirit made a valid point! It would be selfish of me to pray and ask God to deliver me from something and then become afraid to talk about it. I believe that God wanted me to be vocal and share what he delivered me from so that I could show others that the supernatural and transformative power of the Holy

Ghost is real. One of the reasons why this book took years to write is because I wrestled with God about disclosing my secrets—I did not want anyone to know and judge me based off what I did as an emotionally turbulent street rat looking for affection in all the wrong places. Besides the secret of having a pet roach named Bertha as a child, my big secret was none other than the fact that God delivered me from thirteen spirits. In a way, my feelings were just as common as those of the next man. What man would want the whole world to know his deepest, most-embarrassing secrets?

When I let my mind roll back and when I take an introspective look at everything I endured growing up, I can connect the dots and correlate each spirit that I was delivered from to a specific form of abuse I experienced as an institutionalized ward of the court in Texas.

After studying psychology and becoming a mental-health clinician, I was taught that mental abuse is a form characterized by a person subjecting or exposing another to behavior that may result in psychological trauma—including anxiety, chronic depression, or posttraumatic stress disorder. In my case, CPS rescued me from a family of incest and chronic abandonment to subject and expose me to group homes and foster homes, where I was exposed to environments plagued with so much abnormal sex that I suffered mental anguish. Mental-health professionals yelled that I had a genetic predisposition to mental illness because of my mother, but now I know that my vexation, sadness, and perceived mental illness were due to living in a common but abnormal environment.

One of the things I hated about living in the group homes and foster homes was that I was treated as if I were mentally ill. Everyone had an opinion about what was wrong with me. My counselor wrote me off as retarded; the psychiatrists wrote me off as bipolar, schizophrenic, and chemically imbalanced! Even some of my foster parents would yell that I was chemically imbalanced. I firmly believe that my foster parents claimed that I was imbalanced so they could raise my level of care and get more money. Caregivers would provoke me by being mean; then when I yelled back in anger, I was always restrained, isolated to a room, and given a habitual and familiar phrase: "You're getting put out of my house." That phrase was used so many times throughout my childhood as a mechanism of control; it was a means to show me that I was not the boss, to put me in my place. Looking back on this, I'm glad to know that one day, the Lord Jesus will welcome me into a heavenly home where I will never have to worry about being put out.

I grew angry as a ward of the court because the system was teaching me that I was a replaceable number as well. Caregivers and staffs of group homes would write me off as having bad behavior in their progress notes but would fail to explain how they instigated and provoked me. I worry for the foster youths in America who have been labeled bipolar or pegged with having psychotic disorders because psychiatrists have become nothing more than vending machines. If psychiatrists took a closer look, they would see that some children's behavioral problems could very well be normal responses to living in verbally, physically, and emotionally abusive environments. We cannot fault children or even teenagers for lashing out when the people who are entrusted to protect them are just as emotionally unresolved and unstable.

I believe that being forced to take psychiatric drugs as if they were candy and being treated as if I were retarded were charismatic forms of witchcraft and intentional mental abuse, enacted by the system as a mechanism to keep me sedated and docile. To take the mental-abuse issue further, let us look at it from a sociological perspective. Charles Cooley coined the term *looking-glass self*. He postulated that we humans form our identities and self-images through our interactions with other people. In that context, what should we expect children to do in environments where they engage with people who treat them as if they are crazy? What should we expect a child to do in an environment where teenagers think that masturbating in the child's face is a healthy means of regulating their sexual desires? How is the molested child supposed to walk into his purpose, if everyone in his direct environment validates the lie and calls him gay, retarded, chemically imbalanced and mentally ill? We have to remember that children are malleable and that we need to stop intentionally placing children in environments where they are preyed upon and in homes that induce psychosis or mental-health issues. We cannot place them in such environments and then be negligent; we must continually ensure their safety by stimulating them emotionally, spiritually and intellectually.

After all, the Health and Human Services Agency in Texas receives almost a billion dollars in taxpayer dollars. The least we could do is protect these children's innocence and stop seeing them as rent money or a case number.

When I look at the mental abuse from a spiritual perspective, I see that Satan was utilizing people in the system early on in my life to attack my God-given identity, attempting to condition me to believe that I was abnormal. Satan knew that as a child of Jesus, I would one day be in a position to operate as a bright light for Jesus, so he launched a spiritual attack on my mind to gain control of my body. One of the sayings that a pastor drilled in me was "As the head goes, so goes the body." I believe that Satan's objective was to destroy me mentally, so that I would self-destruct someday. Now as an adult, I see that for years I was engaging in full-fledged spiritual warfare without any covering. I have come to recognize that what the world writes off as crazy can very well be spiritual warfare. Let us look at the following statement, which was written by my caseworker.

February 6, 1995

> I contacted Champions Treatment Center to see if Tyrone could have a visitor. The nurse informed me that Tyrone was presently on a one-to-one watch. I asked her why, and she stated that yesterday, Tyrone went to school and was on the second story on a windowsill trying to jump. When little Tyrone was apprehended and asked why he tried to commit suicide, he stated that he heard a voice that told him, "See that dot on the ground? Jump down there, and you will bounce back up when you hit the ground."

This statement shows that on February 6, 1995, while staying at Champions Psychiatric Hospital, I heard a voice that told me to climb to the second floor of the school and commit suicide. From a mental-health perspective, I was experiencing an auditory hallucination, which led the psychiatrists to believe I had entered a state of psychosis. Listen to me carefully! This is not mental illness, this is full-fledged spiritual warfare. This is a child battling demonic forces unknowingly! This experience reminds me of Jesus's experience in the wilderness. In regard to the Word of God, hearing voices is common! Matthew 4:6 talks about how Satan tempted Jesus and tried to get him to kill himself while on the mountain: "If thou be the Son of God, cast thyself down off this mountain."

Does Jesus hearing a voice mean that he was experiencing psychosis? Absolutely not! At what point will mankind and so-called Christians understand that Satan manifests himself through images and thoughts that he places in our heads? Was Moses experiencing psychosis when he saw the burning bush? What about Noah? Did he have a "psychotic snap" when he was instructed to build the ark? Were the disciples delusional and psychotic because they saw the resurrected Jesus pop up and disappear over a period of forty days? Absolutely not! I believe that this excerpt from my case file proves that at the young age of eight, I was deep in spiritual warfare with the enemy and did not even know it! I was under attack by the enemy before I even knew how to utilize the sword of the spirit! This is one of the reasons why it is important for children to have a spiritual covering, whether they are in orphanages or at home with their parents. Sometimes, we never know what our kids are battling with. A question we should ask ourselves today is, who will have enough faith to cover and protect the children who grow up in the bowels of society? Another one is, who will war in the spirit for those considered to be the least, the labeled, and the lost? Who will protect the child in the orphanage that does not know he has a prophetic and apostolic anointing on his life? Who will protect the child that see's angels repeatedly, but is constantly being told he is mentally ill?

The physical abuse I encountered in the system was consistent with a near-death experience. I literally died while being restrained by staff members and died again one night after taking powerful psychiatric drugs. Luckily, Jesus brought me back. According to the regulations set forth by CPS, staff members are only supposed to restrain youths when they become a threat to others or to themselves. That is not what happened in my case! Staff members used restraints to intentionally inflict pain, rather than use techniques to simply hold me. There were many nights in which I lay bloody on the floor while two staff members held me down. One staff member held my feet down while the other sat on me; then they folded my arms behind my back and shoved them up toward my head. "I can't breathe!" I yelled, hollering at the top of my lungs from the pain. I still remember the blood-curdling screams of other children and teenagers who were being physically restrained by staff members for unjustified reasons; for example, children would be violently restrained for being upset at having bad days at school. Recognizing that there were other youths who died due to asphyxiation from this type of abuse, I firmly believe that Satan, as a means to kill me, was working through the staff members of group homes and through the CPS guidelines and policy. One of the worst restraints I ever received was under the psychiatric administration of Dr. Sharon Iglehardt. According to my case file, my caseworker wrote the following: "I visited with Tyrone in Forest Springs Hospital. He was very agitated during the visit. He wanted to remain in the game room instead of coming to the unit where he lived. He did not want to take his medication. He had to be restrained."

This snapshot from my case file shows that I was restrained for not taking psychiatric drugs; however, it does not show how the scene unfolded. Imagine being eight years old and picked up by your hands and feet by hospital staff and thrown into a room with padded walls. In this room, you are scolded for not taking your psychiatric medication and are forced onto a board, placed in a white jacket, and tied down by large brown straps. After thirty minutes of yelling and screaming for help, you then can feel your heartbeat through the temples on the sides of your head. As your snot and tears dry on your face and neck, reality sets in, and you realize that no one is coming to rescue you. You lie subdued and exhausted from the constant movement and struggle to break free. Your constant crying blurs your vision as you stare out of the small window, and you can only long for someone to ease the pain stemming from the attention-starved world that has you bound. My recalling this traumatic event as an adult shows me how Satan uses people and systems to break children's minds and spirits. I firmly believe that I endured intense mental and sexual abuse growing up, because Satan knew that I would one day see angels and Jesus at a young age.

The emotional abuse in the system stemmed from living in environments where caregivers and staff members would tear away my self-esteem by yelling,

"You're the damn foster child!" or by saying things such as "You're chemically imbalanced, bipolar, and need psychiatric medication." There were days when I would have given anything just to have a friend my age to talk to, but instead I was avoided as if I had the plague. My peers in school pointed fingers and laughed in my face, yelling repeatedly that I was a hobo or a faggot, while not even recognizing that I was being molested and beaten the night before. I was fighting just to keep my emotions in check in a world that seemed determined to destroy every fabric of my being.

Looking back on my years in foster care, I see that it was emotionally abusive for foster parents not to allow me to have friends my age. I remember days of getting off the bus after school, only to find a locked house; on those days, I would have to wait two to three hours for my foster parents to let me in their houses. Some days, I would walk around to people's houses in the neighborhood and beg for food because I was hungry. You would think that my foster parents would be understanding; instead, I was punished as if I had done something wrong for trying to make friends in the neighborhood. My foster parents would remind me and say, "The agency prohibits you from staying at strangers' houses."

Many foster youths are emotionally abused while growing up in care because they are deprived of normalcy and treated as if they were a potential liability rather than actual children. When I was a child, caregivers used words such as *attention seeking* and *emotionally disturbed* to describe me. One of the greatest oxymorons in the foster-care system is that children are perceived as "attention starved" in environments that do not provide attention—but the problem is always the children's fault. All children end up craving attention when they are isolated and pushed aside. I remember one of the staff members at my group home pulling me aside to tell me that I should stop being intrusive and that I should stop with my "attention-getting behavior." Most of today's foster youths are being warehoused in group homes and written off as emotionally disturbed (as I was), but no one is bothering to point out that the staff of group homes and many foster parents are abusing these kids—which consequentially triggers the emotional dysfunction. My living in the foster-care system ended up being emotionally abusive because the system failed to place me in environments where I would be free from sexual, mental, and physical abuse.

From a spiritual perspective, I believe that Satan toys with people's emotions, especially vulnerable orphans and foster youths, so he can tear away the fabric of their faith in Jesus. I believe Satan knows that there are some children who are destined to detonate an atomic bomb in his camp to free others from his bondage. Recognizing this, he seeks to launch as many ferocious attacks as possible to kill these children before they are able to recognize who they are and what they are destined to do for the kingdom of Christ.

One of Satan's most horrendous attacks is sexual abuse. What many people fail to realize is that when people are sexually abused, they are being spiritually abused as well—the direct and physical assaults also attack the people's identity of being God's temples. Furthermore, sexual transgressions defy God's instruction and natural order for us to maintain sexual purity. In order to understand this, let us look at 1 Corinthians 6:19 in the amplified Bible: "Do you not know that your body is a temple of the Holy Spirit who is within you, whom you have received as a gift from God, and that you are not your own property?" This passage shows us that our bodies have been set aside as holy abodes for the spirit of Jesus Christ. Because we are vessels of God's spirit, Satan angrily and ferociously launches sexual attacks against innocent children because he is opposed to anything that resembles Jesus Christ.

One of the most important revelations I want sexually abused people to know is that regardless of Satan's trespasses against you, God has already enabled you to transcend your pain, which he has done through Jesus Christ! I was repeatedly abused sexually, but I found the strength that I needed to overcome the collateral damage when I ran to Jesus with my arms wide open. When I embraced Jesus, he delivered me from the thirteen spirits stemming from the totality of the abuse that I had endured as a foster child. Some men would be embarrassed about disclosing the details of their abuse and of what they had to be delivered from as a result of someone else's bad decision. Thanks to my love for Jesus and my intense desire to see people set free and reconciled to Jesus, I happily present to you the thirteen spirits that God delivered me from.

Thirteen Spirits

1. Homosexuality—in order to understand my history in homosexuality, the reader must understand how it began. First, Satan (using my grandfather) attacked and raped my mother, who represented my covering, knowing that she would spiral out of control and abandon me. Then he used an older teenage male to introduce homosexuality by whipping his penis out, wiggling it in my face, and instructing me to suck it. Satan's plan was to appeal to my senses by causing me to see, touch, and smell perversion, with the objective to have me taste perversion at a young age. Then he placed me in group homes with other emotionally unresolved and neglected boys who had sex with each other. "Let me stick this in your butt. I promise it will feel good," they would say with smiling faces as they solicited me for sex. Then he used staff members to do filthy things, such as molest me while restraining me. As a child, I was often restrained by a man named Mr. Harmison. I could never tell whether he used his knee or his penis to hurt me, but after every time he restrained me, my butt and entire body hurt horrendously from the physical abuse. After this, Satan placed me in perverted environments, where boys kept asking to perform oral sex on me, where boys would say such things as "If you don't tap some of this booty or let me suck you up, you're not getting any sleep tonight." One night, I remember just laying there and letting one boy just have his way with me. I grew tired of resisting. After this, Satan used a sexually abused boy to suck on my toes and feel my groin while I was asleep one night. If you, the reader, are a man, I ask you this: what would you do if you were fast asleep in your bed, cuddled up with your wife, and woke to a guy sucking on your toes and fondling your anus? What if the intruder was sucking on your wife's toes or even your children's? I digress. In my case, you would think that Satan and Jezebel would have stopped there, but they used people in my schools to bully me and call me gay. What a slap in the face! I can see Satan and Jezebel sitting on a mountain, like the evil

villains Lord Zed and Rita from the infamous *Power Rangers* cartoon series, and yelling, "Now that we have repeatedly attacked his manhood and molested him, let us get his peers to call him gay and watch his facial expressions as he deals with the mental turmoil!" Finally, Satan launched a full-fledged attack while I stayed at the Covenant House in Texas by causing homosexual young men to constantly pursue me. It is important for us to understand that there are some people who are hunted by spirits intentionally because of the call of God that is on their lives. I did not throw the covers off and stretch my arms one morning and yell, "Today seems like a good day to start sucking penis and eating booty!" I eventually succumbed to perversion after years of repeated sexual, mental, and physical attacks, which spanned from my childhood to early adulthood. In consequence, I eventually had anal and oral sex with men not only because my childhood had been filled with sexual abuse but also because women constantly rejected me when I was a young adult. Although lost and blind, I wanted to feel loved by a woman at a young age; however, I was viciously pursued by homosexual men as an adult, which led to me eventually caving in to their desires when I was only twenty. During my college years, I was so blinded by perversion that I would spend forty-five minutes to an hour sucking a sexual partner's body parts and penis and then another hour biting, sucking, and nibbling on his anus before engaging in full-fledged gay sex. Hear me well when I say this: Satan started off subtly in his attempts to attack my manhood before going in for the kill—that is, before trying to change me into a homosexual. I killed this demon, like David killed goliath and now I am a anointed Eunuch commission to set others free from the chains of perversion.

2. Pornography—I worshipped pleasure and flooded my mind with pornography because I was lonely and void of affection. I did not like how I felt on the inside. I would spend hours exploring the vastness of human sexuality, to the point that I became consumed with sexual deviance. The euphoric feeling of pleasuring myself allowed

me to momentarily engage in complete, selfish affection toward myself, through masturbation. I spent hours looking up sexual videos of what I wanted my sexual partner to do to me. Life had become so bad that I thought masturbating and living vicariously through other people's sexual escapades were the only things I could do to feel better about life. After watching pornography I would cry because I was still lonely.

3. Fetishism—for some reason, feet have been an abnormal part of my upbringing. As I already explained, I remember waking up to another boy sucking and smelling my feet, when I was living at a group home in north Houston. My foster mother made me rub her feet for hours, day after day. Some of the staff members would make me rub their backs and feet at the orphanage as well. While in foster care, I got attention from my foster mother only when I was rubbing her feet and lower back. As a young adult, I thought that it was normal to rub people's feet. As time progressed, I would see boys and girls at school and have a strong desire to rub their feet. I also began to get strange urges to rub, lick, and smell my sexual partners' stinky feet, whether they were male or female! I became addicted to the pheromones released from the human foot and spent hours some nights sucking and smelling men's feet as if I were sucking on barbecued chicken wings and smothered oxtails! I incorporated food in my perverted sexual escapades and would lick cranberry sauce and warm chocolate syrup off of men's toes, nipples and arm pits. I was a raging freak, and my mouth knew no limitations in sex. I became a slave to my flesh in college, and sexual perversion turned into a four-headed hydra: sodomy, foot fetishism, male-on-male oral sex, and anal rim jobs. I'm so happy I'm delivered! How could Jesus accept me into heaven knowing that I exchanged my eternal crown for sucking feet and men's booty holes? I'm so happy that Jesus has set me free and resolved my emotional pain.

4. Rage—after being tossed in and out of foster homes and group homes, I began to grow increasingly angry because I felt out of place and rejected. I grew tired of foster parents using their love and affection

as a mechanism of control. The constant physical abuse and attacks against my sexuality caused me to run from home to home, looking for normalcy. At one point, I almost stabbed one of my foster brothers.

5. Depression—constant rejection, loneliness, and belittling caused me to slip further into the abyss of depression. While in a state of depression, after facing the reality that my biological father was dead, I stopped eating and nearly died from kidney failure and dehydration at Navarro Jr. College.
6. Emotional Turmoil—the instability of my emotions opened my mind to exploring quick fixes that could deal with the internal vexation and pain of childhood abandonment, physical and sexual abuse. For years, I was emotionally deregulated because I struggled with being abandoned by my biological relatives and rejected by my peers. I often felt alone and in a category all by myself, which caused me to run from people my own age, cry, and hide my feelings. I thought I was crazy because I saw angels and felt that everyone hated m.
7. Shame—as a young child, I admired pretty girls and sneaked around the orphanages to try to kiss them. In a spiritual context, it seemed as if Satan himself had instructed agents to plant seeds of perversion through my sexual abuse. It seemed as if he had been trying to slowly and subtly condition my mind to cave in to sexual perversion. As a teenager, I became shameful and embarrassed. I could not understand why I was fixated on feet and pretty girls. At night, I had strange dreams and did not understand what was taking place on the inside of me. The shame from being rejected by my own family does not compare to the shame that I felt deep within after dealing with my sexual problems. The most shameful time in my life was my coming to terms with the fact that for years, I was bound by the one thing that I thought was absolutely disgusting—being gay! After being fully delivered, I had to overcome the shame and embarrassment so that I could adhere to Jesus's command to tell the world about my testimony of deliverance. Jesus was commissioning me like he did

the Gadarene demoniac and I was embarrassed. After all, what man would want to tell the world that he had dealt with gay feelings after being repeatedly molested?

8. Low self-esteem—in high school, I ate my lunch in the bathrooms because students at school never accepted me. I constantly moved from place to place as a foster child, and I was always the new kid on the block and wearing old clothes. The fact that I had to leave class every day at noon to take psychiatric drugs made me feel as if something was wrong with me. I felt retarded because people called and treated me as if I were retarded. I felt chemically imbalanced and mentally ill after my caregivers repeatedly told me so. My peers' rejection and constant bullying reinforced the lies of my caregivers and negatively affected my self-esteem, sometimes creating the desire to kill myself.

9. Alcoholism—alcoholism became the vehicle that helped me sleep at night. The only way to escape the images of my childhood and the reality of my life was to drown myself in alcohol. Alcoholism allowed me to slip into deep sleep without having to relive the images and smells of my traumatic experiences.

10. Marijuana usage—my smoking marijuana was common before I started to engage in sexual encounters with men. In college, I smoked marijuana out of bongs just to fit in with some of my peers. Sometimes I would smoke marijuana before draining men of their seminal fluid in oral sex.

11. Gluttony—to escape loneliness and the reality of my sexual dysfunction, I flooded my belly with Little Debbie snacks, cookies, pies, and chicken wings because they made me feel better. Eating large amounts of food was euphoric because shortly thereafter, I would fall into deep sleep, thus forgetting my pain temporarily. I wanted to be sedated during certain seasons of my life, because I felt the grave was more comfortable than living in a world that rejected and hated me.

12. Idolatry—idolatry is the extreme reverence, love, or admiration of something or someone. As a foster child, I learned to worship my foster mother by rubbing her feet. As a child, I would have done

anything for her attention because I wanted acceptance. As a result of being sexually abused and an attention-starved foster child, I began to seek attention as an adult through the portal of sexual deviance. I worshipped phallic symptoms, such as the feet, anuses, nipples, penises, and vaginas of the physical forms instead of worshipping Jesus wholeheartedly.

13. Murderous spirit—I wanted to kill my grandfather for raping my uncle and my mother. According to my biological relatives, he repeatedly raped my uncle's anus before and after church and was caught nibbling and penetrating my mother's eight-year-old vagina in the wee hours of the morning. It was he who opened the portal of the enemy to wreak havoc on his seed, and I wanted his head on a pike! God changed my heart and filled me with compassion for him and other sexually lost individuals.

Being free from these thirteen spirits fills me with so much joy because Satan and Jezebel can no longer overtake me. Satan knew that I was destined to be an anointed eunuch for Christ, so he attacked my sexuality and manhood ferociously, but now I can live to tell the story and give the testimony of how John 8:36 proved to be true: "Whom the Lord sets free is free indeed." The happiness I feel within also comes from recognizing that the supernatural and transformative power of the Holy Ghost is very, very, very real! Where the world screams that gay people cannot be converted, I yell that deliverance is one of the manifestations of the Holy Ghost! It is impossible to run to Jesus with a broken heart and stay the same—especially when a person's broken heart was not fashioned by his or her own hands. People who are seeking deliverance must understand that sexual orientation according to the world is a lie! According to the world, sexual orientation is the identity in relation to the gender to which people are attracted and involves the fact of being either heterosexual, homosexual, or bisexual. This definition suggests that if people are born with sexual feelings for the same sex, then nothing can change those feelings. The world also says that people can be genetically predisposed to homosexuality! Listen to me clearly; the day people stop listening to the world and turn to God's word is the day that they and their loved ones will be set free from the lie! When people recognize that they are part of a royal priesthood predestined to sit in heavenly places, they then take on the identity of the Savior—Jesus Christ! Many homosexuals and drug addicts are blind, as I was, and are operating in rebellion by refusing to accept Christ's words. God did not create them to be this way, just as he did not create me to be a homosexual! We, as in mankind, have a choice to make, regardless of preternatural, environmental, and genetic influence: live for Christ or live to appease the foolishness of the flesh. One of the things that supporters of homosexuality yell repeatedly is that homosexuality is common among animals, such as dogs, sheep, zebras, and tigers. My rebuttal is that true deliverance takes place when people stop relegating themselves to the status of animals! A dog in the wild will eat its own seed if it is hungry enough; does that mean we as humans should eat our offspring? Absolutely not! A dog will also eat its own feces. Does that mean that we should get a spatula and dig into our best friends' booties and eat their poop? Absolutely not! Most important, animals were not made in the image of the Father, the Son, and the Holy Ghost—mankind was! We were made in his image, by God and for God; thus, we should all step up and yield to the higher standard of being the true sons and daughters that we were ordained to be before we were formed in our mothers' wombs. Stepping up and walking in truth means that we no longer allow the pursuit of euphoria to hinder or prevent us from embracing the royal priesthood or from becoming new creatures in Jesus Christ. The identity that we have in Christ is eternal! You can protect your eternal idenity in Christ by understanding that there are some things you can not do, because the behavior suggests that you are attached to a spirit that is already bound to hell. Come out of addiction! Come out of fornication! Come out of same sex attraction! Come out of the pain of your past and walk into newness of life! God has given us stewardship over a earthly body and we must care for it in a holy manner or we will not be granted a heavenly body.

As I conclude this chapter, all I can think about is two intense desires: I want to help sexually abused people find the healing arms of Jesus, and I want to see everyone become completely transformed in a way that would allow them to clearly see and hear what Jesus Christ is saying in this hour. The road to my complete healing was not easy and was life threatening on numerous occasions, but Christ was always right there. Although I was birthed out of the belly of affliction and endured unspeakable trauma, my thirty years of living have taught me about weathering the vicissitudes of life and braving its winding turns and mountains. Sometimes, the only way to deal with life is by listening to a good gospel song filled with the Holy Ghost. Sometimes, music aids in helping the mind stay positive. The wise understand that between each dip and turn and stormy season, Jesus uses people to plant seeds of love and hope. For the lessons I was forced to learn early on, I am grateful. It would be unfair and out of order for me to conclude this chapter without giving a complete thank-you and standing ovation to the Christ believers who represented a brave sort of love in my life. The truth is that although I felt Mrs. Thibodaux was mean and Mr. Thibodaux was reserved, they saved my life! Yes, they were overbearing and sometimes used their love and affection as a mechanism of control, yet they loved me dearly. My memories show that they prayed over me at night and constantly validated my identity in Christ by speaking the word of God. My foster mother kept us in a spiritually stimulating environment, where I saw men and women praise Jesus as if they were insane. Although Mrs. Thibodaux's ways of parenting were sometimes unconventional, there was not a Sunday that passed by without her hair clip flying off her head from worshipping God as a raging lunatic! I will never know how Mrs. Thibodaux managed to jump around church while wearing stiletto heels. As a grown man of God, I see now that Mrs. Thibodaux was covering me by worshipping Jesus. The Thibodauxs were peculiar ministers, who stood in the gap in a similar manner to Hannah, who prayed for her son, Samuel. Out of all of my foster parents, social workers and staff members, they were only ones who were bold enough to talk to me about Christ. I don't understand why Mr. and Mrs. Thibodaux never embraced me after I explained that I saw angels nor do I understand why they kept me in my room isolated many days. One thing I know for sure, is that without them, I would not be alive and in my right mind today.

Sometimes, foster youths do not appreciate environments where the truth of God's word is being revealed. The best thing CPS did for me was place me in a spiritual foster home, where followers of Jesus validated my identity by prophesying to me and letting me experience the tangibility of God's spirit. I like to use the following analogy: "Jesus is to Tyrone as a net is to a fish." Just as a net can be used to catch fish, Christ was the rescuing force that led to my liberty and transcendence. If I had not met true followers of Christ throughout Texas, I would have never experienced the supernatural and transformative power of the Holy Ghost, which allowed me to see angels repeatedly! I am thankful because at the age of thirty, I recognize that I am a seer with the gift to feel spirits and see angels! This is awesome! From all of my experiences, good or bad, I have learned that we have to accept our purposes in life. My prayer is that people will turn their hearts back to the children to help them understand the truth of God's word.

Declaration of Purpose

My ability to see angels and to experience holy dreams and visions, as well as my being delivered from the thirteen spirits, would have never developed without the presence of Christians with holy boldness. Because such love was shown to me by the followers of Christ, I am now made whole, and I am fully resolved with my past and happily accept my calling to be a eunuch for the kingdom of heaven. Thanks to the direct, face-to-face exposure of the miraculous power of the Holy Ghost, I can fully dedicate my celibacy and life to the deliverer and restorer of my soul, Jesus Christ, who has appeared to me face to face repeatedly and in my dreams since I was a child. My blind eyes are open, the shackles have been removed, and my mind is seared with divine revelation! Therefore, I stand in formation with the body of Christ, happily accepting my commission with my weapon of warfare cocked and loaded in behalf of the afflicted. With the sword of the spirit in one hand and a ram's horn in the other, I shall stand with insurmountable faith and power through Jesus Christ and use my testimony to overcome the enemy and provide global healing in the land.

Satan and Jezebel, the alliances that you have formed and the sentinels of destruction that you have unleashed to sift the young minds of generation Z and Christ's elect shall not prevail!

For using my grandfather to suck the life out of my mother, Jezebel, the Lord Jesus rebuke thee!

For trying to kill me in my mother's womb, Jezebel, the Lord Jesus rebuke thee!

For rescuing me from a home of incest under the guise of ensuring my protection, just to repeatedly sexually molest me, Jezebel, the Lord Jesus rebuke thee!

For viciously attacking me mentally as a child and forcing me to take psychiatric drugs to manipulate the molecular structure of my mind, Jezebel, the Lord Jesus rebuke thee!

For all the beatings and body slamming that brought forth blood and tears, Jezebel, the Lord Jesus rebuke thee!

For operating through child protective services, an institution of degradation and dehumanization that brings forth mental vexation, Jezebel, the Lord Jesus rebuke thee!

For every baby prophet, minister, and gifted youngster that you have killed through charismatic witchcraft, Jezebel, the Lord Jesus rebuke thee!

I declare by the authority vested in me by the death, burial, and resurrection of my Lord and Savior Jesus Christ of Nazareth, with the ability to see and operate in the supernatural, I declare that the young minds of the community that run to Jesus shall live and not die! I declare and decree this day that the generational curses are broken in behalf of the least, the labeled, and the lost, in Jesus' name. Now unto Jesus Christ, who has commissioned me to protect the sanctity of his temple and who is able to send me forth in power and in divine demonstration as an ambassador of heaven, I reverently accept my purpose with holy fear and shout, "Holy, holy, holy is the Lord God almighty, who was and is to come!"

Matthew 19:12 says, "For there are eunuchs who were born that way, and there are eunuchs who have been made eunuchs by others—and there are those who choose to live like eunuchs for the sake of the kingdom of Heaven. The one who can accept this should accept it."

CHAPTER 17

Call to Action

One teen is dead, and another has been charged with murder after a fight at a youth ranch in McLennan County, Texas. The homicide investigation is ongoing, but the suspect has been booked into the Bill Logue Juvenile Detention Center. Investigators were called out to the youth ranch after two teens got into a fight around twelve thirty on a Sunday afternoon. One teen was pronounced dead at the scene, and the other was taken into custody for questioning. Both teens are believed to be sixteen years old.

LEARNING ABOUT THIS TRAGEDY ON October 12, 2014, was so infuriating that I became enraged with anger and not just any anger—righteous indignation. At the time of this incident, I was working for a Christian nonprofit organization that provided services to aged-out foster youths, and I began to question why organizations were not as vocal as they should be for the sake of the orphans. After all, the state of Texas had ample time to get it right, and it seemed as if individuals who were in the child-welfare industry were still blind to the needs of the young people. I became so righteously indignant that I fell to my knees in frustration.

Albert Einstein, the world-renowned German physicist and intellectual genius, said what I view as one of the most powerful quotes uttered by man: "We cannot solve our problems with the same thinking we used when we created them." Often, I wondered whether organizations sought to help foster children or use them as a mechanism for profit. After researching several child-welfare agencies in the Houston area, I was sickened to find out that children were being warehoused in group homes by child-placing agencies for money. I will never forget the reaction I received from an ex-friend, a male, after I explained how society has a way of contributing to the demise of orphans and foster-care children. Before I could finish sharing my thoughts, he said, "Tyrone, it's a noble thing for you to help foster youths, but you need to understand that this whole foster-care issue is a leach on society. This is what happens when parents are irresponsible and freeload off responsible taxpaying citizens."

After he said this, I became angry. All I could think about was how the Bible tells us to care for orphans and widows. I replied, "Just because we have irresponsible parents does not mean that companies should use innocent children as lab rats to test the potency of powerful psychiatric medications!" Unfortunately, our friendship came to an end because he not only refused to show compassion but also was unwilling to engage in the lives of the needy. That conversation taught me that regardless of what scripture instructs us to do, some people will spend their lives focusing only on their families, not including the plight of lost children in their considerations.

Life has taught me that instead of getting angry and yelling and screaming for change, I just have to simplify and work toward executing the concrete solutions that I come up with. Moreover, mentors and colleagues in the child-welfare industry also helped me to understand that lesson. For example, after I graduated college and started to work for CPS, I was lucky to meet several child-welfare champions at a House Bill 915 hearing. That particular hearing focused on preventing the drugging of foster youths in Texas. What a joke! I could not believe that the government had to pass a bill to prevent psychiatric lobbyists from experimenting on foster children. Some of my mentors calmed me down, however. They often told me that I just needed to "take the emotion out and give simple solutions that our legislators can run with." Such advice motivated me to stop, take a breather, and take an introspective look at the positive interactions that helped me overcome the odds when I was a troubled youth. Growth and maturation taught me to highlight negative experiences and to use clear thinking to rectify them, which ultimately generates positive wisdom that encourages others in similar situations.

When I remove every traumatic experience and highlight the three most potent interactions in my life, I am reminded of the times in my life in which I encountered the Holy Spirit, validation, and happy memories.

If our goal is to fix the system or any problems that affect the young minds of the community, we must do three things: validate the children, create happy memories, and create environments where the Holy Spirit can permeate the atmosphere and minds of our children. We must create a new child-welfare model that revolves around Jesus Christ and the supernatural power of the Holy Ghost. After we create this new model, in which Christ is the focal point, the old bureaucratic child-welfare system will eventually become obsolete. I believe the greatest detriment to society takes place when, in regard to certain issues, the Holy Spirit–filled Christians become apathetic and quiet when Christ needs them to be bold, vocal, and visible.

Sometimes as I watch my brothers and sisters in Christ gather to fellowship at church and sing songs, I wonder if they have a clue. How many more children who carry the gift to operate in the supernatural will the church allow to be sifted by Satan's sentinels of perversion? Through the years, I have noticed that many pastors wear long white robes and sip silver chalices and that they use the anointing as a mechanism of wealth accumulation. They drive Bentleys and dwell in mansions while orphan boys in group homes are attacked repeatedly by homosexual demons and manipulated neurologically by harmful psychiatric drugs. They build sanctuaries and preach about the importance of family while the young girls are raped to the point of vaginal and anal prolapse. It seems as if many pastors have no concern for God's word, which tells us to look after orphans and widows. Isaiah 56:10 proves to be true every century: "His watchmen are blind: they are all ignorant, they are all dumb dogs, they cannot bark; sleeping, lying down, loving to slumber."

I firmly believe that Jesus is calling the body of Christ to repentance, for the simple fact there are too many prosperity-preaching, self-titled ministers, prophets, bishops, and arrogant first ladies who lack wisdom, percipience, and the Holy Ghost. If there are gifted children among us—that is, children who were ordained and commissioned by Jesus before the foundations of the earth to execute a specifically supernatural assignment—why is the church, which represents the salt of the earth, participating in the affliction by neglecting to war spiritually for the lost, the least, and the labeled? Why is the church becoming increasingly insipid? Henceforth, if we recognize that 1 Peter 4:17 informs us that judgment begins in the house of the Lord, what judgment and impending penalty should we foresee the church facing, in regard to the innocent children who died while possessing the gift to see the invisible?

I want to use this opportunity to ignite the followers of Jesus to action and to encourage everyone to utilize his or her authority to a greater extent. Sigmund Freud and several colleagues of his coined the terms *alloplastic* and *autoplastic adaptation*. Alloplastic adaptation is a response in which a subject attempts to change his or her environment when faced with a difficult situation. Autoplastic adaptation is a form of adaptation in which a subject attempts to change himself or herself when faced with a difficult situation. The apostle Paul, after the Damascus Road experience, operated in alloplasticity! His experience of using boldness, percipience, and drive to determine the truth still serves as an example to those who have an ear to hear. Jesus Christ, although perceived to be a devil by the Pharisees and religious scholars of his time, took an alloplastic standpoint. Jesus's internal verbalizations were set, and he never lost sight of his primary objective. If Jesus had pursued autoplastic adaptation and altered who he was to fit into his environment, no one would have access to heaven. My point is that as the body of Christ, we must recognize that someone's life could be dependent on our ability to change the environment and not succumb to adversity. The spiritual well-being of our children necessitates that we change the environment and be the light that we were ordained to be.

The Bible says in Acts 1:8 that after the spirit has come upon us, we shall receive power and will become Christ's witnesses throughout the entire world. If we recognize that America is home to so many Holy Spirit–filled Christians, then we should recognize that the five hundred thousand foster youths in America should be the recipients of love from these shepherds, who should be eager to protect the youths' innocence. Perhaps the world is inundated with Christians but not enough Holy Ghost–filled Christians who can tend to our orphans. The Holy Spirit is needed because if we harness it, we gain the power to effect significant changes.

    I firmly believe that one of the reasons why I am the man that I am today is because I had imperfect foster parents who were full of the Holy Spirit. Dana and Stan Thibodaux were not perfect; however, I would be a fool to deny the power of Jesus that was evident in their home. Their having the Holy Spirit enabled them to engage in spiritual warfare on behalf of my soul, and I say this because there were many nights when I felt as if I were going to die, but my foster parents would lay their hands on my head and speak the word of God loudly and boldly, which would ease my fear. Regardless of their shortcomings, Dana and Stan Thibodaux never hesitated to pray. I firmly believe that we followers of Christ need to stand up and care for orphans as the Bible instructs us to do. If we believers allow the government to perpetuate its harsh treatment of foster youths, we will forever see orphaned children drowning in crises. My foster parents allowed the Holy Spirit to permeate the atmosphere by keeping me in a spirit-filled church that was nondenominational and by speaking the truth boldly.

    Validation is important because it leads to individuation. Psychologist Carl Jung described this process by which the individual unconscious and the collective unconscious are brought into consciousness together to reveal a person's whole personality. In short, it is the process of self-actualization. All children in America need as much validation as they can get until they are old enough to start making responsible decisions for themselves. One of my most-cherished memories occurred while I was living with the Thibodauxs. In it, our pastor laid her hands on all the children, but she paid extra attention to me and validated my identity as a prophet and individual who would one day operate in the supernatural. The memory leads me to contemplate how much better the lives of children would be if everyone focused on each other's family units and validated and encouraged each other. I believe validation is an integral part of children's growth and development because it helps children enter the world with a clean mental state. Without verbal encouragement and validation, children are left to fall victim to whatever they see and hear in their environments. If my foster parents had refused not only to minister to me but also to confirm my identity in the word of God, I would have believed the lie and bloomed into a psychopathic homosexual with numerous drug addictions and uncontrollable fetishes, both of which would have landed me in jail or, perhaps, even killed me. I am alive and in my right mind because imperfect foster parents made the decision to instill the word of Christ in me.

Reader, know that one happy memory has the potential to overwrite a litany of negative ones. Although I dealt with a lot of negative memories, I learned as a young adult to cherish and hold on to the memories that made me smile. I will never forget how my first-grade teacher's entire family got involved in my life when I was staying at an orphanage. Ann McClelland's college-age son, Michael, bought me a toy airplane and a fire truck and taught me how to play with them. I also remember being showered with gifts and love from Mrs. McClelland's whole family. All the trips to the rodeos, movies, and Easter egg hunts replaced memories that could overwhelm me with sadness if I were to dwell on them. Although I felt as if the Thibodauxs were hard on me, some of my happiest memories with them involve watching my foster mother sing songs around the house in her bathrobe and watching my foster dad cook and listen to music. They did not have all the money in the world, and to be honest, it did not matter. One of the most beautiful things I got to do was watch their dancing to BeBe Winans after dinner. Life has taught me thus far that sometimes, the only way to make it to the next checkpoint in life is by being grateful for the people who unselfishly decided to come alongside you to steer you in the right direction. The happy memories that I have force me to be humble and extremely grateful because Jesus not only used people all over Texas to help raise me but also appeared to me in dreams and even face to face while I was reading the book of Revelation as a teenager. For this reason, I will forever say that the good outweighed the bad. Through it all, life has taught me that there is more to this world than what is seen with the naked eye.

CHAPTER 18

Along the Way

~~~

Note To Reader:
WRITING THIS MEMOIR HAS BEEN a rewarding experience. I decide to conclude this book with poems and snapshots of prayers that have helped me grow. May my prayers in this final chapter and words of wisdom aid you as you blaze the trail of life.

CHILD-WELFARE PIE

Who will take action and enact spiritual warfare on behalf of the little girl's vagina and anus that were brutally pummeled by her father and by the staff member of the group home, which was entrusted to provide love, protection, and affection?

Who will war in the spirit for that little boy, now a man, who sits at the bus stop like a vagrant, with no clear direction?

You have aged out of the system, they say...

It is your time now, and do not forget to reach for the sky!

Seems like the joke was on me! There are numerous organizations that fail to pray for us. They prey on us and stuff themselves with money, giving themselves second and third helpings of child-welfare pie.

BIG BRENDA

You remember Big Brenda? Big Brenda was the one with the bad attitude, always rolling her eyes. No one could tell her anything. I ran into her last week at the bus stop after I left street church. Her anger has turned to rage, and her hurt has turned to bitterness. Yet behind the dense forest of her emotions, I still saw her, that little girl who had been raped by her father and in a group home and then forced to take psychiatric drugs to mollify and sedate her pain. Yeah, I was face to face with the teenage girl whose tears had filled the crevices of the marble floors, after she was restrained for trying to run back to a home that no longer existed. She has three kids now, and I hope she finds true love out there, even though some would say she is too thick. My prayer is that she falls in love with Jesus and not with the next man who says, "If you love me, come ride my stick."

After the Restraint
"I'm tired of you staff members always restraining me! I hate this place! I'm running away…"

After you get up off the floor, go to your room and stay…

"That's the guy—he hit me with a stick…"

Stop being a tattletale; go back to your room and stop being a little bitch…

"Don't you see this isn't fair? I want a real family!"

Welcome to the school of hard knocks, boy. Life doesn't always give you what you wish, you see.

"They're talking about my stuttering! I didn't do anything! This is s-s-something that they started…"

Shut up, lil' nigga. You know your ass is mildly retarded!

"Can I at least go to church and meet my Savior?"

Didn't I tell your dumb ass to sit down? Going to church is contingent on your behavior…

The purpose of the poem "Pinpointed" is to explain how I was targeted before I was born to be afflicted. The ending of the poem shows how through Christ I have overcome the many attacks of the enemy.

Pinpointed

As for this one, this one right here, let's start with his mother. Let's have her father nibble on her genitals and destroy her innocence and purity; while we're at it, let's do the same to her brother.

Yes, this will prevent him from having family, love, and affection. Let's institutionalize him and place him in an environment where he will be sexually abused, rejected, and void of protection.

As the head goes so goes the body—that mind of his we must destroy! I know! Let's manipulate the molecular structure of his mind through psychiatric drugs and place him in hospitals—our doing so will surely kill this boy.

By playing on the memories of his trauma and abuse, surely we will succeed! If he makes it to adulthood, let's poke at his sexual abuse; he'll become one with homosexuality! Surely that will cut him off at his knees.

No friends and family for him; let him sit at the sideline and wallow hopelessly in depression. When he tries to win the love of a woman and aspires to be married, give him front-row seats at watching others go before him! Let's even laugh at his facial expressions!

Wait a minute, we have a problem. After all this, why haven't our sentinels of destruction succeeded at tearing him to pieces? This can't be happening; the stronghold is weakening, and he's pleading the blood of Jesus!

It is I, Tyrone, the one you tried to destroy! This message is to serve as a reminder that according to Luke 10:19, I have authority over you. Satan, the Lord Jesus rebukes you, and just in case you forgot, hell awaits you! Through the emotional, physical, and sexual abuse, I've learned to watch, fight, and pray! Jesus, I felt pinpointed for years, but thank you for enduring a crown of thorns for me; my mind is renewed, and now I can live to see a brighter day.

Strip Tease

> You see, I was beaten and restrained into submission; all I wanted was normalcy.

In the system, there is no spiritual covering; God help us—oh,
the perversity!
Smell my balls, little boy! They taste just like cherries! Bend over now; trust
me, it will feel good.
For a five-year-old child in kindergarten, I needed protection, someone like
Robin Hood!
How precious they are; why are so many rejected and molested?
Although they are stripped of their innocence and teased as children, I must
war in the spirit for their protection!

Tyrone's First Psalm

Note—along the way, I felt the need to write my feelings to the Lord, when I was in a spiritual wilderness, alone and by myself. I wrote it after recognizing the pride and arrogance of my heart. It was a desperate cry for mercy, written after I was charged with a crime and facing two to ten years in state jail.

Jesus, for the past seven months, I have been on my knees and striving to approach even closer to you. With boldness, I prayed the following: "Lord, expedite the process! Allow me to go through everything I need to go through to become the man that you have called me to be! Show me the error of my heart so that I may grow in you." Through this prayer, Lord, you have shown me the error of my heart, and now I am sad! It stinks to high heaven! Have mercy on me, Jesus, and place my feet back on the path toward purpose and destiny. How foolish of me to believe that my physical self would rectify every situation! How arrogant of me to think that I can say whatever my heart feels! Lord, I see now that worshipping you in spirit and in truth means that I must remain free of pride. To operate within the arms of the Holy Spirit shall be my heart's desire for the length of my days. Oh Jesus, my heart feels disgusted after recognizing the error of my ways! Purge me, and allow your spirit to permeate my mind and heart. Lord, is there any hope for me? Please, do not allow me to rot in prison and watch other people be used by you in a phenomenal way! Have mercy upon me, oh Lord, and allow your prevenient grace to shield me from delay and destruction. As your son, I have repeated many times, "No weapon formed against me shall prosper." Jesus, do not allow me to be the weapon formed against myself. Before I was conceived in the womb, you had a unique plan for my life. Yes, you chose me to be a vessel of signs, wonders, and miracles. Remember the prophecies that you spoke over my life, dear Lord, and forget not the visions you have shown me. From this day forward, I will be careful to prevent pride and arrogance from compromising your purpose and promises for my life. Allow me to run free toward my assignment like a gazelle in an open field. Hide me from the criminal system that is trying to destroy my life before I can start my mission. Now that I am pride free, dear Lord, provide a miraculous way of escape so that I may serve you all the more. My love for you has increased, for you loved me enough to show me my faults. I am reminded of the Hebrew boys in the Bible who were thrown into a fiery furnace for not bowing to the golden image. My prayer is the same as my elder brothers'. If it be so, I know that you can deliver me from this fiery furnace and out of the hands of the criminal-justice system. However, if this is not your will, oh Lord, I still choose to never bow down to the spirit of pride.

A Psalm of Repentance from Sexual Perversion

My Lord and Savior, Jesus Christ, have mercy on me during this hour of spiritual growth and development! As you hold my face to the mirror to show me the error of my ways, my knees buckle in shame. I do not feel worthy to be used by you after seeing the filth that you are removing from deep within my soul. Can you use someone as filthy as I was? Was it my fault? Oh Lord, thank you for picking me up, turning me around, and placing my feet on solid ground. What type of love is this that you would call me son and commission me to be a royal priest? There is no excuse for my behavior, for I have experienced your power firsthand and have seen you face to face. Were you the angel that I saw? Listen, oh Lord, to my cry of mercy! Draw near to me as I draw near to you in this hour of transformation! Embrace my supplications, and look intensely at the sincerity of my heart. As a child, Lord, my innocence was attacked repeatedly by that old and dirty wasp called homosexuality. I could not defend myself against its attacks, nor could I remove its stingers.

Jesus, I believe right now, in this hour, that your presence alone can remove the numerous stingers of perversion that have attempted to infect my soul. Because of your blood sacrifice at Calvary, I have been redeemed and bought with a price! You endured a crown of thorns so that I could access the helmet of salvation! You allowed yourself to be beaten and whipped to the point of exhaustion so that I could utilize the breastplate of righteousness! For this reason, I bow in submission and choose to walk in the authority of your sacrifice. Your Word says in John 8:36 that whomever you set free is free indeed! Lord, I magnify your holy name, thanking you today with a pure heart because my sexual abuse will no longer stand in the way of my purpose and destiny! Yes, I refuse to allow my sexual abuse to hang me by the neck, Jesus. Your word is my only line of defense, and I choose to stand on your word instead of feeding my childhood trauma. Jesus, your word clearly means in 1 Corinthians 6:14 that God raised you up by his own power and that he will raise me up as well to ascend into heaven. Surely, if I have the faith to believe that you have the power to supernaturally raise me up in the final hour, I can put my faith to work and believe that you have the power to raise me up out of homosexuality. Thank you for complete deliverance and divine transformation.

—December 20, 2015

Tyrone's Second Psalm

Note—the following was written when I was experiencing severe loneliness and frustration in the wilderness.

Jesus, where are you? How long will I feel isolated from everyone? As an orphan, I endured years of unbearable isolation and abuse! Is your plan for me to be lonely as an adult too? My belief that somehow my latter years would be better than my former years is slowly dwindling to doubt. When will you restore me and give me blessings for everything that the locust and the cankerworm devoured? Where do I belong, oh Lord? I don't have any friends, and people scoff at my belief in you. How can I bear witness to someone and disciple them to the kingdom if I'm in a constant state of isolation? I can't help but to feel frustrated. Can I go to heaven now?

Tyrone's Third Psalm

Note—this was written after I recognized the flawed perceptions of the Christian family, and it provides an interesting connection to understanding spiritual warfare.

What's going on in the world today? So the child who was ordained to be a prophet and eunuch before the foundations of the world has to live a life of constant pain? Now that I have killed the Jezebel spirit that was trying to destroy me, I have to deal with Christians who perceive me to be arrogant, self-righteous, and evil? With fake smiles and slanted eyes, they say, "He needs to be humbled. It's not his time; he needs to sit down and shut up." Lord, it seems as if the church takes a hands-off approach to dealing with serious societal issues. Why am I constantly around church members who observe people going through spiritual warfare but refuse to intervene? Jesus, you crossed a raging, stormy sea just to heal the Gerasene demoniac, but my fellow Christians choose to sit back at a distance? It seems as if my brothers and sisters in the faith can be just as cruel as people in the world. "Don't even entertain him," they say with slanted eyes. Jesus, where were they when I was being body slammed by staff members at group homes? Where were they when the psychiatrist had unhindered freedom to manipulate the molecular structure of my mind? Where were they when I was beaten and placed in straitjackets because I was hyperactive? They were nowhere near me when I was being repeatedly molested and warehoused like a wild animal! I have figured out the source of my affliction: Jezebel was trying to kill me over and over again, but the church only sat around, playing patty-cake as I struggled to breathe. Lord, your word says that judgment starts with the church. Help me understand something: if judgment begins with the church, then will my brothers and sisters recognize at one point that they are pushing people away from the faith through their apathy and lack of involvement? Lord, no one seems to understand that if an orphan is subjected to mental, sexual, physical, and spiritual abuse in a region of Christians, the responsibility to address the abuse falls back on us! Lord, it seems as if the joke was on me. If we are all spiritually connected, why didn't Christians smother me with love and support? I'm not acting entitled; I'm just worried about the next orphan who ages out of foster care after being raped, overmedicated, and beaten! How long will the prophets sit back and remain uninvolved while Jezebel and demonic spirits freely oppress your chosen ones? It is cruel for people to see afflicted orphans going through hell but only sit back and observe the orphans' facial expressions. Orphans and widows should be uplifted, not marginalized and looked upon as the scum of the earth.

Lord, you know my heart. I am sad at how Satan, after I was molested, used people to laugh, point their fingers, and yell, "He's gay!" Is that how Jezebel works? What type of spirit would possess a man to wiggle his funky penis in the face of a child who still sucks his thumb, in hopes that he would suck it? Wait! That's not all. It's hurtful to remember that after I was written off as mentally ill and forced to take strong psychiatric drugs, Jezebel used people to laugh, point fingers, and say, "He's crazy!"

It angers me to remember, Lord, that after you anointed me to be a man of God, Jezebel used people to step back with extreme caution as they yelled in their minds, "He's demon possessed!"

Now that I am free, I look forward to being the light that you have called me to be, despite the folly of Christians in the faith who do not understand the anointing and my purpose and destiny. Send me undetectable and behind the scenes so that I can do a mighty work for the children that the church has marginalized. My Christian brothers preach down to me fervently about tithes and offerings as they monetize the anointing, but they refuse to teach me how to use the spiritual gift that they prophesied I would operate in. Lord, help your church! Help us all so that we can fulfill your promise to do greater things—only then will we operate in the greater today!

Tyrone's Fourth Psalm

Lord, what in the world is going on! Deception and idolatry have crept their way into the church and are deceiving millions. I hear numerous sermons about tithes, offerings, and family, but the pastors look over the children who are being sifted and afflicted in the orphanages? What about the eunuchs for Christ? How can my brothers in Christ focus on tithing and reject the calling and instruction to look after orphans and widows. How can they prophecy to people when they're living a lie and have become self-deluded by their desire to accumulate wealth? Too many ministers are milking parishioners to build larger temples and sanctuaries and forgetting the young temples that are being afflicted right under their noses. Is the body of Christ focused on wealth accumulation or focused on protecting the innocence of the children who are destined to operate in the supernatural?

How many children who carry the gift to operate in the supernatural will the church allow to be sifted by Satan's sentinels of perversion? They wear long white robes and sip silver chalices while using the anointing as a mechanism of wealth accumulation! They drive Bentley's and dwell in mansions, while orphan boys in group homes are attacked repeatedly by homosexual demons and manipulated neurologically by harmful psychiatric drugs! They build sanctuaries and preach about the importance of family while the young girls are raped to the point of vaginal and anal prolapse! Lord, your orphans are suffering! Jesus, please send Michael the Archangel in defense of the orphans so they don't suffer like I did. Jesus, please deal with the fake, prosperity-preaching, self-called ministers, prophets, bishops, and arrogant first ladies who lack wisdom, percipience, and the Holy Ghost:

Lord, I understand that there are gifted children in the world who were ordained and commissioned by you before the foundations of the earth to execute a specific supernatural assignment, Why is the church, which represents the salt of the earth, participating in the affliction by apathy and negligence in warring spiritually for the lost, the least, and the labeled? Why is the church so insipid if we are the salt of the earth? Lord, 1 Peter 4:17 informs me that judgement begins in the house of the Lord. Have mercy on us and forgive us for the innocent children who died while possessing the gift to see the invisible.

Tyrone Obaseki

Jesus's Response to the Pain and Turmoil of Tyrone

Fear not, my son; I was with you from day one.
Your cry as an infant and your screams as a child and vexed heart as a teenager were not out of my direct line of view.
The angels assigned to you have pleaded your cause, and I feel the pain of each and every one of you.
Your prayers for other orphans have not gone unnoticed; trust me at my word, and know that I care for each and every one of you.
You see, my purpose and plans exceed the thoughts of man, and I have called you, Tyrone, to stand and plead the cause of the homeless, the orphans, and the widows.
My eyes do not grow tired, my son, and because of my love for humanity, I am slow to anger.
Stand up, get out of your bed of affliction, and prepare to execute your assignment!
Tell my church that I used the parishioner to get an introspective look at the heart of the pastor.
Tell the psychiatrists that I used the ones who were perceived as mentally ill to debunk their false logic and reason.
Yes, I used the test subject to get an introspective look at the test facilitator.
I am not pleased! Warn them that I come quickly, and remind them that judgment starts with my church.

An old, retired mental-health therapist decided to take a stroll through Central Park in New York. As he watched the autumn leaves fall from the trees, he relished the simple blessing of enjoying the cool breeze. As he took a long sigh and gazed at the clouds slowly moving in the sky, he recalled memories and quotes that had helped him move forward. He decided to write a letter with random quotes that had helped guide him through life.

Dear World,

As you blaze this trail of life, remember these sixty random quotes and words of wisdom. These words have guided me through many trials and tribulations. If you pay close attention, these words may turn your life around. Life has taught me that regardless of the ups, downs and turnarounds, you must move forward to make the world a better place. Some seasons in life may bring forth intense feelings of brokenness; others may bring forth overflowing joy. Whether happy or sad, remember that everything is centered around Jesus Christ. If you trust him, he will resolve all of the pain, worry and frustration that this life can create. The test in life involves your ability to defend your crown and empower others to do the same. Recognizing that God made us new creatures and a royal priesthood, make sure that you don't abdicate you eternal crown for pleasure and comfort that lasts only for a season. This crown that He has bestowed upon you reigns throughout all perpetuity.

- The day you start paying less attention to people's faulty assumptions and more attention to God's promises will be the day that you will step into a greater anointing.

- When the spirit of the Lord shows you where you are going, believe him!

- When Jesus calls you into the deep, leave reason and logic at the shore.

- When life becomes a tease, keep praying; it'll make sense in due season.

- Some people will spend so much time talking about you while you are struggling in the valley that they will refuse to see you when God elevates you to the mountain.

- The pain I endured as an institutionalized child does not compare to the excruciating pain felt deep within after coming of age and recognizing that the system itself is the greatest detriment to our children.

- This world does not owe you anything, not even your parents!

- Wise people understand that learning is contingent on their ability to watch and listen.

- Retire your attitude! The day you stop blaming the world for what you did not receive as a child will be the day you start experiencing new life!

- First, they rescue you from your parents; then they abuse you and label you. After you defy the odds and dispel the stigma of growing up institutionalized, they get intimidated and ostracize you.

- Just because life continuously places you in an environment where you are relegated to the status of a dog does not mean you have to start barking.

- Faith is when you stand toe to toe with the enemy and declare God's promises, even when your immediate environment is conducive to you throwing in the towel and screaming, "Forget it!"

- Sometimes, all it takes is a made-up mind. The day I refused to lean on Zyprexa and started to lean on faith to regulate my emotional and cognitive functioning was the day I experienced transcendence.

- When I became old enough to discern spiritual matters, I recognized that as a man of God, I am required to remain focused on Christ's promises rather than on a mental health diagnosis.

- Psychiatrists look at your history and your current mental-health status to assess congruency. If you look at the etymology of the word *psychiatry*, you will see that it means "the medical treatment of the soul." Don't be confused—Jesus is the only being who can provide treatment for your soul.

- The day you stop seeking natural remedies to heal what was created by the supernatural will be the day you are set free from the lie of mental illness.

- The Lord liberated me from the pain of my past, validated my identity as his son, and vindicated me from the lies of my naysayers.

- The Lord will liberate you from apathetic Christians, will validate the anointing deep within, and will allow his grace and favor to shield you as he propels you toward destiny.

- Who will fight for and protect the little girl who was raped to the extent of vaginal and anal prolapse?

- When I was addicted to alcohol, I reasoned like an alcoholic because I was preoccupied with being victimized. When I became a man, I put away childish reasoning and became less focused on being a victim and more focused on walking in victory!

- Alcohol afforded me the opportunity to cross into deep sleep without seeing and reliving my sexual and physical abuse. The euphoric effects of alcohol were stronger than the images of being slapped by a teenager's penis when I was only six years old.

- Validate and accept your daughter today so that she does not seek validation and acceptance between a man's legs.

- Validate and accept your son today so that he does not validate his masculinity by exploiting the purity of women.

- Your destiny and purpose take precedence over fear and uncertainty.

- Never allow obstacles to slow down your expedition!

- Crossing the finish line is contingent on your ability to press toward the mark of the prize in Jesus Christ!

- Come hell or high water, destiny and purpose are yours! If he called you to the mountain, surely he will equip you to climb it! Take the mountain!

- You have your path. I have my path. As for the right path, the correct path, and the only path, it would behoove us all to turn to Jesus.

- Needs take precedence over wants! It's not about how bad you want it; it's about how bad you need it!

- Just because a person doesn't believe that your persona exudes a Christian lifestyle does not mean you are not a Christian. Jesus was considered to be crazy by his family and was perceived to be a devil by the religious leaders of his time, yet he kept his focus on his mission!

- Your destiny takes precedence over the faulty assumptions of your naysayers.

- Where you are going is more important than where you started.

- Just because someone doubts whether or not you're qualified does not mean you're not chosen.

- The extent to which you are elevated in life is contingent on your ability to defer gratification.

- Beware of people who constantly find enjoyment at seeing you in a state of need.

- When my time in this realm has reached its end, I pray that all those who came in contact with me will run toward Jesus all the more.

- The problem in today's society is that people have their priorities mixed up. When wealth accumulation becomes the priority, orphans and widows are exploited and cast aside.

- In the higher echelons of leadership, you will be faced with envy from people who are intimidated by your visibility, vocality, and volition.

- The life of the apostle Paul confirms that walking in faith enables us to access the promises required to utilize the power needed to change the world.

- As you strive for upward mobility, understand that success is not given; it's earned.

- Tenacity and mental dexterity are the primary factors in your ability to cross the finish line.

- Resilience is tantamount to the food you eat.

- Intestinal fortitude is needed to overcome obstacles.

- Vituperative people will only slow down your momentum.

- Energy should be devoted toward bringing your dreams to fruition.

- The worst feeling in the world has to be the point in which you reflect and realize that you spent your life as an apathetic quietist in regard to what Christ commanded you to be vocal about.

- I wonder what would happen if people's hearts were as beautiful as America's megachurches?

- People can try their best to destroy your purpose, but they won't prevail.

- Don't be swayed when people try to destroy you with their words; keep standing on God's promises!

- Foolishness is believing that being human is synonymous with carnality. Just because I am a man does not mean that it's natural to screw everything in pumps and a miniskirt.

- Some people deal with stressful situations and relationships because they are foolish. When God pulls back the curtain in the natural and shows you what you've been feeling in the spirit, believe him! Remaining preoccupied with people who don't understand your purpose and destiny only debilitates your momentum. How is it that you have enough faith to believe that your paycheck will hit the bank every two weeks but do not have enough faith to escape from parasitic relationships? Your destiny and purpose is too important!

- If you find yourself facing resistance every step of the way, remember to stay in a mind-set of prayer each and every day.

- Science reveals that when a caterpillar goes through the chrysalis phase, the intense heat causes it to go from a solid to a liquid prior to morphing into a butterfly. Although the process seems extremely uncomfortable, it is irreversible and complete.

- Just because something hasn't manifested in the natural doesn't mean that Jesus hasn't released it in the spirit!

- Faith is being able to keep your gaze set on the mark of the prize, despite the principalities in high places.

- Faith allows us to stand on God's promises. These promises, in return, give us the power to exercise dominion in the earth realm.

- Jesus will give you crazy favor in exchange for your crazy faith, just to show the world that the resplendence of his glory is greater than your crazy past! This is your manifested time!

- What people see with the naked eye is no comparison to who you are in the kingdom of heaven.

- Protect your thoughts, for your thoughts dictate your behavior. Guard your heart, for it influences your spirit. Meditate on the words of Jesus, lest you be deceived to entertain the lies and strong delusions that tether you to a spirit that is condemned to hell. Choose heaven, and be liberated by Christ's love.

- Along the way, I recognized that the anointing is uncongenial to the temperaments and dispositions of the world. Protect it!

Eighteen Years of Slavery

This was a good day! I was preaching a powerful sermon until I started stuttering the sermon. Jesus has a sense of humor. Didn't Moses have speech problem?

Special thanks to Texas CASA (Court Appointed Special Advocates) for letting me inspire the crowd!

On this day, I empowered over 100 teachers and principals that work for Houston Independent School District.

Ambassador Tyrone Obaseki before the Texas Legislature.

Eighteen Years of Slavery

This picture was taken at a staff development day for Sumter School District! Over 75 teachers and principals were in attendance! I hope to go back to South Carolina one day!

Protesting in front of the Texas Capitol in Austin, Texas.

On this day, I gave a speech before the Citizens Commission on Human Rights!

Motivating and empowering 200 students at Roberson Middle School in Spring, Texas.

Eighteen Years of Slavery

Leading a army of religious leaders and foster youth to the capitol to speak about foster care reformation.

Press conference with Fox 26 News Anchor Damali Kieth.

On this day I gave a speech before the members of the Citizens Commission on Human Rights.

Photo shoot with Andrea Sparks to support Texas CASA.

Eighteen Years of Slavery

On this day I had the opportunity to inspire 50 foster youth who were about to start college at my Alma Mater (Texas A&M University- Commerce)

In this picture I was interviewed at the Texas Capitol by Univision Broadcasting Company. Univision is an American Spanish language broadcast television network. Isn't Jesus wonderful? He's preparing me to reach the masses! I'm so excited!

In this picture I gave a speech to 50 students at Remington College.

On this day I was awarded a clock by the Houston Police Department for mentoring incarcerated juveniles. Life is but a vapor, so we have to get busy helping people trust Jesus!

Eighteen Years of Slavery

In this picture I gave a speech at Abundant Life Cathedral in Houston, Texas! Never in a million years would I have dreamed of having this opportunity.

In this picture I had the opportunity to motivate students at Sam Houston State University.

Tyrone Obaseki

On the phone with one of my mentors, Dr. Elwyn Lee. I was working on a speech for Texas A&M University – Commerce.

In this picture I was at the home of my 1st grade teacher, Ann McClelland. I spent Christmas at her home with her daughter Jill McClelland. Happy Memories!

On this day I attended one of my little mentee's stage play's. Here I am pictured with Logan Obrien and his mother and father, Christie and John. John and Christie, are one of the numerous families that have allowed me to spend time with them. I'm happy to be Logan's big brother!

My biological mom and dad

My graduation picture from Texas A&M University- Commerce

On this day I provided a speech to the teachers and administrators of Sumter South Carolina School District.

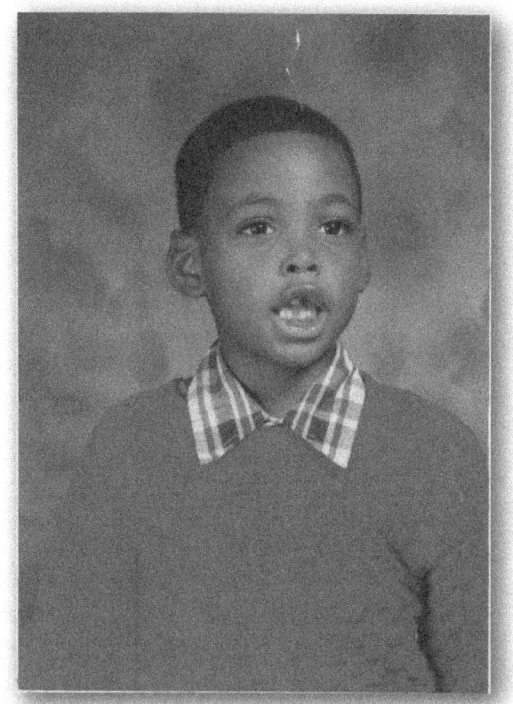

My first grade picture at Smith Elementary School in Spring, Texas.

My mughsot after being arrested for fighting in college.

On this day I was interviewing and providing a statement after one of my childhood psychiatrist's was arrested for fraud.

Providing a compelling speech in Dallas, Texas.

Eighteen Years of Slavery

Speaking before students at Sam Houston State University.